Haile Selassie I's Ethiopia, Volume One:

The Rise of the Priestly Warrior Kings

Kwasi Bonsu, Esq.

**BOOKMAN
EXPRESS**

Edited by Dutty Bookman.
Cover illustration by Joavan Puran.

ISBN: 9780985375508
Library of Congress Control Number: 2021943938

Published by Bookman Express, LLC.
For publishing inquiries, email works@bookmanexpress.pub.
For general inquiries, email info@bookmanexpress.pub.
www.bookmanexpress.pub

BOOKMAN
EXPRESS

| BEX0007 |

To: Tamrat Medhin

I pray this work is worthy of the great legacy of Ethiopia! It is an honor to present this work to some one who has given their life for the glory of Ethiopia

Contents

Foreword by Dr. Aklilu Habte
Former President, Haile Selassie I University, 1969-74
(Appointed by H.I.M. Emperor Haile Selassie I)

Kwasi Osei Bonsu, Esq. has set out to write a comprehensive, multi-volume history of Emperor Haile Selassie I at national, regional and global levels. This is an ambitious but timely and welcomed treatment of the emperor's contribution during his leadership era in Ethiopia, Africa, and the world.

Several books have been written in different international languages, including Amharic and Ge'ez - both local languages - but most of them tend to be generally one-sided depending on the writer's political views and, too often, religious persuasions, unfortunately depriving them of balance. Kwasi's approach promises to escape from several of these earlier deficiencies, largely because of the material and the information covered, as well as the Afro-European and Afro-American political and cultural relationships that have influenced and prevailed over global history.

Kwasi's treatment of the emperor's birth circumstances shows that, though deprived of his mother's love beginning at a very early age, he was very fortunate that his father was placed as the first civilian governor of the province and the walled city of Harar, internationally recognized as the fourth holiest city in Islam. The future emperor and, indeed, Ethiopia were both lucky to have been associated in such a manner as though anticipating what was to come in the long and difficult civic life of the emperor.

What seems miraculous is the continued affirmation and perpetual recognition of the kingship era of Ethiopia. The nation's later contributions to the African

i

continent and globally, even after a disastrous invasion by Italy and the merciless destruction of the country and the environment (including using internationally forbidden poisonous gas), stand as testaments to the tradition of inner leadership strength exemplified by the emperor until his demise from the political scene at the onset of the Derg era. The positive and unwavering contribution to the request of the United Nations by sending his elite combat forces to Korea and the Congo, even after the disastrous position the League of Nations took against his country at the Geneva meeting, heralds concretely the humane and collaborative character of the country's leadership.

It did not take much time or require additional evidence to expose the negative positions taken by so-called civilized Europe against the lonely but determined African nation, and to prove that truth and justice prevailed – an important lesson exposed by Kwasi. I look forward to learning more, in this volume and the subsequent ones, about the negative impact of European colonial domination in Africa, the determined position taken by Emperor Haile Selassie I and the love for freedom embraced by the people, which restored Black people's dignity and identity.

Dr. Aklilu Habte
Virginia, USA.

Foreword by H.I.H. Prince Ermias Sahle Selassie
President, The Crown Council of Ethiopia
(Grandson of H.I.M. Emperor Haile Selassie I)

The latter part of the 19th century prior to 1892 witnessed the American civil war, the Austria-Prussian war, the Franco-Prussian war and the assassination of Abraham Lincoln. The same period also witnessed advances in technology such as the invention of the first practical telephone, the phonograph, the light bulb as well as modern photographic film. It was also filled with larger-than-life personalities who left their mark in history, such as Bismarck, Lincoln and Queen Victoria.

Shortly after the birth of Lij Tafari Makonnen in 1892, Germany emerged as an important imperial power in Europe. The rise of Germany culminated in the Berlin Conference of 1884-1885, which erased any semblance of African independence and carved the continent amongst competing European powers. Few states, such as Ethiopia and Liberia, were able to escape this fate but there were ominous signs that this was not going to be the case for much longer.

It was against this backdrop that the prophesied birth of Lij Tafari Makonnen took place according to Ethiopian tradition in 1892. Lij Tafari was the only surviving son of his parents Ras Makonnen and Woizero Yeshimebet. Eight of his siblings died shortly after childbirth. The young Tafari was never able to see his mother and this must have deeply affected his early childhood.

Ethiopia, as one of the oldest civilizations, entrenched in its traditions and faiths, remained isolated from the rest of the world. Yet, by 1892, events were about to change and Ethiopia was beginning to embark on a journey that would forever change the country and the perception of Africa around the world.

Ras Makonnen, the father of Lij Tafari, was a devoutly religious man, an able general and a diplomat. Unlike many other nobles of his generation, he was able to travel and represent his country on the world stage. This exposure and experience must have ingrained in him a desire to see and shape Ethiopia's independent development. It also instilled in him the importance of complementing his son's traditional education with modern languages. In this regard, he was helped by Jesuit missionaries, offering the young Tafari a taste for discipline and intellectual curiosity. Above all else, Tafari developed a strong moral compass and a spiritual devotion to his ancient faith.

The victory of Ethiopia, under Emperor Menelik II, against the Italians in 1896 at the Battle of Adwa also elevated Ethiopia to become a symbol of Black pride and resistance against subjugation and colonialism. The young Tafari, raised at Menelik II's palace and surrounded by his father's loyal followers, quickly became a strong and able administrator. He witnessed firsthand and studied the character of his people and how to apply the dispensation of justice. Tafari was unaware at this juncture how much this would shape his future destiny and work. Certainly, it developed in him the courage to confront both personal and national challenges, a courage which would serve him well in his many years of service to his people.

Kwasi Bonsu, Esq., as a firm, practicing Rastafarian, an educator and a researcher, has achieved a remarkable glimpse that he shares with us of the early moments of young Tafari Makonnen's life in this volume. He is able to synthesize history and world events, bring the ancient world to life and challenge us to reflect on topical subjects, such as the fight against institutionalized racism, that continues to plague us to this day. In reading this first volume, it is my hope that a younger generation of readers and thinkers will appreciate the challenges that the young and growing prince was confronted with on his way to becoming one of the 20th century's giant leaders.

H.I.H. Prince Ermias Sahle Selassie Haile Selassie

Washington DC, USA.

Author's Preface

The role of the storyteller or the griot is a tradition that runs deep in African cultures, both on and off the continent. How this tradition has translated to the diaspora is something that fascinates me. As a Jamaican-born Ras Tafari who grew up in Toronto, I am very familiar with the oral tradition. My home, a gathering location for friends and families, was filled with vividly told stories. This is how the culture of Jamaica is maintained for many children residing in the diaspora and how it is preserved from generation to generation.

During my university days in Washington DC, I had the privilege of spending countless hours listening to Ras Tafari elders speak about Jamaica and Ethiopia. Their historical recall was nothing short of remarkable. It has always been my desire to emulate these elders' gifts for storytelling by adding to the historical narrative in written form. In this work, it is my aim to share with the coming generations the pleasure I experienced reasoning with those living archives. It is not lost on me that young people in the digital age spend increasingly less time reasoning (storytelling) and more time consumed by media via the internet. By condensing the contents of several books about Ethiopia along with some oral tradition into one work, and adding some storytelling flair, I hope to provide youths with a work that will open the door of inquiry and introduce them to the wonderful world of Ethiopia and its most impactful King of Kings, Emperor Haile Selassie I, the father of Africa.

This work, with its many limitations, is an attempt by the author to add to the foundation of the story of Ethiopia's greatest and, in some circles, most controversial emperor. Instead of a dry history, I have approached the history as an African storyteller would. The assertion that history can ever be objective is a fiction. From time immemorial, authors of history have brought their biases in regard to the facts within their narratives. It will be quickly apparent to the reader that this work is no different. I have provided citations where possible and, even where I have strongly presented facts in my own view, I have tried to present alternate theories or versions of history within the narrative, where I am aware such alternate versions exist.

In some instances, this work also presents the emotions or thoughts of the historical figures I write about. While it is impossible to know what one was actually thinking in cases where there is no documentation of same, I have tried to use a reasonable person standard. That is, I asked myself what a reasonable person would feel under the circumstances presented, given the available facts. In my opinion, this provides for better storytelling and a more compelling narrative as I attempt to place the reader in the shoes of the historical figure. That being said, I have tried not to overindulge in this technique.

This work revolves around the birth of H.I.M. Emperor Haile Selassie I in 1892. Thus, any facts or occurrences that happened after that year are not included in this first volume. The Almighty willing, subsequent events will be addressed in later volumes. At the time of publication of this volume, I have already started working on *Volume Two*, which will address Emperor Haile Selassie I's life from 1893 until 1906 when he was given the title of Dejazmatch. *Volume Three* will cover 1907 until 1916 when Dejazmatch Tafari was crowned as Ras Tafari. *Volume Four* will cover 1917 until 1928 and will examine his time as Ras Tafari until his crowning as Negus. *Volume Five* will cover from 1929 until 1941 and look at his coronation as Negus Negast (King of Kings) and the subsequent Italian invasion. *Volume Six* will cover from 1942 and the rebuilding of the empire until 1963 and the founding of the Organization of African Unity (OAU). Finally, *Volume Seven* will cover 1964 until the coming of the Derg and the disappearance of Haile Selassie I from the world stage in 1975.

In addition to covering Ethiopia and the life of the emperor, this work introduces a Pan-African perspective, contrasting other happenings around Africa and the diaspora with the developments in Ethiopia. It also addresses the rapid development of Europe during the corresponding period.

One of the challenges I faced was not being able to read Amharic, therefore having to rely on source materials written in English. I hope to correct this limitation in future volumes as well as release updated editions of this and other volumes written without the benefit of my not being able to read Amharic. Despite this limitation, I am thankful for the large number of Ethiopian authors who have begun to publish works in English. Their inside information and cultural perspective have been invaluable to this work.

At the time of this writing, the Disney/Marvel movie, *Black Panther*, sits as the third largest grossing movie in United States history. The movie inspired a renewed focus on Africa by African-Americans and other African descendants around the world, injecting new life into discussions about Africa's relationship with its scattered diaspora and the trauma of being separated from one's history and culture. Popular opinions surrounding *Black Panther* fail to point out the fact that there is indeed a real-life unconquered nation in Africa or draw the parallel between Wakanda and Ethiopia, both unconquered

African nations shrouded in secrecy, surrounded by mountains and ruled by a majestic, benevolent king.

It should be noted that when the New York-based authors, Stan Lee and Jack Kirby, created the *Black Panther* character and the kingdom of Wakanda in 1966, it was only three years after the Ethiopian emperor, the Conquering Lion of the Tribe of Judah, Emperor Haile Selassie I, visited New York and received the largest parade in the city's history since World War II. New York was celebrating the emperor's historic address to the United Nations (UN), which made him the only world leader to address both the United Nations and its predecessor, the League of Nations. The emperor was also bringing with him the charter of the newly established OAU, a major victory for his diplomacy in Africa. A portion of that speech would later be immortalized in Jamaican Ras Tafari reggae artist, Bob Marley's song, 'War.'

While Stan Lee and Jack Kirby chose to make their character a panther king and not a lion king, it would be hard to believe that the spark of inspiration for their main character and his African stronghold was not connected to Ethiopia and her world famous emperor. The fact that the authors were of Jewish heritage (Jew being short for Judah) further leads to the conclusion that they were, at a minimum, aware of Ethiopia and the emperor at the time of *Black Panther's* creation. As the 225th ruler in the line of King Solomon, Emperor Haile Selassie I was beloved in the modern state of Israel that had been created by UN mandate in 1948.

In light of these considerations, it is important that the young people of the diaspora continue to read accounts of the history of Ethiopia and Emperor Haile Selassie I so that they will not have to rely on a fictional country like

Wakanda for a sense of pride. They can read this book and many others that address the subject matter, and realize that the light of freedom in Africa was never completely extinguished. Ethiopia remains unconquered.

I must thank my loving mother, Norma Clarke, for her assistance in the initial editing of this work. Special mention also to my father, Paul Clarke, and brother, Osei Clarke, for their reviews and comments as well. I must also thank my beautiful, intelligent and supportive wife, Sherine Bonsu, for her support and belief in my ability to complete this work along with my many other projects. I pray this work will be read by my children, Yaa Asantewaa Serwa Bonsu and Tafari Kwaku Osei Bonsu, who are my inspiration and energy, and who inspire me to continue to tell the still unfolding story of African people. I have had the privilege to sit and listen to many Ras Tafari elders – Elder Ras I-rice, Elder Nana Farika Berhane, Elder Ras Marcus, Elder Brother Jack, Elder Irie Ions, Elder Bongo Wato and the many others – whose hours of relayed history have shaped the person I am today. This work would not be possible without them. Youthful elders and masterful orators such as Ras Ivi also impacted my love for the historical reasoning and storytelling exemplified in this book. I would also like to thank my colleague, Dr. Nebiyou D. Tessema, Esq., for recommending and then lending his personal copy of Professor Bahru Zewde's book of the history of modern Ethiopia, which was very helpful. There are many others who deserve mention; however, it is such an extensive list that this preface would not be the appropriate place. I would like to thank filmmaker Haile Gerima for introducing me to a critical analysis of Ethiopian history and introducing me to so many Ethiopian elders who helped shape the narrative. I must give special thanks to H.I.H. Prince Ermias and Dr. Aklilu Habte for reading the work and contributing forewords.

The honor of their time and attention cannot be expressed in words. Finally, I would like to thank Dutty Bookman and Bookman Express for the editing and publishing of the final version of the work.

I fully acknowledge that, as Ras Tafari, I ascribe to the view that H.I.M. Haile Selassie I is the physical manifestation of the Almighty – fully human and fully divine – with all the baggage that this view carries in the eyes of academia and religious orthodoxy. However, while my telling of the story of the life of Haile Selassie I is undoubtedly animated by that sentiment, I have stayed to the facts presented by history in telling this story. It is my view that the facts speak for themselves.

Finally, any errors in this work are my fault and I will endeavor to correct those that I can in future editions of this work. I am particularly interested in the response of native-born Ethiopians, including scholars, after reading this work. I have been inspired by Ethiopia and I pray this work reflects the love and adoration that I have for the land and its people. I pray everyday for the unity of Ethiopia, knowing that it is critical for the overall unity of the African continent.

Kwasi Osei Bonsu, Esq.
Washington DC, USA.

WORLD MAP SHOWING THE LOCATION OF ETHIOPIA

KEY

Ethiopia

A - Africa
B - Europe
C - Arabia
D - Syria-Palestine (Judea)
E - United States of America
F - Jamaica & other Caribbean Islands

MAP OF ETHIOPIA SHOWING SOME PROVINCES AND LOCALES

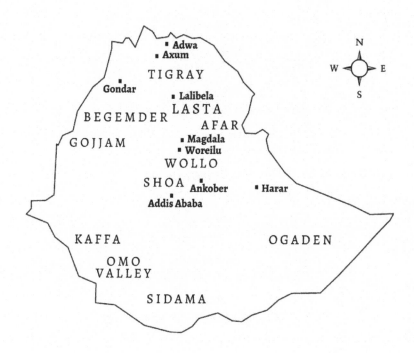

GLOSSARY OF ETHIOPIAN RANKS AND TITLES[*]

Negus Negast
King of Kings (Emperor)

Negus
King

Ras
General

Dejazmatch
Lieutenant General / Keeper of the Gate

Fitawrari
Major General / Commander of the Center

Kegnazmatch
Brigadier-General / Commander of the Right Wing

Meridazmatch
Colonel / Leader of Shoa (until 1813)

Shalaqa
Colonel / Commander of a Thousand

Balambaras
Lieutenant Colonel / Commander of a Fort

Basha
Commander of a Rifle Squad

Wagshum
Leader of Wag

Lij
Boy of Noble Birth

Agafari
Superintendent of Banquets / Chief of Protocol

---

[*] See a more extensive list by the Crown Council of Ethiopia at:
https://ethiopiancrown.org/imperial-and-traditional-ranks-and-titles/

CHAPTER ONE

The Evil Days

"For unto us a child is born, unto us a son is given: and the government shall be upon his shoulder: and his name shall be called Wonderful, Counsellor, The mighty God, The everlasting Father, The Prince of Peace." **– Isaiah 9:6**[1]

His first cries were drowned by thunder. The thunder signaled the triumph of his birth. He lived! He survived the perils of childbirth. All his brothers and sisters had been miscarried, delivered stillborn or died shortly after their birth. Eight children conceived, eight lives claimed. The angel of death would not claim this child.

No one witnessing his birth could have known his battle against death was only beginning. However, in this moment, the moment of his birth, he was victorious. Death did not prevail. The women who surrounded his mother and the hundreds of people who anxiously awaited his arrival were witness to a thunderous welcome for the boy child. Their anxiety was partially because it was believed the boy's mother's previous misfortunes with childbirth were caused by a curse.

---

[1] The King James Version of *The Bible* is quoted throughout this book.

Almost immediately after his birth, the baby boy was taken away from his mother to distance him from any curse that may have inflicted her. No one could have known the power of this child or that he would forever change his ancient realm and kingdom into a modern nation. No one present could have known that he would inspire billions of people, be praised by some as the living manifestation of the Almighty, hated by some as a tyrant, or that he would forever change Africa and the world.

For a moment – the moment of the birth of the baby boy – the angel of death was defeated and evil was forced to retreat. On July 23, 1892, in that mountainous land, in the midst of a crippling drought, the heavens opened and released life-giving water. The land scorched by the seemingly omnipresent sun was granted relief. The rain fell relentlessly from the sky and replenished the Earth.

AN END TO THE "EVIL DAYS"

There is a land that is far away from the modern centers of power, where the sun has always dominated; a land of thirteen months of sunshine; a land of towering mountains that, until the modern era, was shrouded in mystery; a land more ancient than recorded history. This land is the land of the people with sun-kissed faces – the land known as Ethiopia.

The ancient Greek historian, Homer, referred to the majestic realm south of Egypt as the land where the gods love to feast.[2] The inhabitants of the land in 1892

---

[2] Homer, *Iliad* (1,423).

called it Abyssinia. During the drought, the gods of Homer's writings were nowhere to be found as famine showed the land no mercy. The angel of death reigned unchallenged.

All the kingdoms of the realm were affected. The famed leaders from the great houses and their august sovereign had no answers. The kingdoms of Gojjam, Begemder and Shoa were forced into submission. The kingdoms of Tigray, Wollo and Yejju, were pummeled with punishment. Even the Kingdom of Kaffa and the Kingdom of Gondar, the capital of ancient kings, were brought to their knees. The drought had plagued Ethiopia, and the city-state of Harar in particular, since 1888.

The coming of the rain was not a sudden event. Days earlier, black rain clouds had slowly amassed in the sky, signaling the coming relief to the years of drought. The sky grew dark. Rain showered the earth. The falling rain was bringing an end to the Evil Days.

Those Evil Days, or *Kifu Ken* as the people throughout the kingdoms called them, had arrived with drought. The days and then years of the *Kifu Ken* made Ethiopia a demons' paradise, as if the omnipotent Almighty had forsaken the land where the gods loved to be. It was as if the Angel of Death's forces of darkness had been permitted to reign over the Almighty's peculiar treasure. The Lord of the Flies let loose his armies – parts of the land were seized by suffocating swarms of tsetse flies, while caterpillars and locusts destroyed most edible crops.

A menacing plague accompanied the drought, killing 90% of the cattle in Ethiopia. In some places, the bodies of dead cattle seemed to stretch to the horizon and the stench of death stifled the air. The dead cattle provided the perfect habitat for numerous native diseases to thrive – smallpox, typhus, cholera and influenza – and it was not long before human bodies were added to the landscape. Disease impartially searched the crevices and corners of crowded cities, encampments and villages alike. There were mass migrations across kingdoms as people uprooted from their ancient dwelling places to seek refuge from the relentless famine.

The scene was apocalyptic in proportion. Had the kingdom of hell become manifest and unleashed its armies against Ethiopia? Was the sun that blessed Ethiopia with 13 months of sunshine now being used as a weapon to bring about the destruction of the realm? Was suffering to become the status quo? For four years the Angel of Death stood triumphant over Ethiopia's kingdoms.

It is estimated that one third of the people of Ethiopia lost their lives during those Evil Days. The smell of death brought mother nature's morticians out of their hiding places. Lions, hyenas and leopards feasted on the banquet provided by the Angel of Death.[3] The hyenas, in particular, feasted until they could barely move. Some of the fattened hyenas then became prey to hungry humans, some of whom were forced to pick through animal droppings for edible pieces of straw.[4] Vultures were ever-present markers of death in the Ethiopian skies.

---

[3] Fesseha, Senait. "The Rinderpest Factor in the Great Famine of Ethiopia." 2002. CCT 640, University of Massachusetts, Boston, p. 4.

[4] Prouty, Chris. *Empress Taytu and Menilek II: Ethiopia 1883-1910.* 1986. The Red Sea Press, 2016, p. 100.

THE EVIL PLAGUE

It would later be discovered that the cattle plague was a foreign invader, which had previously wreaked havoc in Europe. The deadly pathogen hitched a ride on Italian cattle to infect the isolated land of Ethiopia. It was the dreaded rinderpest, which worked its way from the coast into the highlands. Known for its habit of following war, rinderpest was an untimely and unwelcome guest in Ethiopia. It was a virus that mercilessly killed both cattle and oxen, which were the principal animals used by Ethiopian farmers as tools to prepare their fields for the growing season. Virtually all cattle and ox-driven agriculture ceased in the land, making the famine worse.

For a land dependent on agriculture for survival, the impacts of famine were far reaching. Ethiopian agriculture persisted throughout countless centuries of pre-recorded history. The famine of 1888 CE meant that the Cradle of Man could no longer protect, feed and nurture its ancient population.

THE REALM OF ETHIOPIA: THE RIFT VALLEY AKA "THE CRADLE"

Archeological discoveries point to Ethiopia being the birthplace of mankind, earning her the right to be known as the Cradle of Humanity. Her mountainous terrain forms the walls of a volcanic cradle and are part of the Great Rift Valley. The rift valley marks "a giant breach in the crust of the earth where the African continent slowly splits into two parts."[5] It starts in Syria and extends all the way into central Mozambique. It includes the Jordan and Nile rivers. It runs southwest through Ethiopia, dividing in two Ethiopia's eastern plateau of Harar from the central plateau famous for providing habitation to the Tigray and Amhara kingdoms.[6]

The people of Ethiopia, true to the country's name and like her fertile soil, come in all shades of brown. It is as if a sampling of all the peoples of Africa were placed on display. Ninety languages are spoken in the realm and all manner of cultures and religions have been practiced since time immemorial. Christianity, Islam and Judaism are dominant, however hunter-gatherer societies and nomadic herdsmen also share the land. The nation's use of the Julian calendar gives the country 12 full months and an extra month a few days long – Ethiopia's famed 13 months of sunshine.

The massive energy contained in the shifting geology of the rift valley formed Ethiopia as a land of mountains, rolling hills, steep valleys, high plateaus and endless grasslands; a land so diverse that it contains both arid deserts and lush tropical rain forests. Its wildlife is equally diverse. It is the land of apex predators such as lions, leopards, cheetahs and even a rare species of African wolf. It is also the home of other warm-blooded killers such as hyenas, wild dogs, foxes, jackals and caracals. Its consistent warm and, for the most part, sunny climate and

---

[5] Vestal, Theodore M. *The Lion of Judah in the New World: Emperor Haile Selassie of Ethiopia and the Shaping of Americans' Attitudes toward Africa*. Praeger, 2011, p. 8.

[6] Vestal, Theodore M. *The Lion of Judah in the New World: Emperor Haile Selassie of Ethiopia and the Shaping of Americans' Attitudes toward Africa*. Praeger, 2011, p. 8

abundant prey species ensures it is also the home of some of Africa's largest cold-blooded killers such as Nile crocodiles and African rock pythons. Ethiopia also enjoys numerous species of snakes, turtles and lizards.

As a result of its lush grasslands, it is home to many herbivores, such as zebras, African buffalo, rhinoceros, giraffe, Oryx, gazelles, wildebeest and many species of antelope. The mountains of Semien are home to the rare Ethiopian Ibex. In 1892, Ethiopia was still home to mighty herds of African Elephants that helped maintain the landscape for the other herbivores. The Somali wild ass also survived in small herds in the lowlands. Ethiopia's rivers were full of not only Nile crocodiles but hippopotamus as well. While the hippopotami gladly kept river channels free of vegetation the males were fiercely territorial and had to be given wide birth by the inhabitants of the realm. Primates were also common in the form of lemurs and baboons, like the world-famous Gelada baboons, which lived in large social groups high up in the Semien mountains. Ethiopia was also home to hundreds of species of birds, such as pelicans, cranes, ibis, flamingos, eagles, blue winged geese and several species of vultures.

All of Ethiopia's wildlife had to contend with the effects of the Evil Days. The herbivores, particularly, did not benefit. Meanwhile, scavengers and other species were able to flourish.

The scavengers came in many forms. A few years before the start of the Evil Days, the external enemies of Ethiopia had conceived a plan to ensure that Ethiopia emerged from the Evil Days in bondage. Though the falling rain had started to loosen the grip of the Evil Days and disperse the ever-present vultures in the Ethiopian skies, it would be too late to save Ethiopia from facing the vultures controlling the nation states rising against her.

The Italians used the chaos caused by the Evil Days to claim land on Ethiopia's coast for the Roman government. In their minds, Africa was a resource rich carcass and they wanted their portion. On July 23, 1892 a weakened Ethiopia had been long on the road to conflict with Europe and its philosophy of colonialism and white supremacy.

THE NEWBORN

The baby boy born on that day was not concerned with any impending conflict. In 1892 it was not yet an accomplished fact that the government and his people's freedom would rest on his shoulders. It had not yet been written that he would be forced to wage war against the encroaching Italians for his land and people. The baby boy was not yet old enough to engage in geopolitical struggles. Even his mother's struggle to push him out through her narrow hips were of no concern. The baby who survived the odds did not have time to bask in the warmth and affection of his mother. He would not suckle from her warm bosom. He was immediately removed from her loving arms by the attending women who were under strict instructions to do so. The previous fruit of her womb had perished. The baby must be protected from the evil eye or any other curse attached to his earthly mother. The life-giving falling rain was surely joined by tears of the baby boy and by tears of a mother who was not able to spend the night with her baby boy, her only living child.

CHAPTER TWO

Divide and Rule

"Why do the heathen rage, and the people imagine a vain thing? The kings of the earth set themselves, and the rulers take counsel together, against the Lord, and against his anointed, saying, Let us break their bands asunder, and cast away their cords from us."

– Psalms 2:1-3

The baby boy's father's eyes were surely holding back tears at the sight of a healthy baby boy. Just as water was falling from the heavens, so did water fill the eyes of both parents at the birth of their son. The baby boy's father's emotions were colored by his life experience. He had lived a hard life but a good life. He was an Ethiopian with special knowledge for his time. He had sailed on the sea, traveled outside of the realm and visited distant foreign capitals. He had seen the wonders and terrors of the industrial age. He knew firsthand the dangers that would face his baby boy should he live to be a man.

CONFERENCE IN EUROPE

The year was 1884. Snow fell silently on the dark streets of Berlin. On Saturday, November 15, the city was blanketed with the cold, white substance. That afternoon, the historic West Africa Conference, or Berlin Conference, would begin. It had snowed each night that week, piling snow higher and higher on the sidewalks, turning to slush by the time the delegates from fourteen great and lesser powers dismounted their carriages to gather to decide the fate of Black Africa.[7]

The gathering was the culmination of the rise of the conquering European in the annals of the human story. The warring tribes of Europe conquered, divided themselves into nation states and collectively rose to the top of the global food chain. With the help of superior military technology, Europeans had managed to defeat non-European peoples almost wherever they encountered them. Like the Egyptians, Babylonians, Persians and Mongols before them, the Europeans used war to carve themselves an empire outside the borders of their native territory. The philosophy of white supremacy emerged and erected a façade of Christianity and commerce to provide intellectual and spiritual foundations to the rising edifice of European global domination.

White supremacy would seemingly unify the fractured tribes of Europe in their quest for African land. The philosophy that the white race was superior to all

[7] Pakenham, Thomas. *The Scramble for Africa: White Man's Conquest of the Dark Continent from 1876 to 1912.* 1992. Perennial, 2003, p. 239.

others was meant to prevent the Germans from fighting the Italians, or the English from fighting the French, during their quests for colonies and resources. For while Europeans had grown powerful, their biggest impediment in their hour of global expansion was the greed of the other European States and kingdoms. After all, it was the Germanic tribes that were responsible for the fall of the mighty kingdom of Rome!

It was the might of a united Germania that also convinced the other European powers in the utility of European unity. In 1871, Prussia completed their military victory over the French Empire and brought the German princes under one government. During the German siege on Paris in January of 1871, the southern states of Germania were united under King Wilhelm, the absolute ruler of the Kingdom of Prussia.

On this snowy day in Berlin, it was the Germans facilitating the call for unity. The Germans were winning the industrial revolution. German engineering had become the epitome of quality. The Berlin Conference was further evidence of the growing power of the newly emerged united German State.

Nineteen plenipotentiaries with fifteen assistants (representing the fourteen powers) answered the German call. The host of the conference, the engineer of Germany's success and faithful servant of King Wilhelm, was the Prince of Bismarck. Otto Eduard Leopold von Bismarck. The world would put respect on his name.

Though it was the skill of the Prince of Bismarck that made such a monumental gathering of European powers possible, it was not the Prince of Bismarck who pulled the strings. That honor belonged to a monarch who preferred to remain in the shadows.

The countries present were France, Portugal, Spain, Belgium, Austria-Hungary, Denmark, Germany, Great Britain, Italy, the Netherlands, Russia, Sweden-Norway (unified from 1814-1905), Turkey, and the United States of America. As far as Africa was concerned, Great Britain, France, Germany and Portugal were the major players in the conference, having conquered the most African lands.

Despite the imbalance in military technology, European colonies had yet to penetrate the interior of Africa and were mostly in control of the coastal areas. The rapid pace of progress of the industrial age would start to change this. Skirmishes over which European country controlled which African territory increased and the conference was intended to present solutions to the growing problem of intra-European conflict.

The Europeans' determined solution took months of negotiation. The conference went from November 15, 1884 to February 26 1885. At the conclusion, they had agreed to the principle of effective occupation. Effective occupation had three pillars: one, that the European powers had treaties with local rulers; two, that they flew their flag openly in the territory; and three, that they established some level of administration with a police force to govern the territory.

The principle of effective occupation was initially opposed by powers like Germany. Recognizing that it was late to the Scramble and feeling like the principle was a little too loose, Germany favored control to go only to powers that exercised effective political control. In the end, it was agreed that the powers would need to have some type of base on the coast. Britain and France's perspective that effective control of the interior was not a necessary requirement won the day and the terms for the Scramble were set.[8]

There were no African countries present at the table. The concept of the modern nation state was not yet a reality in Africa. The remaining independent kingdoms and empires of Africa were not invited. The European powers were hungry for land and the empire of Ethiopia was on the menu.

INDUSTRIAL REVOLUTION

In 1789, the continuous rotary steam engine was invented and Europe was thrust into the industrial age. Beasts of burden like oxen and horses were replaced by iron and steel. In 1804, shortly after the freedom fighters of Haiti liberated themselves from the yoke of slavery, the first steam engine journey began in the United Kingdom on February 21. By 1883, engineers were able to create machines capable of delivering 10,000 horsepower. By the time of the Berlin Conference, the transportation of goods had long been revolutionized and the growing cities in Europe required more and more consumer goods. The shift in human priorities did not come without great sacrifice. Europe's great need for consumer goods created an insatiable need for raw materials. Europe's rapid rise had been fueled by the slaving of African bodies and theft of African labor and, now, to sustain their increasing appetites, bodies alone would not suffice. Europe now

---

[8] Herbst, Jeffrey. *States and Power in Africa: Comparative Lessons in Authority and Control.* Princeton University Press, 2000, pp. 71–72.

wanted African land. The abundance of raw materials reported from Africa only increased Europe's hunger.

EUROPE'S HUNGER

The creation of the Suez Canal in Egypt in 1869 created access to a critical trade route, bringing raw materials out of Africa and, once again, making Egypt the most valuable real estate on Earth. The race to satisfy Europe's hunger for raw materials was escalating. While Great Britain did not support the building of the canal, it was a British ship that was first to travel through it.

The English prime minister, Benjamin Disraeli, went on to acquire all of Egypt's shares in the canal for Great Britain in 1875, through a loan from the powerful Rothschild family.[9] Having invested so much capital in this African territory it was decided that further action by England was needed. In 1882, two years before the Berlin Conference, the British flexed their muscle and took effective control of Egypt. The conquest of Egypt gave the British immediate interests in Sudan and Somalia. Egypt's former colonizers, the Ottoman Empire, maintained garrisons in Sudan and Somalia and with the fall of the Ottomans in Africa, the British took their place. It just so happened that, at the precise time that Britain took control of Egypt, the entire horn of Africa was under the grips of a Mahdist uprising led by Islamic fundamentalists.

The Islamic forces were inflicting heavy losses on all who opposed them and, as a result, Britain came to the Berlin conference ready to negotiate. War in Africa was

---

[9] Lee, Stephen J. *Gladstone and Disraeli*. Routledge, 2005, p. 107.

costly and the returns uncertain. The sunny land of Ethiopia was an enigma. In the years prior to the conference in Berlin, Britain had marched an army that included Indian elephants through those mythic mountains to liberate British citizens that had been taken captive by the Ethiopian Emperor. The British did not march through those mountains unaided and they knew that an attempt to control Ethiopia would not be easy. The British had marched against an Emperor who had lost the support of many of his people and, as a result, they received substantial Ethiopian assistance on their mission. For the British, Ethiopia's importance stemmed from the fact that Ethiopia bordered areas that Britain deemed to be of strategic importance. Ethiopia was not on the British menu. Britain was happy to use Ethiopia as a negotiating tool at the conference to protect her other slices of the Africa cake.

THE BRITISH INTEREST

By the time of the Berlin Conference, the Mahdists had grown in strength and had managed to isolate and pin down the Egyptian forces stationed in Sudan. This was not unique to the British. Many of the other stakeholders at the table in Berlin were also facing uprisings in the territories that they held. Europeans were smart enough to realize that they could not fight each other as well as combat local resistance.

Europeans were not yet strong enough on the ground in Africa to rely solely on their own military forces or that of other European armies to enforce their rule. After all, maintaining an army so far from home was expensive and the taxpayers in Europe would not stand for it. At least not before the colony proved itself to be profitable. A public-private partnership that harnessed the business interest of private companies was the answer. The template for colonial commerce, the British East India Company (established December 31, 1600) was a success. Thus, the Imperial British East Africa Company was established in 1888, four years after the Berlin Conference, as the best option. This way there was no need for taxpayer accountability and any mistakes could also be disavowed by the government.

The policy of divide and rule was also instituted. The policy was simple: enlist the assistance of friendly tribal chiefs and arm them against their rivals, or other villages, tribes or empires not friendly to European interests. This strategy was employed with Ethiopia. In order to secure the lives of their subjects trapped in Sudan at the time of the Berlin Conference, the British begrudgingly decided to turn to the one African leader that could help them against the Mahdists: Ethiopian Emperor, the King of Kings, Lion of Judah, Yohannes IV.

While the British delegate sat around the large table in Berlin conspiring against Ethiopia's future, the Ethiopian Empire was preparing to go to war against the Madhists to help free the besieged Egyptian/British forces. Such was the colonial age. The Ethiopians and the British had signed a treaty of friendship, the Treaty of Adwa, and the Ethiopians were eager to show their ability to fulfill their obligations under the treaty. The treaty provided five main provisions:

1. that all negotiations regarding Egypt would be done through the British;

2. that the Ethiopians would facilitate the withdrawal of Egyptian troops from their besieged Sudanese bases;

Ethiopia with its drought and Italian cattle-borne disease. The Evil Days only added to the looming problem of European expansion facing the ancient empire of Ethiopia. It was a cruel twist of history that only a few short years after the Europeans had gathered to conspire to control Africa, Ethiopia was hit with the Evil Days.

The Berlin Conference would change Africa for all time. It largely removed the possibility of war between the great European states over Africa and gave them the opportunity to share information about what was happening on the ground in Africa. It provided the European powers with the license that they needed to carve up the great African cake among themselves.

By 1892, the end of the Evil Days, the Ethiopians were surrounded by the English, the French and the Italians. All had been present at the Berlin Conference. All had negotiated actively. Few, if any, Ethiopians could imagine the level of coordination against African self-determination that took place in distant European conference rooms. Ethiopians could not concern themselves with European dreams of domination. Instead, Ethiopians had to concern themselves with survival during those relentless Evil Days.

Given the threat of foreign conquest and the constant presence of death that gripped the Ethiopian highlands, the Evil Days were certainly not a good time to conceive a child, much less attempt to bring a child into the world, even a child of noble birth. Yet, the baby boy was born.

CHAPTER THREE

Islam's Holy Harar

"Let Ishmael live before Me, and I will make him a great nation, and he shall beget twelve nations and shall reign over them."

– **Kebra Nagast**[12]

A baby boy had been born to noble parents during the Evil Days. His father ensured his birth was in the best conditions available in the realm. He was born in a time when many died. The Evil Days had claimed countless lives. This baby boy lived. Then he was immediately taken from his mother without experiencing her motherly affection. He did not have the blessing of suckling from his mother's warm bosom. He also would not spend his first night in the arms of his father. His first sustenance came from a stranger, a wet nurse. These were not happy times. No one could truly be certain that the Evil Days were gone. Survival was the priority.

The baby who conquered death was born in the mountains near a city that was not of his forefathers. His father was the reason his family lived in the city. His parents had only recently arrived in the region to live in

---

[12] Brooks, Miguel F., comp., ed. and trans. *Kebra Nagast: The Glory of Kings.* 1995. Red Sea Press, 2002, p. 119.

the infamous city. With the consent of his father, the baby boy was removed from his mother and likely taken to a temporary location near the city, not far from his mountain birthplace. The city would become the boy's first home. The city itself was ancient and had a story of its own, a story that would only be enhanced by his arrival.

THE CITY OF HARAR

In the eastern highlands of Ethiopia, seated high on a hill, there was a famous walled city. The city was called Harar. Inside its high walls, the Evil Days made a hard life even more difficult. The 1880s ended in misery. In addition to the drought and flies, incessant swarms of locusts and caterpillars left no crops in Harar's vineyards or terrace gardens. Many people starved to death. Malnutrition was accompanied by the weeping and mourning heard throughout the city. At the start of the *Kifu Ken*, hyenas served as Harar's unofficial sanitation service as they meticulously searched for opportunities to feed, growing fat and lazy as their numbers swelled.

Then, four years after the Evil Days had arrived, just when it seemed like the land, animals and humans could take no more, something changed.

SHOWERS OF BLESSINGS

Towards the end of July 1892, great black clouds gathered above the flat-topped mountain Kondudu, which dominated the Harar landscape.[13] The entire mountain side began to darken under the shadow of the great canopy of rain clouds. The sound of thunder roaring like a lion in the heavens humbled the countryside, and lightning danced in the sky. Rain began to fall, quickly filling the cracks in the soil caused by the years of drought, while a warm breeze slowly dispersed the smell of death and decay characteristic of the *Kifu Ken*.

The black clouds then cast their shadow over Harar itself. Soon, rainwater quickly filled the narrow, once dusty streets, twisting and turning and flowing towards the city's lower elevations. The life-giving water from the heavens blanketed the entire place. It covered the once cultivated fields to the east of the city.[14] It covered the terraced ridge of orchards to the west.[15] It covered the numerous tombs of Harar's cemetery in northern part of the city.[16] It covered the little dome in the southern corner of the city that marked the final resting place of Shaykh Umar Abadir al-Bakri, the patron Saint of Harar.[17] It covered the five large gates that allowed the traveler access to the high walled city. It covered the oval towers that supported the city's massive walls. It covered the *gambisa* thatched cottages of the poor and the apartments and courtyards of the rich.[18] It covered the many mosques and

---

[13] Sandford, Christine. *The Lion of Judah Hath Prevailed*. 1954. Research Associates School Times Publications, 1998, p. 25.

[14] Burton, Richard F. *First Footsteps in East Africa*. Frederick A. Praeger, 1966, p. 177.

[15] Ibid.

[16] Ibid.

[17] Ibid., 186.

[18] Ibid.

drenched the joyous faithful whose voices rang throughout the atmosphere with their call to prayers.

HARAR AND ISLAM

The desperately needed rain was falling on an ancient and important city. Harar was famed for being the fourth holiest location in the Islamic faith, sitting comfortably in the heavens at 1885 meters (6,184.38 feet) above sea level. The walled city was home to a resilient people who had seen more than their fair share of trials and tribulations.

Harar's elevation was of military importance as well. Its strategic position in Ethiopia's eastern highlands made it an unlikely target for invading armies. Even Ethiopia's proud Christian rulers who, for hundreds of years, had been reluctant to take on the might of Harar's independent Islamic armies, had to respect such an advantageous location. Its famous wall was erected by Amir Nur, the successor of Harar's most famous son, Imam Ahmad Gran (or Imam Ahmed Gran or Ahmad ibn Ibrahim al-Ghazi). Amir Nur was not only credited as the builder of the wall of Harar but he was also canonized by his Muslim brothers after he succeeded in bringing the head of Ethiopia's Christian Emperor to his wife-to-be as a memento of his love.[19] Needless to say, there was historic tension between Islamic Harar and Christian-ruled Ethiopia.

Harar's Islamic roots were so deep that even after it fell to the rulers of the realm in 1887, it remained the center of Muslim life in Ethiopia. According to Arabic oral

---

[19] Ibid., 183-184.

tradition, Harar was established by Arabic speaking invaders who, in the 7th century, conquered and colonized the lowlands between the Red Sea and the Christian dominated highlands.

It was described by the first European "explorer" to ever visit as being, "The ancient metropolis of a once mighty race, the only permanent settlement in Eastern Africa, the reported seat of Muslim learning, a walled city of stone houses, possessing its independent chief, its peculiar population, its unknown language and its own coinage, the emporium of the coffee trade, the head-quarters of slavery, the birth-place of the Kat plant, and the great manufactory of cotton-cloths…"[20]

Harar's leaders were very independent minded despite its historical association with foreign invaders. The Emirs were men who prioritized commerce and Harar was, at its heart, a commercial city. Unfortunately for the tribes less acquainted with modern warfare, some of its commerce involved the buying, selling and enslaving of peoples. The Zangaro, Gurage, Alo and Oromo all fell victim to the scourge of slavery.[21] Their sons and daughters were sold as labor in Harar's once famous slave markets. Other trade items included "ivory, coffee, tobacco, safflower, Thobes (Islamic style robe), woven cotton, mules, holcus, wheat, bread, honey, ghee (clarified butter), gums (myrrh), and sheep fat."[22]

Although predominantly ethnic Somali-Ethiopians inhabited the area – Oromo tribes traditionally farmed the land outside the gates – foreign traders were numerous

---

[20] Burton, Richard F. Preface. *First Footsteps in East Africa or an Exploration of Harar*, by Burton, 1856. Echo Library, 2006.

[21] Ibid., 139.

[22] Ibid.

behind the city walls, coming from all around to hear stories of the latest intrigue in Arabia and Yemen. These travelers were Muslim for the most part, or they practiced various indigenous religions, but very few Christians entered the gates of Harar prior to 1887.

EGYPTIAN OCCUPATION OF HARAR

In 1875, the same year that the Rothschilds were making sure that Great Britain had the resources to invest in the Suez Canal, Harar was occupied by the Egyptian army under the orders of Khedive Ismail Pasha. The well trained Egyptian military force was led by Rauf Pasha.[23] They landed in Zeila in September and made their way inland without facing much opposition. Their easy passage was interrupted when they entered the territory of the Oromo, Afran Quallo confederation (four sons of Quallo).

The leader of Harar, Amir Muhammed Ali was an important ally of the Afran Quallo and as word of the approaching foreign army approached, the Afran Quallo gathered their armies and prepared for war. The battles were bloody and many brave Oromo lost their lives. They were no match for the canons and howitzer artillery fire of the Egyptians, who were able to enter the walled city with their superior firepower.

Inside, they encountered factions of Harar residents who were opposed to Amir Muhammed Ali and who were disgusted by his alliance with the Afran Quallo. These enemies of the Amir informed the Egyptians of his

---

[23] Hamid, Jilcha. "The Ten Year War: Egypt's attempted colonization of Eastern Oromia (1875-1885)." *The Gulele Post*, 18 Apr. 2013, https://oromialandinfo.wordpress.com/2013/04/18/the-ten-year-war-egypts-attempted-colonization-of-eastern-oromia-1875-1885/.

whereabouts and he was immediately killed. However, the powerful Egyptian forces, like many invaders before and after them, soon discovered that Ethiopia was not an easy realm to conquer. Soon, they found themselves under siege within the walls of the ancient city.[24] They dug in their heels and fortified their position with their howitzer guns, preventing any frontal assaults. However, outside the range of the guns, the Oromo cavalry controlled the land.

Knowing that their supplies would eventually run out, general Rauf Pasha organized negotiations with the Oromo leadership. While negotiations were taking place, he used the opportunity to bring in supplies and reinforcements. Once they restocked, they continued their war of occupation, this time extending it to the north. The resistance was fierce and they were ultimately limited to conducting raids on the surrounding Oromo states for supplies.

When the British conquered Egypt, the British administrator, Charles Gordon, removed Rauf Pasha from his post and installed a new Emir, Mohammed Nadi Pasha. The new leader of Harar was much more welcoming to European traders and lifted the previous ban on the arms trade imposed by the Egyptian government.

The overall trade in Harar exploded during the period of Egyptian control, which expanded to include 12,674 villages and hamlets. These provided them with the supplies to run their administration and included 60,000 ardebs of wheat and barley, 1,977 litres of millet, and between 25,000 to 26,000 Egyptian lire in annual taxes.

The Egyptian commercial success – the traditional 4 or 5 caravans leaving Harar every year expanded to approximately 75 – was detrimental to the traditional

---

[24] Ibid.

systems of the Oromo. The increased supply of goods from Harar provided an alternative to the Oromo traders and their representatives lost their former power over the villages. Word of Harar and its economic opportunities spread throughout the eastern world. As a result, European, Arab and Indian businessmen began to arrive in pursuit of fortune.

Despite the commercial success of Harar, the new British appointed Emir ran into the same problem as the old Emirs: the cost of defending against the guerilla warriors of the Oromo resistance was too much. The Egyptians ended up withdrawing their forces by 1885, the same year that the Europeans met in Berlin. The Europeans were making strategic decisions about their presence in Africa, and Britain decided that, with the constant threat of war, Harar did not justify its expense. It was just not worth keeping a commercial foothold in Ethiopia.

After the Egyptian withdrawal, Harar returned to the control of its own noble families. The Oromo resistance was successful in causing the Egyptians to leave, yet they would not be a match for Ethiopia's Christian rulers when they turned their attention to the walled city. Christianity was not the monopoly of any one ethnic group, and many Oromo and other kingdoms within Ethiopia accepted the faith. This made the Christian rulers and their forces particularly powerful. Traditionally, few, if any, Christians were to be found behind her walls. However, by 1892 this had started to change.

The Muslims and Christians of Ethiopia maintained a complex relationship throughout the centuries. In 615 CE, the Prophet Mohammed himself sent his early followers to Ethiopia, including a woman who was to become his wife, along with his cousin, to escape the persecution of the leading tribes of Saudi Arabia. He instructed them that they must seek out the ruler there who believed in "one God," and that he would give them refuge. Many Muslims hold Ethiopia in high esteem as a result of this action by the Prophet.

ISLAM AND THE BABY BOY

Islam would play an important role in the life of the baby boy born just outside of Ethiopia's most important center of Islam. The baby boy's mother started her life in a Muslim home, and he himself would grow up in Harar, a place inhabited almost exclusively by Muslims. The holy Islamic city would be his first refuge from the Western World closing in on Ethiopia.

The beginning of the relationship between the land of Ethiopia and the faith of Islam is often viewed as the first account of refugees in the modern era. That relationship, like the life of the baby boy born near Harar, was complex. Islam would begin with a prophet with a vision of one God. The holy Prophet's vision would spark hope in the hearts of the people of Arabia, hopes of a life free from the persecution of a ruling, idol-worshipping elite. Once the faith took root in Arabia, it spread to Mesopotamia. It then spread throughout Africa, driven by that desire for freedom from slavery and oppression. Islam spread the radical belief that every believer was a free man, and that the followers of Islam could not enslave their brothers in the faith. This message of freedom from slavery was powerful in a world where the powerful routinely enslaved the powerless. The desire for freedom and self-determination would lead the early Muslims to the mountain kingdoms of Ethiopia.

CHAPTER FOUR

Land of Sunburnt Faces

"But the hoopoe stayed not long and said, 'I have encompassed [in knowledge] that which you have not encompassed, and I have come to you from Sheba with certain news. Indeed, I found [there] a woman ruling them, and she has been given of all things, and she has a great throne.'" – **Quran 27:22-23**

In the old world, for a father with no legitimate heir, the birth of an heir lifted a great weight from his shoulders. As a wise father, the father of the baby boy born near Harar knew that weight would now rest on the shoulders of his son. He was born a Christian boy destined to grow up in a Muslim city. As a son of noble birth, he would have to learn quickly how to maintain the balance between the two religions.

ETHIOPIA AND EARLY ISLAM

Islam was no stranger to Ethiopia at the time of the baby boy's birth. The Quran identifies the queen who ruled over the land of Sheba as a woman of great power, and gives details of her interaction with the famous King

Solomon. The author of the Quran, the Prophet Mohammed, through his divine inspiration, held the queen in high regard. This great respect, along with the fact that the history teaches that the queen also ruled Ethiopia, likely influenced the Prophet Mohammed's decision to suggest Ethiopia as a refuge for his early followers.

According to the story, as it appears in various Islamic traditions, the early followers of the Prophet Mohammed were forced to flee persecution in their native Arabia. He sent them to Ethiopia, where they were very cordially received by the Christian Emperor, the Negus Negast (King of Kings) of Ethiopia.

It was a wise move by the Prophet Mohammed and demonstrated his knowledge of the powerful and prosperous Christian kingdom. It was not by coincidence. A renegade Ethiopian army, equipped with war elephants, invaded Mecca during the year of the Prophet Mohammed's birth. The Ethiopians were well known to the people of Arabia as their former conquerors, plus a major trading power.

It was Ethiopia's power that prompted the followers of Islam to seek her shores for refuge. The early followers of Prophet Mohammed were running from the Quraysh, the leading elite in Mecca. During the Prophet Mohammed's formative years, it was the Quraysh who exercised control over the mysterious Kaaba stone in Mecca.

Islamic tradition states that biblical patriarch, Abraham, and his son, Ishmael, first laid the foundation for the Kaaba, a structure that would become the holiest site in Islam. They intended to build a house of worship to the creator of heaven and earth, Allah. Once the house was completed, an angel brought them the black stone, which fell from the heavens, and that black stone was fixed to the wall of the Kaaba by the Prophet Mohammed. In 1892 the Kaaba still held a sacred place for Muslims as the first house of God in history.

ETHIOPIAN INVASION OF ARABIA

Prior to the birth of the Prophet Mohammed, Ethiopia's Christian Emperors extended their domain and conquered Arabia on two separate occasions. The first was under Emperor Ezana and the second era of conquest occurred under Emperor Kaleb. During the latter's reign, a rebellious general named Abraha carved a place for himself in the history books when he took advantage of the great distance between himself and Emperor Kaleb. A competent military commander, Abraha gained the loyalty of a faction of Emperor Kaleb's highly skilled soldiers. His military success further emboldened him to break from Emperor Kaleb and declare himself King of Arabia, waging war against the unconquered portions of Arabia with his superior Ethiopian fighting force.

Abraha grew so powerful that he organized a march against the Quraysh and the rest of the pagan tribes controlling the region surrounding the Kaaba stone. The year was 570 CE, the year of the Prophet Mohammed's birth, known in Arabia as *am al-fil* ("year of the elephant") in recognition of the war elephants that allegedly accompanied Abraha on his march.[25] It is said that the elephants stopped in their tracks and refused to enter Mecca, a miracle attributed to the power of Allah and thereby confirming the holiness of Mecca. According to

---

[25] Ullendorff, Edward. *The Ethiopians: An Introduction to Country and People*. 4th ed., Headstart Printing and Publishing Company, 1998, p. 54.

Islamic sources, Abraha himself was killed by a flock of birds carrying stones. They attacked his army, mortally wounding Abraha as he tried to invade Mecca. This failure to conquer Mecca did not stop the independence of Abraha's army, which continued without their leader and successfully resisted Emperor Kaleb's attempts to reassert his control over Arabia. They remained a rogue Ethiopian presence in Arabia until, finally, they agreed to submit and pay tribute to Emperor Kaleb's successor.

By the time the Prophet Mohammed reached adulthood, the Ethiopians were not a significant factor in Arabia, having been pushed out of Yemen by the Persian Empire's expansion into the area.[26] Still, Ethiopia was a well-known power in the region. Its people's belief in one God, which would have been peculiar to the pagan tribes of Arabia during the days of the invasion, was of great interest to Mohammed himself.

THE PROPHET MOHAMMED AND ETHIOPIA

After the Prophet Mohammed received his divine revelation, a new faith spread like wildfire. Once disparate tribes began to unite under the banner of Islam. His new religion made him a threat to the authority of the ruling Quraysh and their idols, which had brought them tremendous wealth. They were not about to let a lone, desert-dwelling tribesman, talking about an all-powerful God, disrupt their traditions and power. The Quraysh wanted the Prophet Mohammed destroyed. However, the Prophet Mohammed was a resourceful man. The Quraysh

---

[26] It would be useful to study if some of the hostility that some Arabians express against Black Africans is a result of the memory of being colonized by their Western neighbors from Ethiopia.

were not able to hurt him directly. All the same, the Quraysh were also resourceful, and they found and tortured the poor and less fortunate of the Prophet Mohammed's disciples. Meanwhile, his more prominent followers and those with wealth were boycotted, isolated and some were restrained in their homes.

The Prophet Mohammed witnessed this persecution of the early Muslims. Filled with divine inspiration, he devised a plan to get some of the more vulnerable followers out of the reach of the Quraysh. Having heard of the justice of the Ethiopian Negus Negast and his belief in one God, the Prophet Mohammed trusted that his followers would find protection under him. It is said the Prophet instructed, "…if you are in Abyssinia, you will find a king under whom no one is persecuted. It is a land of justice where God will grant you relief from your troubles."[27] The year was around 615 CE.

Word of their escape and destination reached the Quraysh, who were not about to let these rebels find a sanctuary and multiply only to come back and try to take over their beloved city! The Quraysh conceived a plan to convince the Negus Negast to return the fugitives to their custody. Since the Persian Empire's expansion had ultimately driven Ethiopia from Arabia, cutting off their domination of Red Sea trade, the Emperor might have been motivated to connect with a powerful partner in Arabia to gain a new advantage over the Persians.[28] Although the economic resources of the Quraysh could not

---

[27] Elfasi, M., editor. *General History of Africa III: Africa from the Seventh to the Eleventh Century*. United Nations Educational, Scientific and Cultural Organization, 1988.

[28] Ullendorff, Edward. *The Ethiopians: An Introduction to Country and People*. 4th ed., Headstart Printing and Publishing Company, 1998, p. 54.

match that of Ethiopia, they nevertheless decided to disregard the wealth imbalance and present the Emperor and his generals with gifts they could not refuse. Knowing how much Ethiopians were reputed to love leather, all types of leather works were prepared.

The Quraysh sent two trusted men and told them to speak to the generals of the Negus Negast. The emissaries followed their instructions and were able to win the assistance of some of the Ethiopian generals with the help of their considerable bribes. They petitioned these generals by saying:

> "Some foolish young men and women of our people have taken refuge in this kingdom. They have left their own religion, not for yours, but for one they have invented, one that is unknown to us and to yourselves. The nobles of their people have sent us to your king on their account, that he may send them home. So when we speak to him about them, counsel him to deliver them into our hands and have no words with them."[29]

THE EARLY MUSLIMS AND THE NEGUS NEGAST OF ETHIOPIA

The Quraysh emissaries repeated their story for the King of Kings, a wise and just leader and a man who feared the Almighty greatly. His name was King Armah.[30] He was not so quick to follow the words of these strange men

---

[29] http://www.cyberistan.org/islamic/negus.html

[30] El Fasi, M., ed. *General History of Africa, Volume III: Africa from the Seventh to the Eleventh Century.* University of California Press, 1988.

bearing gifts. King Armah's kingdom had its own coins bearing, on one side, his image sitting on a throne, and a cross on the other. He had no fear of the Quraysh as his armies were more powerful and he knew his predecessors had once ruled over their lands. He said:

> "Nay, by God, they shall not be betrayed - a people that have sought my protection and made my country their abode and chosen me above all others! Give them up I will not, until I have summoned them and questioned them concerning what these men say of them. If it be as they have said, then will I deliver them unto them, that they may restore them to their own people. But if not, then will I be their good protector so long as they seek my protection."[31]

The Negus Negast ordered the followers of the Prophet to report to his royal chamber, also sending for his bishops. When the Prophet's followers entered his chambers, it is said that they inspired the awe of their Christian brothers. Among the exiles were powerful members of the Mecca Muslim community, including a man named Ja'far and his wife. It was Ja'far who, being extremely eloquent, was chosen to represent the community interests.

The stage for an interfaith showdown was set.

---

[31] See: http://www.cyberistan.org/islamic/negus.html

EARLY MUSLIMS DEFEND ISLAM

The Negus Negast surveyed the room in royal fashion, waited for all to settle, then asked:

> "What is this religion wherein ye have become separate from your people, though ye have not entered my religion nor that of any other of the folk that surround us?"[32]

Ja'far answered him humbly:

> "O King, we were people steeped in ignorance, worshiping idols, eating unsacrificed carrion, committing abominations, and the strong would devour the weak. Thus we were, until Allah (The One True God) sent us a Messenger from out of our midst, one whose lineage we knew, and his veracity and his worthiness of trust and his integrity. He called us unto God, that we should testify to His Oneness and worship Him and renounce what we and our fathers had worshiped in the way of stones and idols; and he commanded us to speak truly, to fulfil our promises, to respect the ties of kinship and the rights of our neighbors, and to refrain from crimes and from bloodshed. So we worship God alone, setting naught beside Him, counting as forbidden what He hath forbidden and as licit what He hath allowed. For these reasons have our people turned against us and have persecuted us to make us forsake

---

[32] Ibid.

our religion and revert from the worship of God to the worship of idols. That is why we have come to thy country, having chosen thee above all others; and we have been happy in thy protection, and it is our hope, O King, that here with thee we shall not suffer wrong."[33]

Though he could not understand a word that his guest had said, as Ja'far spoke in Arabic, the King listened intently. The royal translators then translated his argument. The Negus Negast was intrigued! The bishops were also intrigued. As a student of prophecy, the Negus Negast was interested in the spiritual elements of his guests' faith and requested they share with him some of their Prophet's revelation.

Ja'far was ready for the challenge. He answered:

"And make mention of Mary in the Book, when she withdrew from her people unto a place towards the east, and secluded herself from them; and We sent unto her Our Spirit, and it appeared unto her in the likeness of a perfect man. She said: I take refuge from thee in the Infinitely Good, if any piety thou hast. He said: I am none other than a messenger from thy Lord that I may bestow on thee a son most pure. She said: How can there be for me a son, when no man hath touched me, nor am I unchaste? He said: Even so shall it be; thy Lord saith: It is easy for Me. That We may

---

[33] Ibid.

make him a sign for mankind and a mercy from Us; and it is a thing ordained."[34]

The royal court wept as a result of the passion and force of Ja'far's delivery; and, again, they all wept when the passage was translated to the Ethiopians' native Amharic.

The Negus declared, "This hath truly come from the same source as that which Jesus brought."[11] To the envoys of the Quraysh, Negus Negast Armah said firmly, "Ye may go, for by God I will not deliver them unto you; they shall not be betrayed."[35]

The well educated Quraysh, not so easily defeated, decided to expose what they thought to be a key distinction in the faith of the Negus Negast's guests: they believed Jesus to be a slave! The following day, they said, "O King, they utter an enormous lie about Jesus the son of Mary. Do but send to them, and ask them what they say of him."[36]

When re-summoned, Ja'far humbly replied, "We say of him what our Prophet brought unto us, that he is the slave of God and His Messenger and His Spirit and His Word which He cast unto Mary the blessed virgin."[37]

The Negus Negast was now even more convinced in his duty to protect his guests. He picked up a piece of wood and exclaimed, "Jesus the son of Mary exceedeth not what thou hast said by the length of this stick."[38] He continued to address Ja'far and the group of exiles, stating,

---

[34] Quran 19:16-21

[35] See: http://www.cyberistan.org/islamic/negus.html

[36] Ibid.

[37] Ibid.

[38] Ibid.

"Go your ways, for ye are safe in my land. Not for mountains of gold would I harm a single man of you."[39]

To his generals he commanded, "Return unto these two men their gifts, for I have no use for them."[40] The Negus Negast was already wealthy and did not need to accept these gifts. The most important fact, however, was that the Negus Negast controlled the armies of many kings and had no fear of his Arabian neighbors. The Negus Negast feared only the wrath of God.

THE CLAIM OF ARMAH CONVERTING TO ISLAM

Emperor Armah's great act of kindness also marked the beginning of a quiet tension between Ethiopia's Christians and Muslims. According to the Islamic accounts, so powerful was his defense of the exiles that the word quickly spread throughout the Ethiopian realm. In particular, word spread about how readily he had agreed with his Muslim guests' view of Jesus, stirring up rumors that he had secretly adopted this new religion.

The Negus Negast, who possessed a very capable information gathering system, recognized the possible danger if his firmly Christian people believed that he had left his faith. Despite his claim by blood to the throne, it was only the true believers of Christ that could hold the throne in Ethiopia. No king could rule without the Church, a fact still true centuries later, at the fateful moment of the baby boy's birth in 1892.

---

[39] Ibid.

[40] Ibid.

The Islamic sources state that Emperor Armah instructed his guests to be ready to flee by sea, if necessary, before going to address his people. Although he was Negus Negast and had ruled his people justly, he now had to defend himself to them. In preparation for the meeting, he wrote on a parchment his understanding of the beliefs of his guests:

> "He testifieth that there is no god but God and that Muhammad is His slave and His Messenger and that Jesus the son of Mary is His slave and His Messenger and His Spirit and His Word which He cast unto Mary."[41]

To his people, Armah said, "Abyssinians, have I not the best claim to be your king?"

They agreed.

"Then what think ye of my life amongst you?"

"It hath been the best of lives," they answered.

"Then what is it that troubleth you?" he pressed on.

"Thou hast left our religion," they said, "and hast maintained that Jesus is a slave."

He asked, "Then what say ye of Jesus?"

"We say that he is the son of God," they answered.[42]

According to the Islamic tradition, the Negus Negast put his hand on his breast, pointing to where the parchment was hidden, and testified to his belief in "this," which they took to refer to their words. The assembled people were satisfied and went about their daily lives, only

---

[41] Ibid.

[42] Ibid.

needing to be reassured by a just and benevolent ruler whose governance pleased them. Confident that the rumors had been refuted and that people were again on his side, the Emperor sent word to Ja'far and his companions. They were instructed that they could return to their dwellings.

THE PROPHET MOHAMMED'S MARRIAGE TO AN ETHIOPIAN EXILE

The relationship between Negus Negast Armah and the Prophet Mohammed did not end with this incident. In 628 CE, Umm Habibah, one of the exiles, became a widow upon the death of her husband. Mohammed sent word to Armah requesting that he stand in for him in the marriage of the widow. At the ensuing ceremony, they solemnized the pact of the Prophet to the widow and held a grand feast to which all Ethiopia's Muslims were invited.

Being as wise as he was, the Prophet realized that the Negus Negast could be a powerful convert. So, in a letter requesting passage for exiles who desired to return home (including Ja'far), Mohammed also asked that the Negus Negast accept Islam. Conscious of the history of his throne, the Negus Negast declined the invitation. However, his love for his guests did not diminish and he provided them with two boats to aid them in their journey home.

Ethiopia's historic act of kindness caused Muslim numbers to swell within the realm. The faith spread among Ethiopia's many non-Christian tribes. In particular, Oromo peoples (at times victimized by the Christian imperial government's plans to expand and secure

Ethiopia's borders) abandoned their traditional gods and embraced the new faith. Conversion to either Christianity or Islam gave less equipped nations a better chance to avoid the slavery which was thriving in Ethiopia as a result of the Arab demand for servants, human laborers and concubines.

BILAL: FROM SLAVE TO SERVANT OF ALLAH

One of the prominent early followers of Islam, Bilal ibn Rabah was known as an Ethiopian, being born to an Ethiopian mother. Bilal was held in high regard by the Prophet Mohammed and is credited with being the first person selected to perform the *adhan* (or muslim call) to prayer.[43] This prayer was chanted throughout the Ethiopian realm in 1892. Bilal became the poster child for Islam on the African continent. Though he was born a slave, he rose to a position of high importance in the early Islamic world. In fact, he was appointed treasurer of Medina by the Prophet.[44] Bilal was proof to Africans that Islam was a religion that would liberate them from bondage.

ISLAM CLASHES WITH CHRISTIAN NUBIA

The rise of Islam gave Arabia and many disparate tribes inhabiting the fertile crescent a reason to unify. A unified Arabia pushed out the Persians and, soon after, the

---

[43] Adamec, Ludwig W. *Historical Dictionary of Islam*. Scarecrow Press, 2nd ed., 2009, p. 68

[44] Charbonneau, Joshua, comp. *The Suffering of the Ahl-ul-bayt and Their Followers (Shi'a) throughout History*. J. M. Charbonneau, 2012.

mighty Persian Empire embraced the faith. Their proximity to Europe and Asia gave them access to guns and gunpowder. Once united, they swept into Africa from the fertile crescent and Arabia with their new faith. Egypt was soon brought under the banner of Islam.

In 641 CE, the Islamic armies pushed south and, after fierce fighting with the Christian Nubians,[45] agreed to the treaty of Baqt.[46] The Nubians had once been subjects of the Ethiopians but had grown independent. This treaty obligated the Nubians to send 360 slaves of the highest quality to Egypt every year. The treaty mandated that the slaves had to be half male and half female. The enslaved peoples would serve the insatiable demand for servants, laborers, and concubines that was growing in the thriving centers of Islamic commerce.

History relies solely on the Islamic accounts of the treaty, which themselves differ. One account relates that Egypt was also obligated to send grain and other provisions south in exchange for the Nubian slaves. The treaty was unique among the kingdoms that encountered Islam during the period. The fact that the Nubians were not forced to convert to Islam speaks to the treaty being more of a negotiated accord of equal powers than a set of rules imposed on the Nubians. The Nubians, the original inhabitants of Egypt and an ancient people were skilled in the art of war and diplomacy and would not have been an easy conquest, even for the rising tide of Islam. However,

---

[45] The Nubians were descendants from the ancient Kushites and were based in modern-day Sudan. The royal court of the kingdom converted to Christianity around 545 CE.

[46] Spaulding, Jay. "Medieval Christian Nubia and the Islamic World: A Reconsideration of the Baqt Treaty." *The International Journal of African Historical Studies*, vol. 28, no. 3, Boston University African Studies Center, 1995, pp. 577–94, https://doi.org/10.2307/221175.

by 1892 the glorious history of the Nubians had receded into the sea of human forgetfulness.

Similar to the differing accounts of the Egyptian treaty with Nubia, the Christian account differs substantially from the Islamic account in regards to the conversion of an Ethiopian Emperor to Islam. There is no record in Ethiopia of the Ethiopian Emperor ever converting to Islam. Notwithstanding that disagreement, it is agreed by both Christians and Muslims that an act of kindness occurred, and that both Christians and Muslims would now call Ethiopia, the land with 13 months of sunshine, home.

The founding of the walled city of Harar was a result of the Islamic foundations that had been laid in Ethiopia. It was into this reality near the walled city that the baby boy would be born.

FROM MUSLIM TO CHRISTIAN

The mother of the boy born in the mountains outside of Harar that fateful day in 1892 had begun her life as a Muslim. A quiet woman, she was the daughter of a prominent Muslim Chief. The mother and her Muslim heritage were part of the legacy of that historic act of kindness from the Ethiopian Negus Negast.

The boy's mother was born in a highland district called Bete Giorgis, located in the region of Bete Amhara.[47] Located in southern Wollo, Bete Giorgis, or Woreilu as it would come to be named, was predominantly inhabited by

---

[47] Beresford, Deena-Marie. *Gurage! Gurage! Gurage! The Story of a Wollo Princess: Woizero Yeshimabet Ali AbaJifar*. Yeshimabet's Books and Things, 2019, p. 15.

the Oromo. The kingdom of her birth was once the center of Orthodox Christianity until the time of the infamous Imam Ahmad Gran and served as part of the political center for Ethiopia's early Christian Emperors.

Following the fall of Imam Ahmad Gran, the power of the Christian Imperial throne grew and some of the prominent Muslim families in areas controlled by the throne were forced to convert to Christianity. On the day of the birth of her baby boy, the mother was no longer a Muslim. She was an Orthodox Christian married to a noble man who was also Orthodox Christian.

As in the days of the Prophet Mohammed, Ethiopia's Negus Negast went by the title the King of Kings and while some demonstrated considerable religious tolerance, the Emperor that reigned during the childhood of the young mother would not tolerate Muslims among his governors, or as heads of his vassal states. The heads of the prominent Muslim families were given the choice to convert to Christianity or lose their land and titles. Many chose to embrace the Christ rather than lose their family wealth and legacy.

The woman, the baby boy's mother, left the house of her father and converted to Orthodox Christianity and was married by her family to an Orthodox Christian man of status. A man that would be able to secure her families interests in relation to the throne. The baby boy's mother married young and moved to Harar on the invitation of her husband, shortly after it was incorporated into the land of the King of Kings. Her husband spent a lot of time away as he was a soldier, a man of war and trusted advisor to the King of Kings. Her husband was given the task of governing Muslim Harar, and though not a native daughter of Harar, she too would become part of it's great legacy.

On that fateful night of July 23, 1892, in the midst of her sadness over being robbed of the opportunity to bond with her baby boy, a child she had struggled with for nine months, she could not have known that she had given birth to a child whose name would reverberate through the ages. Her son would be venerated by nations and peoples far beyond the borders of her native Ethiopia and above all of the kings and emperors of Ethiopia. That future was hidden from her and the present was filled with joy and sadness – the joy of a successful birth and the sadness of a mother separated from her only child.

CHAPTER FIVE

The Jihad of Imam Ahmad Gran

"For they have consulted together with one consent: they are confederate against thee: The tabernacles of Edom, and the Ishmaelites; of Moab, and the Hagarenes; Gebal, and Ammon, and Amalek; the Philistines with the inhabitants of Tyre."

– Psalms 83:5-7

In Christian-ruled Ethiopia, Islam started as the faith of outsiders. In the baby boy's father's case, as the head of a Christian household, it was he who was an outsider in Islamic Harar. He had done his best to endear himself to Harar's population. Having seen in Europe the advancements in public health, he was inspired to establish Ethiopia's very first modern hospital in Harar. He ensured that the new facility had medicine and even imported a trained modern doctor from the Caribbean.[48]

The baby boy's father knew the importance of public relations. His position in the empire demanded his awareness. Through his mother's lineage, he also

---

[48] Mosley, Leonard. *Haile Selassie: The Conquering Lion.* Weidenfeld and Nicolson, 1964, p. 16.

happened to share royal blood with the Christian Negus Negast who had played host to the early Islamic refugees. Despite this connection, he was not the heir to the throne and whether or not he would sit on the throne of the realm was far from certain. Even as whispers circulated that he was a possible contender for the throne, his baby boy knew nothing of such rumors. In fact, at the moment of his birth, the baby boy knew nothing of the many wars that had been fought for the throne, or that his life would one day be caught up in such intrigues. For the time being, he was resident in a city that had just seen the end of the Evil Days, a once independent city state that was the staging ground for a great and historic civil war. It was a war that would forever shape the city itself and Ethiopia at large. Islam and Christianity may have started on good terms, bound by a historic act of kindness, but human nature ensured that these two branches of the Abrahamic faith would clash on the battlefield.

THE CLASH OF CHRISTIANITY AND ISLAM IN ETHIOPIA

Not long after the time of the Prophet Mohammed, the Persians joined the Arabians in adopting the new Islamic faith and began asserting control over the region. They cut off the coastal city-state of Axum's control of the Red Sea trade, pushing the Ethiopians further into the highlands. Soon, Ethiopia's Christian Church was cut off from its spiritual headquarters in Coptic Egypt. The center of Imperial rule gradually shifted and settled for a time in the northern kingdom of Gondar. The once powerful kingdom entered into a period of isolation from the rest of the world, fading into the pages of history.

Ethiopia, once a place of refuge for Islam, now found itself surrounded by Islam on all sides. Muslims in the highlands swelled in number and Islamic leaders expanded their kingdoms. Not by any measure passive inhabitants of the land, they rose up at various times against Ethiopia's Christian Emperors who, isolated as they were, waged war and raided the autonomous Muslim tribes throughout the land.

Though nestled deep within Christian Ethiopia, Harar had managed to maintain its independence as an Islamic city-state until 1887. Thus, when the baby boy was born in 1892, Harar still had a firmly Muslim character that was solidified for the ages during a turbulent period in Ethiopia's history. It was a period marked by a clash of religions, the climax of which occurred during the reign of Harar's most powerful Islamic leader: Imam Ahmad Gran.

"GRAN THE LEFT-HANDED"

It is one of history's paradoxes that the center of Muslim life in Ethiopia gained global renown for being the birthplace of the baby Orthodox Christian boy born at the end of the Evil Days. Long before then, Harar was known throughout the realm due to the exploits of another Ethiopian who embodied the greatest challenge faced by the Christian emperors. He was the Emir, Imam Ahmad ibn Ibrahim al-Ghazi, or Ahmad Gran.

Despite the bond of kindness forged between Ethiopia's Christians and the Prophet Mohammed, a time came when the call for Jihad (holy war) echoed throughout the mountainous realm. The call was loudest from Harar's Imam Ahmad Gran. Bloody raids against Muslims by professed Christians, and the accompanying feelings of helplessness, had motivated a deep hatred of Christians in him, and justice would only be served by Jihad.[49]

Imam Ahmad Gran built a reputation as a knight trained under the Muslim Emir of Harar, Garad Abun. It is said that he was "endowed with intelligence and foresight [and he] consulted in his youth and in his prime, the inspiration of God the Most High in regard to the commission that God willed should be entrusted to him."[50] His service to the Emir earned him the Emir's love and admiration. The Emir imposed strict Islamic law on the land and outlawed alcohol, "games, and dances accompanied by drums." He also managed to reduce highway robbery, thus further endearing himself to his zealous servant, a young, ideal Ahmad Gran.

The Emir's reign in Harar was not long-lived. His enforcement of Islamic law impacted many people's pockets. A purported descendant of the renown Sa'd ad-Din, the Sultan Abu Bakr, did not find it difficult to rise rebellion against the Emir.[51] He recruited Somalis and waged war against Harar.

When the Emir was killed and his government was overthrown, Imam Ahmad Gran and some of the Emir's other knights fled to the countryside. Instead of fading into obscurity, he began establishing his military legend,

---

[49] 'Arabfaqīh, Shihāb al-Dīn Aḥmad ibn 'Abd al-Qādir, and Pankhurst, Richard. *The Conquest of Abyssinia: 16th Century*. Tsehai Publishers & Distributors, 2003, p. 11.

[50] Ibid., 9.

[51] Ibid.

defending the honor of his Muslim brothers and sisters against plunder by nearby Christians.[52]

Emerging as a natural leader, Imam Gran was able to mobilize a force capable of retaliating against the Christian incursion. His victory against the Christians won him fame among the region's Muslims. His victory also drove fear into the heart of the new Sultan, who fled Harar with his Somali army. Over the next few years, the Sultan and the Imam battled for supremacy over the region. On the eve of an epic battle between their two forces, Muslim elders in the region managed to mediate between the two leaders and negotiate a peace treaty.

Following the mediation, he met with the Sultan who had amassed "a vast army from the country of the Somalis and beyond."[53] The Imam was not afraid. It is said:

> "A swarm of bees flew by, like a black cloud that overshadowed his head, until it concealed the eye of the sun from the place called Samanjud to the house of the sultan. Upon the imam's entering the Sultan's presence they greeted each other and exchanged pleasantries. In the meantime the swarm of bees remained at the door, until the imam Ahmad withdrew, whereupon the bees swarmed above his head, causing harm to no one, until he reached his home. The swarm then returned to the tree. This was a portent for the imam,

---

[52] Ibid., 11.

[53] Ibid., 17.

being good news to him from God the Most High."[54]

News of the incident with the bees spread throughout the countryside and the Imam's legend grew as he won the hearts and minds of the people. Meanwhile, increased tensions between the Imam and the Sultan, including an attempt on the Imam's life, resulted in Ahmad Gran eventually killing the Sultan. He began his reign over Harar at that moment, wisely appointing the Sultan's brother as an administrator. Imam Ahmad Gran was planning a bigger fight – he would conquer the entire realm of Ethiopia!

IMAM AHMAD GRAN VS. ETHIOPIA

The chronicle of Imam Ahmad Gran, the famous Futah Al Habasa states:

> "In the time of Sa'd ad-Din, and in the time of those who governed Harar after him, and even up to the time of Garad Abun, the infidels [Christians] made incursions into the country of the Muslims and laid it waste many times; so that some of the Muslim towns even paid them the karaj [tax]. This was the situation until the imam Ahmad ruled."[55]

In the time of Ahmad Gran, the goodwill between Christians and Muslims had deteriorated. The enormous

---

[54] 'Arabfaqīh, Shihāb al-Dīn Aḥmad ibn 'Abd al-Qādir, and Pankhurst, Richard. *The Conquest of Abyssinia: 16th Century*. Tsehai Publishers & Distributors, 2003, p. 18.

[55] Ibid., 22.

mobile tent cities of the Imperial court exacted a heavy toll on the population as it moved through the countryside collecting tributes and taxes, and subduing rebellions. Some of the powerful Christian kings, subjects of the Emperor, would also launch attacks into Muslim territory for slaves or supplies. The Muslims outside the reach of the Emir and his knights were at the mercy of these raids, so many Muslim peoples paid tribute to the Imperial throne for protection.

Ironically, Christians did not pose the gravest danger for these Muslims. Other Muslims did. Lacking a central authority, Muslim society, like all others, was full of power struggles and intrigue.

Imam Ahmad Gran was determined to unify Ethiopia's Muslims and to avenge the wrongs committed against Islam by Christian overlords. Greatly disgusted by the situation, he began short incursions into Christian villages, even ordering their churches destroyed, such as the church named Zaharaq, belonging to the ancient kings, which he burned to the ground. This pattern continued with all churches encountered.

Ethiopia burned. The earlier kindness paid to Islam by a Christian king was forgotten.

Imam Ahmad Gran's Jihad threatened the traditional balance of power between Christian Ethiopia and her Muslim residents. Before Harar's famous high walls were constructed, Imam Ahmad Gran organized a militant confederation of Somali warriors and other Islamic tribes. He then devastated Ethiopia from 1528-1542, starting with his small raids. However, after consolidating his power with Adal, another Muslim stronghold, he expanded his military campaign.

He was not alone.

THE ARMIES OF AHMAD GRAN

Imam Ahmad Gran's armies marched across Ethiopia with impunity. Village by village, they brought the mountainous terrain, still lush with vegetation and wildlife in the sixteenth century, under their control. During one march, his troops witnessed a "cloud of dust… filling the sky so that they could not see the mountains or the trees for the amount of dust." At first glance they thought it was the armies of the Christian king pursuing them but scouts soon informed them that the "dust cloud [was] not caused by a troop of infidels, but by the tramping of herds of elephants and wild antelopes."[56]

Ethiopia was not rich in animals and vegetation alone. The land was also abundant in gold, silver and precious stones. Being a people staunch in their spiritual faith, Ethiopians continued the Hebraic tradition of storing wealth in their houses of worship. This wealth, known throughout the realm, likely motivated the Imam's desire to decimate the churches as well as the desires of thousands of Mujahidin (guerilla warriors) who reported to Harar to answer the war cry. The spoils found upon pillaging those holy places helped fund the war effort.

The Somali tribes were the first to answer the call. "They encamped in a place called Qāsa in the heights above the valley of Harar. They showed off their equipment and their weapons, and paraded their horses."[57]

It was not long before the Muslims lined up on the battlefield against their Judeo-Christian nemesis. The

---

[56] Ibid., 40-41.

[57] Ibid., 43.

Muslim chronicles described their enemies noting, "Their adornments were unmistakable. With their banners raised aloft, they raced like a lighted flame, protected by coats of mail like David's, by obstructive helmets. In their hands were razor sharp swords and piercing spears."[58]

The Christians' razor sharp swords and spears would not save them from defeat. Imam Ahmad Gran's stunning victories against a much more powerful adversary continued to spread through the Muslim world. In one battle, "He killed so vast a number of them in the middle of the river that the river water was turned red by the blood."[59] A multitude of faithful Muslims poured into Harar to participate in the Jihad.

One thing that Imam Ahmad Gran relied on was the pan-Islamic importance of his city. He was able to employ Arab mercenaries from Mocha and benefited from the assistance of Yemeni Turks who arrived with a team of trained Janissaries well equipped with artillery.[60] The Janissaries were the special forces of the Ottoman Empire, the strongest sons of non-Muslim subjects who were taken into custody and given to Turkish families. These well-disciplined young boys were schooled in the ways of war and in Islam. The Ottomans used them to form the first standing army since the Roman Empire. Known for their use of firearms, and generally being a terror on the battlefield, the Janissaries formed an elite class within the Ottoman Empire, more than willing to bring their skills to Ethiopia in service to Imam Ahmad Gran's Jihad.

---

[58] Ibid., 60.

[59] Ibid., 66.

[60] Burton, Richard F. *First Footsteps in East Africa or an Exploration of Harar.* 1856. Echo Library, 2006, p. 180.

THE BATTLE OF SEMBERA KORE, 1529 CE

Early one morning, both Muslim and Christian troops arose to recite their respective morning prayers. By midday the two armies were facing each other for the Battle of Sembera Kore. The tide would be in favor of the Muslims that day.

An alleged former Christian member among Imam Ahmad Gran's followers recalled:

> "The number of the king's cavalry that took part in the engagement of Sembera Kore was sixteen thousand knights, each of whom had a mount from the Arabian sea-coast. The foot-soldiers, more than two-hundred-thousand of them, these carried shields and bows, that is to say, they were archers with poisoned arrows; and they carried glistening spears. And as far the Abyssinian cavalry, their forces were so vast as to be innumerable and uncountable. They blended one with the other like a well compacted construction with no spaces left between its various parts."[61]

The battle that ensued was bloody and there was great slaughter on both sides. Three thousand Somalis died at the hands of the house of David.[62] It is said:

> "...the dust clouds grew so dense that none of the Muslims could recognize his

---

[61] 'Arabfaqīh, Shihāb al-Dīn Aḥmad ibn 'Abd al-Qādir, and Pankhurst, Richard. *The Conquest of Abyssinia: 16th Century*. Tsehai Publishers & Distributors, 2003, p. 74.

[62] Ibid., 82.

companion, and none of the infidels could recognize his companion; nor could brother see brother."

A witness remembered one instance where:

"The patrician was wearing protective armour, but the sword sliced through the armour and coat of mail, and cut him in half.[63] The top half flew to the side while the other half remained on the horse, and finally tumbled off."[64]

It was stated that, "Around ten-thousand of the distinguished people from Tegre were killed."[65] When the dust settled:

"The Muslims collected booty of horses, swords, chain-mail and weapons of war so numerous as to be uncountable. They captured one of the most distinguished patricians, Takla Madhen, the brother-in-law of the king whom they took with them to their own country, whence he was ransomed for five-hundred ounces of red gold. Then the imam turned round and returned to his city of Harar, happy, rejoicing, victorious, triumphant, wearing the victor's crown, exultant, in the course of the month of Rajab in that year."[66]

---

[63] A patrician is an aristocrat or nobleman.

[64] 'Arabfaqīh, Shihāb al-Dīn Aḥmad ibn 'Abd al-Qādir, and Pankhurst, Richard. *The Conquest of Abyssinia: 16th Century*. Tsehai Publishers & Distributors, 2003, p. 83.

[65] Ibid., 85.

[66] Ibid., 86.

After each of his military campaigns, Imam Ahmad Gran would return to Harar, horses overflowing with the spoils of war. No doubt, this helped to spread Harar's fame throughout the Muslim world. Before each campaign, the tribes would camp outside the city with banners blowing unfurled in the wind. Thus, the legend of Imam Ahmad Gran grew, and he flourished.

THE PERSONAL ARMY OF AHMAD GRAN

The Imam reserved the strongest and bravest men for his own army, which was described by Islamic chroniclers as consisting of "men of strength and valour who were nicknamed 'The Sea,' because of the number of their swords."[67] Feeling destined to conquer the whole realm of Ethiopia, "[he] swore an oath that either he would not return from the country of the Christians, or he would die a martyr."

By 1528, Imam Ahmad Gran had taken possession of Shoa and overrun the Amhara tribe as his power grew with each stunning victory. By 1529, his armies were hunting the remnants of the Christian Ethiopian Empire. The Muslim armies, emboldened by such success, continue to plunder what they could. "Small and great among the Muslims became wealthy, and there was no longer any poverty amongst them,"[68] the records state. Imam Ahmad Gran used this considerable, newfound wealth to relentlessly strengthen his Jihad, like when "he sent to Zayla to have weapons of war, swords and the like, procured for him. He also ordered them to buy for him

---

[67] Ibid., 125.

[68] Ibid., 167.

some cannon[s] because he wanted to take them with him on the raid into the Abyssinia. They bought him what he desired and brought back to him seven cannon[s]."[69]

For the most part, the Imam's troops remained loyal to his policies, such as that of destroying churches. On one occasion, when a soldier was found negotiating peace with the monks of a church, he was overruled by a fellow warrior who proceeded to burn the church, justifying his action by saying, "The imam did not command us to do anything but burn it down. He did not commission us to make peace for the sake of treasure."[70] Upon hearing about the disagreement between his soldiers, the Imam stated, "There was nothing wrong in burning it down. After all, wasn't *burning it down* what I ordered you to do, from the very outset – since it meant much more to them than anything else?"[71]

THE DESTRUCTION OF THE MAKANA SELASSIE

One of Christian Ethiopia's major losses was the destruction of the royal church at Bet Amhara. Had it survived to the present day, or even to 1892, it might have been named one of the wonders of the world. The church was named Makana Selassie, meaning *house of the trinity*, and was described glowingly:

> "There was a church in Bet Amhara that had no peer in Abyssinia. King Nā'od [Zara Yaqob], the father of king Wanag

---

[69] Ibid., 122.

[70] Ibid., 192.

[71] Ibid.

Sagad had built it. He exhausted himself in its construction, in its planning and in every detail of the work. He adorned it with gold, and spent thirteen years in its construction. He never saw the work completed, because he died after thirteen years. His son Wanag Sagad [Emperor Lebna Dengal] became heavily involved in it and took over its construction, after him. He took more pains over it than his father. He spent twenty-five years until he had completed it. It was entirely plated in gold leaf; it blazed like a fire. He made for it vessels of gold and silver. Its breath was one-hundred cubits, its length was one-hundred cubits and its topmost height was one-hundred-and-fifty cubits: wholly covered in gold, inlaid with gems, pearls and corals."[72]

The Imam was stunned by Makana Selassie's beauty and grandeur when he first encountered it, "almost blinded by its dazzling brilliance" and "stupefied by the workmanship."[73] Stupefying workmanship would not save the historic church in the end. True to form, Imam Ahmad Gran plundered and burned it to the ground. It was never to be seen by future generations, among whom would be the mother of the baby boy born near Harar. Although she herself was born in the same region where the church was located, never would she get the chance to lay eyes on that wonderful church whose glory survived only in the writings of Arab invaders.

---

[72] Ibid., 220-221.

[73] Ibid., 246-247.

Imam Ahmad Gran's legendary hatred for Christians – he even killed the famous Ethiopian monk, Gabriel, with his own hands[74] – intensified the passion of his armies. A great deal of Ethiopia's history was lost in all the plunder and pillaging. Important manuscripts were burned and artifacts destroyed. In the end, Gran the left-handed left behind a legacy of Muslim strength and dominance over Christianity in Ethiopia. Even the baby boy, as a man long after 1892, would mention in his memoirs the name of "Ahmed Gran [who] emerged from the east of Ethiopia" to do irreparable damage to the "history and culture" of the empire.[75]

Fearing the fall of Zion, the Christian Emperor was forced to seek support from the Portuguese, who were searching for gold and a mythical Christian king to help them to contain the spreading Muslim threat in Europe. (Recent Moorish conquest was still fresh in the Portuguese's minds.) They landed at the port of Massawa on February 19, 1541, and were welcomed by the forces of Emperor Asnaf Sagad I, also known as Gelawdewos.

The Portuguese had arrived in the midst of an epic Jihad. The modern military equipment they brought, which included 400 musketeers, helped to balance the scales for Christian Ethiopia against the Imam's Ottoman Empire-supported forces. On April 1, 1542, the Portuguese and Imam Ahmad Gran's forces faced each other on the battlefield. In a twist of history, the originators

---

[74] Burton, Richard F. *First Footsteps in East Africa or an Exploration of Harar.* 1856. Echo Library, 2006, p. 130.

[75] Selassie, Haile, I. *My Life and Ethiopia's Progress: The Autobiography of Emperor Haile Sellassie I, King of Kings, Lord of Lords, Conquering Lion of Judah,* vol. 1. Frontline Distribution International, 1999, pp. 81-82

of the trans-Atlantic slave trade stood beside what would be the only unconquered African empire.

It was not long before they engaged an incredible Islamic force on the battlefield. Noting the involvement of the Portuguese, the Imam was sure to arrange for reinforcements from Arabia and the Ottoman Empire. Some 2000 musketeers answered the call from Arabia and 900 highly trained soldiers arrived from the Ottoman Empire.[76] The Muslim world had decided that Ethiopia should become its possession.

The Islamic world's investment in Jihad in Ethiopia initially yielded results as the Portuguese commander was taken captive in a battle and later killed. However, Ethiopia never depended on foreigners for their independence. Ethiopian forces rallied, along with the surviving Portuguese soldiers, and eventually turned the tide.

Imam Ahmad Gran was killed at the Battle of Wayna Daga on February 21, 1543. It was rumoured that he was killed by a Portuguese solider who charged through the Muslim front lines and managed to shoot the Imam to avenge for the death of his famous commander, Cristóvão da Gama.[77] Once word spread on the battlefield that Imam Ahmad Gran had died, his army scattered to the winds.

---

[76] Whiteway, R.S. *The Portuguese Expedition to Abyssinia in 1541-1543 as Narrated by Castanhoso*. Hakluyt Society, 1902, p. 41.

[77] Meredith, Martin. The Fortunes of Africa: A 5000-Year History of Wealth, Greed, and Endeavour. PublicAffairs, 2014, ch. 11.

northern, southern and western Africa. The anti-slavery movement was gaining popularity in Europe and the abolishment of slavery was a frequent sentiment in foreign conversations about Ethiopia. Europe was using the fight against slavery as a pretext to annex African kingdoms. Slavery was still a part of day-to-day reality in Ethiopia and the baby boy's father was committed to ending the institution on Ethiopia's terms.[80] He was sharp and had no illusions about Europe's love for Africa or Africans.

Ethiopia was a target in 1892. Beyond its slowly expanding borders, a looming threat was closing in on the realm. European nations had promised themselves a divided Africa at the conference in Berlin but independent Ethiopia was in the way of their master plan. Since they viewed Africans as inferior beings, all Ethiopians – Christians and Muslims alike – were seen as chattel waiting to be ruled over. Regardless of religion, things would not fare well should the imperial government, including the baby boy's father as foreign minister and governor of Harar, fail to overcome the peril on the horizon.

EUROPE AND AFRICA

The historical relationship between Europe and Africa was not always antagonistic, nor was there always a master and chattel dynamic. Ethiopians, in particular, did not feel inferior in any way to Europeans. Shortly before the baby boy was born, his father traveled to renowned

---

[80] Marcus, Harold G. *The Life and Times of Menelik II: Ethiopia 1844-1913*. Red Sea Press, 1995, p. 73.

cities in Europe, carefully observing the technological advancements made there during the centuries of Ethiopia's isolation. His awe was undeniable but such sights did not shake his world view. He was taught that human life began in Ethiopia and that Adam, the first man, was an Ethiopian. Many educated Ethiopians were taught that it was African culture that shaped the European gentiles and changed Europe's conception of itself.

After the fall of Rome in 410 CE, Europe was dominated by a foreign religion: Christianity. Its rise meant that history as recorded in the Hebrew Bible began to be prioritized over their own stories and the legacy of the ancient European tribes soon receded into the background. One by one, the mighty gods of Europe were defeated by the Christ of Nazareth. Thor and Odin fell. Abandinus and Latis were forgotten. Zeus and Jupiter were ditched. Priests and scholars manipulated the stories of the ancient Hebrews and Egyptians, and taught that they were about Europeans.

The mighty Roman empire no longer worshipped Jupiter. Instead, it rebranded itself under the banner of the Catholic (meaning *universal*) Church. The headquarters of this new religious organization, called the Vatican, asserted that the throne of Peter (an apostle of the anointed messiah, or Christ, Jesus) was the throne of supreme authority until the Christ returned to Earth. It also asserted that Peter's throne was located in Rome and his representative would be the Pope. Thus, the Catholic Church became the central, spiritual shadow government of the rising European superpowers, influencing the affairs of all her obedient subject nations. Colonialism and imperialism became the vehicles to spread this interpretation of the "good news" to the so-called "heathen" masses of Africa.

THE RISE OF THE MOORS

In order to maintain its iron grip, the Catholic Church forbade education among the working masses of Europe, plunging the continent into a period of darkness known as the Dark Ages. It was an era of the church's greatest power. Ironically, the first serious challenge to the supreme power of the Pope came from Africa. In the 7th century, shortly after Ethiopia gave the first Muslims sanctuary in her holy mountains, a tidal wave of African and Arab Muslims invaded southern Europe and turned things upside down.

In some European circles, the word "Moor" was synonymous with "dark-skinned African." William Shakespeare would write Othello, his famous interpretation of *Un Capitano Moro (A Moorish Captain)*, in 1603. Othello was the story of a black general's love affair with a wealthy European white woman. The popular play was written long after the Moors left Europe and illustrated some of the Europeans' perceptions of their Muslim invaders.

Muslim Moors from Morocco conquered Catholic Spain and they had no intention of slowing down their expansion. This was cause for concern among the neighboring Christian states whose southern borders were suddenly threatened by the ambitious generals pushing their invasion north. After some time, the northern advance hit a wall when the Catholic Franks were able to defeat the Moors at the Battle of Tours in October of 731 CE, containing the spread of Islam in Europe. However, the Moors managed to maintain their stronghold in Spain for a long time and there was no way to stop their cultural influence from there. They proceeded to leave an indelible mark on Europe. The Moors' love for education broke the Catholic Church's stranglehold on information, eventually giving rise to the European Renaissance.

THE PROTESTANT REFORMATION

The first European power to break away from Papal influence was that of the Germans. It was fitting that they would be the ones to break the spiritual and imperial monopoly of the Roman Pope since German tribes were previously responsible for ending the former Roman Empire. The spiritual rebellion against the Catholic Church, known as the Protestant Reformation, began with the rise of Martin Luther in 1517 CE. This coincided with the death of Imam Ahmad Gran's father-in-law, the governor of Adal, which sent Harar and Adal into anarchy. While Harar struggled with the chaos, Martin Luther's uprising in Europe culminated with the rise of the Church of England. The head of the Church of England, King Henry VIII, officially severed ties with the Catholic Church in 1534. As Imam Ahmad Gran rampaged through the Ethiopian highlands slaughtering the realms Christian soldiers and burning her churches, King Henry VIII was cutting ties with his Catholic overlords. This split would prove monumental to world history as England soon emerged as the world superpower.

EUROPEAN EXPLORATION AND CONQUEST

Europe had already begun its age of exploration shortly before the German-instigated period of religious upheaval in 1517. In 1492, the African Moors of Morocco were defeated at the Battle of Granada by Europe's most powerful queen and servant of the Roman Pope, Queen Isabella. With Queen Isabella's blessings and funding, Christopher Columbus embarked on his fateful journey to the Western Hemisphere that same year. While Africans had long known about the lands across the Atlantic, for Columbus, he had discovered a new world. Columbus's voyage would spark a European race to exploit the rich resources of the new world.

By 1555, seven years after the death of Imam Ahmad Gran, on the other side of Africa, the first Africans were brought to England as slaves. John Hawkins, an English businessman and sailor, ran the first commercial operation that year, making substantial profit from the trade of African lives. He gained fame as a slaver after he violently captured Africans from Sierra Leone and transported them to the Spanish colonies in the new world for trade. In return for the terrorized and enslaved Africans, Hawkins received pearls, hides and sugar from the Spanish. Wealth and prestige were the result of his terrorist mission and the Queen of England, Elizabeth I, wanted in on the spoils. His subsequent voyages were sponsored by the Queen, who ensured that he was well supplied with guns, supplies and ships. For his loyalty, John Hawkins was gifted with a coat of arms depicting a bound enslaved African. Millions of Africans paid the price for their unholy alliance.

ARAB SLAVE TRADE

Certainly, the English were not the first Europeans to enter the trade. The Moorish impact in Europe, and subsequent Renaissance, had caused an increase in European wealth and power, and this newly acquired power led to a thirst for African inspired luxury.

Subsequently, it led to an insatiable appetite for free labor through the brutal conquest of new lands. Historically, the majority of slaves in Europe had originated in Bosnia. The word "slave" was derived from the ethnic Slavs who inhabited the area. Between 730 CE and 1000 CE, the trade in enslaved Europeans flourished and it continued until it was crushed when the region was conquered in 1463 by the Ottomans during the rise of the Ottoman Empire. With the European source of slaves cut off, the stage was set for Africa to become the replacement.

It was the Muslim Moors who introduced previously unimaginable wealth to Europe and it was to the Muslim world that Europe would look to for another source of people to enslave. The enterprising Arabs had long established an extensive African slave trade centuries prior and, in some instances, served as the middlemen ushering Europe into the trade.

Roughly 200 years after the Prophet Mohammed sent his followers to Africa for refuge, the Arabs began looking to Africa for human slaves. From the 9th century onward, it is estimated that they enslaved millions of Africans between the north and east coasts of Africa as well as the Middle East.[81] Between 650 CE and 1600 CE, an estimated average of 5,000 Africans per year were kidnapped and enslaved by the Arabs. Another 1.4 million Africans were shipped out of Africa by the Arabs from 1600 CE to 1800 CE.[82] The trade proved lucrative and slave markets sprang up in various Muslim settlements. It was at a Muslim-controlled slave market where the first

---

[81] "Africa | Focus on the Slave Trade." *BBC News*, BBC, 3 Sept. 2001, http://news.bbc.co.uk/2/hi/africa/1523100.stm.

[82] Pavlu, George. "Recalling Africa's Harrowing Tale of Its First Slavers – the Arabs." *New African Magazine*, 31 July 2018, https://newafricanmagazine.com/16616/.

recorded Africans enslaved by Europeans were reportedly purchased by servants of Catholic Portugal, and with that began the arguably ugliest phase of recorded human history.

THE TRANS-ATLANTIC SLAVE TRADE

Slavery is older than written history. It had long been a feature of many ancient societies but the Europeans' enslavement of Africans took on a different quality than all the previous forms of slavery. The Europeans' insatiable demand for free labor made them justify the dehumanization of the enslaved and create a new trans-Atlantic slave trade. The theory of white genetic superiority, and that Africans were lower than animals and possessed no souls, gained popularity around this time.[83] The foundation of the trans-Atlantic slave trade was based on this race theory, also referred to as White Supremacy. The Moorish conquest of Europe likely implanted the seed of fear and hatred against dark-skinned people.

Whatever the impetus, there was no hope of being integrated into the tribe that enslaved you, as had been the common practice. There was no assimilation of any kind. Black skin granted a perpetual status as a slave. Africans were to be treated only as subhuman chattel, unworthy of justice.

---

[83] Welsing, Frances Cress. *The Isis Papers: The Keys to the Colors*. Third World Press, 1991, p. 7.

IN SEARCH OF LEGEND

Prior to the Moors' expulsion from Spain, many in Europe had heard tales of a Christian king in Africa by the mythical name of Prester John. No doubt, gradual whispers of a Christian stronghold in Africa surfaced following Ethiopia's 7th century act of kindness to the first Muslims. Places like Portugal would have been hearing rumors via Rome.

Portugal's Prince Henry, who was then looking for allies to fight against the Muslims, who were close to his borders, set out to determine whether the legend of a Christian king and kingdom in Africa were true. If so, this African king could give Christian Europe the strategic advantage it needed. He could attack the Muslims from the south while the Europeans attacked from the north. That was the prevailing thought among the Europeans who were passionate about finding the Christian African king.

Prince Henry's motives were neither purely defensive nor patriotic. He was a shrewd businessman interested in increasing his wealth and he was confident that financing expeditions to that mysterious land mass, Africa, would help him achieve this. Gold was already making its way from that continent into Europe, intriguing the latter's ruling elite of which Prince Henry was a vanguard member. In 1441, he was quick to mobilize two of his employees who sailed to the African coast in search of the mythical Christian king and the gold.

The prince got more than he bargained for. His men returned not only with the anticipated gold but also with twelve enslaved Africans purchased from Muslims at a slave trading market in Cape Bianco, in present day

76

Mauritania. While the African Moors ruled next door in Spain, Portugal went on the offensive against the people of the continent that had brought conquerors to Europe's shores and managed to bring enslaved Africans into Europe. By the 1480s, the search for the Christian king was put on the back burner. The Portuguese were busy making fortunes from gold and enslaved humans from places like Senegal and Ghana. Two-thirds of the world's gold supply came from West Africa during the Middle Ages.[84]

THE REAL PRESTER JOHN

Prince Henry failed to locate the mythical Christian kingdom and its legendary king. His failure did not mean that the myth of a Christian king was completely false. At the same time that Portugal put the search for the legendary Christian king on the back burner, the real life Christian throne in Ethiopia did not fail to make its presence known to Europe. Indeed, there was a Christian king in Africa, already a legend in his own land, claiming descent from King David, King Solomon, the Queen of Sheba and Menelik I. His name was Emperor Zara Yaqob.

Emperor Zara Yaqob, full of religious zeal, was trained in the art of war. He proudly ruled Ethiopia since 1434, though formally crowned in Axum in 1436, continuing a tradition of his ancestors - a tradition of warrior kings. More than that, he was also trained in a monastery and became a writer of religious works. He was a priestly warrior king. Emperor Zara Yaqob was a

---

[84] Pakenham, Thomas. *The Scramble for Africa: White Man's Conquest of the Dark Continent from 1876 to 1912.* 1992. Perennial, 2003, p. 16.

powerful ruler who exercised his power skillfully among the global powers of his day.

In 1441, the same year that Prince Henry's servants initially set out to West Africa, Emperor Zara Yaqob heard that the Sultan Jaqmaq destroyed a Christian monastery in Egypt. He wrote a letter of protest to the Sultan, informing him that Muslims were treated fairly in his realm, adding that, as Emperor of Ethiopia, he had the power to divert the waters of the Nile river and wipe Egypt off the map![85] Having no intention of using his realm's limited resources to do such a thing, the pragmatic and cunning Zara Yaqob made it clear in the same communication that he would not take such an extreme action due to the potential human suffering. Yet, his statement served its intended purpose: to make clear to the Sultan that, powerful as he may be, Egypt exists because Ethiopia allows it to exist. The Sultan responded by sending gifts to the Emperor, though he refused to rebuild the monasteries.

The same year, Zara Yaqob also sent a delegation of Ethiopian clerics to the Council of Florence in Rome.[86] On August 26, 1441, his clerics arrived to join their Christian Orthodox brothers from Greece, Turkey, Russia and Armenia. The representatives of these Eastern Orthodox Churches were concerned about the expanding Muslim armies threatening their borders. The Catholic Church, by this time a major power, dangled the hope of financial and military assistance in front of them and they allegedly signed an agreement admitting the Filioque, purgatory, and the Papal primacy. This included the

---

[85] Tamrat, Taddesse. *Church and State in Ethiopia, 1270-1527.* Oxford: Clarendon Press, 1972, pp. 262–263.

[86] Silverberg, Robert. *The Realm of Prester John.* Ohio University Press, 1996, p. 189.

Ethiopian delegation, although it is unlikely that they had Emperor Zara Yaqob's permission.

It is clear that the declaration had no effect on Ethiopia. Ethiopians continued to practice their ancient form of Christianity without desire to follow decrees issued from Rome. They were unaware that their realm was causing waves in distant Europe, where they now had confirmation of a Christian King of Kings – the real Prester John! This did nothing but inflame rumors of the African Christian empire. Hearing descriptions of some of Ethiopia's larger churches, including those built by Emperor Zara Yacoq himself, covered with gold plating and adorned with precious gems, could have only increased the Europeans' yearning to see the legendary highlands themselves.

THE SCOURGE OF SLAVERY

The Roman Catholic Church's first priority had nothing to do with the daily religious practice of the Ethiopians. Following the success of Prince Henry, enslaved Africans were flowing by the thousands, not only into Portugal but into several European countries. The church's loyal subjects were paying their tithes and building more churches with the wealth accumulated through the free labor. This only increased the influence of Rome.

The wealth generated from African lives encouraged and funded more European exploration. The more Europe plundered, the richer they became. The Portuguese, meanwhile, ever the faithful servants of the Vatican, reignited their hope of locating the kingdom of Prester John. The knowledge of the Christian kingdom had been confirmed by the Ethiopian delegation to Rome and it was only a matter of time before they confirmed the delegates' stories for themselves. In 1520, they sailed around the southern tip of Africa and visited the highlands of Ethiopia for the first time. This was during the reign of Zara Yaqob's son, Lebna Dengel, who they helped to fight Imam Ahmad Gran and preserve Christianity in the African highlands.

It was also the Portuguese who first discovered for Europe the way to India and China around the tip of South Africa. With the riches from their African plunder, the Europeans were able to fund their voyages to India and China and load their ships with exotic commodities. One by one, the European powers joined the trans-Atlantic slave trade, empowered with a growing knowledge of world geography and ocean navigation. One by one, African peoples fell victim to these external forces that were tearing their land and ancient ways of life apart. The trade continued for hundreds of years and all of Europe benefited in some way from the spoils.

SLAVERY IN THE NEW WORLD

As Europeans expanded their global footprint, slavery was established in the Americas. The historic Spanish-funded voyage of Christopher Columbus created a Spanish foothold in the new world. In 1517, while the Catholic Church was reeling from the rebellion of Martin Luther, a Spanish Catholic priest, Las Casas, who was stationed in Jamaica, wrote a letter to Spain requesting African slaves to replace the murdered Taino population.[87]

---

[87] Sherlock, Philip and Bennett, Hazel. *The Story of the Jamaican People*. Ian Randle Publishers, 1998, p. 74.

His request led to the Spanish crown sanctioning the importation of 4,000 Africans from West Africa. The first recorded Africans in Jamaica arrived in 1509 as servants of their enslavers. By 1534, the population had grown to include 30 Africans kidnapped from the Canary Islands, who were knowledgeable in sugar production. Sugar would prove to be the commodity that would attract European business interest and shift the balance from African enslaved servants in favor of African enslaved field laborers.

The first census ever taken in Jamaica, in 1611 by the Spanish, revealed 523 Spainiards, 558 slaves and 107 free blacks, 74 Taino herdsmen, and 75 newcomers.[88]

The small numbers of Spanish forces led to the Spanish defeat by England. On July 1, 1655, England formally took possession of the island. The Spanish had not managed to generate much wealth and the limited resources that the English managed to plunder were the results of the works of the Africans living on the island. Some of the Africans managed to escape the Spanish and join with already established Indigenous settlements in the mountains of Jamaica. With the coming of the British, their numbers increased.

A British officer described the situation as follows:

> "The Negroes...live by themselves in several parties, and near our quarters, and do very often, as our men go into the woods to seek provisions, destroy and kill them with their lances. We now and then find one or two of our men killed, stripped and naked, and

---

[88] Ibid.

these rogues begin to be bold, our English rarely or seldom killing any of them."[89]

With internal conflict as well as the threat of war from Spain and other European competitors in the Caribbean, the British turned to English pirates such as Henry Morgan to defend their Caribbean interests. Henry Morgan was so effective in protecting British interest that he was appointed as governor general in Jamaica. Jamaica became a mecca for pirates from all over the Caribbean and the town of Port Royal was known as the wickedest city on Earth until it sank in the infamous earthquake of 1692. The earthquake may well have been divine retribution for the tortured souls of Africans who had to endure the lawless society.

Between 1655 and 1807, over 747,506 kidnapped Africans were imprisoned and enslaved in Jamaica.[90] In 1787, the white population was 25,000 and the African population was 210,894. The philosophy of the English slavers was to maximize production by working their slaves to death and importing more as needed:

> "It is evident that few plantations could remain productive for long without imports for replacement. It is paradoxical that high profit were not necessarily incompatible with high mortality not a few contemporaries pointed out, as did Lord Brougham, that so long as a slave market exists, men find their profit in working out a certain number of their slaves, and supplying the blacks by purchase rather than by breeding. Slavery, as a profitable

---

[89] Ibid., 80.

[90] Ibid., 93.

institution, thus depended on the constate recruitment of cheap labour by importation from Africa."[91]

The success of the English slave plantation in Jamaica ensured that it would spread to England's other colonies. By the 1700s, enslaved Africans were pouring into "South Carolina from Barbados."[92] The South Carolina slave codes were largely imported from Barbados in the Caribbean and laid some of the legal foundations that would justify the continued enslavement of Africans into the modern era.

By the 1800s, over 12 million recorded Africans were taken from their homeland to the New World. Millions more were transported through the black market and the Arab slave trade. Countless others perished in resistance or during transport.

Africans, no longer seen as human, were paraded around Europe as sideshow attractions, such as Sara Bartman who, in 1810, was brought to England so that the European population could stare at her bottom. In 1875, as Egyptian forces occupied Harar, a popular Nubian exhibit (a zoo-like attraction featuring live Africans) toured throughout France. The popular culture of Europe became fascinated with Africa and the demand for African colonies, and the potential wealth they could provide, grew among both the business class and common people of Europe.

---

[91] Ibid.

[92] James, Winston. *Holding Aloft the Banner of Ethiopia: Caribbean Radicalism in Early Twentieth-Century America*. Verso, 1998, p. 11.

THE REIGN OF BISMARCK

So great was the demand for enslaved people that it almost led the European powers to war among themselves. Ironically, the only thing that prevented an all-out conflict over African resources in Europe was a hulking figure of a man, described as demonic by his contemporaries: none other than the infamous Otto von Bismarck.

Bismarck had proven his ability to win decisive victories on the battlefield as well as bring together the German tribes and kingdoms. Thus, he emerged as the leader of a unified Germany, the most powerful European nation since the Roman empire. It was the dream of generations of Germans and Bismarck made it real. He did not fear war but he saw that he could manage the Scramble for Africa differently. He had a plan.

POST-OTTOMAN EMPIRE HARAR

Bismarck's plan evolved into the Berlin Conference. Slavery had become unpopular and expensive with the rising number of rebellions by Africans in the colonies, so Europe needed another strategy to sustain their newly attained levels of wealth. Spain ended slavery in 1820 and France ended slavery in all their colonies in 1847. England ended slavery in 1834 after sustaining major losses in Jamaica as a result of the Sam Sharpe rebellion in 1831-1832. The Berlin Conference would allow Europe's powers to devise the best way to continue to exploit Africa's resources.

While Bismarck and his European contemporaries planned and plotted the future of Africa at the conference in Berlin, Harar was returning to the rule of her own Harari people. In 1885, the British, after their recent conquest of Egypt, were not prepared to finance an Ethiopian city-state in the face of an emperor whose power was growing and an Oromo resistance in the surrounding countryside. Plus, the negotiations at the Berlin conference had further solidified that Ethiopia was not to be an English protectorate. When they left Harar, the powerful Harari families that ruled prior to the Ottoman/Egyptian invasion filled the vacuum and were restored to full control of the walled city.

Those families did not rule longer than two years. As it turned out, the British had made the right decision not to hold on to Harar. Shortly after their withdrawal from the city, Harar fell into the sights of a powerful adversary, who the British once assisted but could not control: Ethiopia's King of Kings, Emperor Yohannes IV.

Harar was an economic stronghold after trade expanded there during the Egyptian occupation. Emperor Yohannes IV now saw it as a priority to prevent another foreign power from controlling such a valuable city-state in the middle of his empire. Therefore, he gave his blessings to one of the kings of his realm to conquer Harar. This happened in 1887, two years after the end of the Berlin conference.

The king entrusted with accomplishing the task was one of the most powerful kings in the realm, the emperor's former schoolmate and rival, King Menelik II, the King of Shoa. King Menelik II was looking for a reason to bring Harar and its trade under his control, so he was a more than willing participant. Possessing the training of a priest, he was a warrior king at his core, and he led the battle for Harar himself.

King Menelik II organized one of the seminal battles of modern Ethiopian history with the help of his most trusted general and advisor, his younger cousin, Ras Makonnen. Aside from his tactical skills and competence, Ras Makonnen was also soon to be the father of the baby boy born fatefully in the mountains of Ejersa Goro on Harar's outskirts. The conquest of Harar and Ras Makonnen's subsequent appointment as its governor would shape both the future of Harar and the life of the baby boy himself.

CHAPTER SEVEN

King Solomon's Blood

"Judah, thou art he whom thy brethren shall praise: thy hand shall be in the neck of thine enemies; thy father's children shall bow down before thee." – **Genesis 49:8**

As Ras Makonnen paced outside the house where his son was born, he was well aware that the loyalty of Harar's inhabitants was not assured. As the new governor, a lot was riding on his success in Harar. The revenues from the city were needed to help fund the growing empire. In order to govern effectively he needed good information. Was he moving his newborn heir and wife into a dangerous situation? Could he trust the Hariri who were given positions of power? How strong was the Egyptian and Arab influence in the city? These questions and more swirled in his mind, preventing him from dwelling too long on the triumphant birth of his baby boy.

THE RAINS END THE EVIL DAYS IN HARAR

Precisely because of her strong sense of identity, rooted in faith, Harar was able to resist non-Muslim outsiders for centuries and endure the hardships of the Evil Days. In 1887, a year before the Evil Days began, Muslims lost control of the city-state for the first time in centuries. Harar's resilience was tested.

On July 23, 1892, the blood red soil of Harar was alive with color.[93] Dry patches of land transformed into red mud, then filled with gigantic puddles resembling pools of blood. Unlike in 1887, these were not actual blood from Harar's fallen soldiers but pools of life-giving water raining down from the heavens. Soon, isolated pools connected with each other and the once dry stream beds began to flow again throughout the parched countryside. The bright red streams appeared like blood rich veins coursing through a body.

The herds of wild Somali ponies that grazed atop the large plateau of the Kondudu mountain had sensed the rain hours before a drop touched the ground.[94] They now rejoiced, seemingly dancing in unison with the lightning, knowing that the much-needed rain would restore the lush green hills with yellow daisies that nourished them for generations.

The ponies were not the only elated animals. The area around Harar was rich in wildlife. Many were dispersed by the drought but returned with the coming of the rains. In 1892, Harar was still lion country where prides of the Ethiopian Black-Maned Lion reigned among the beasts in the region's unsettled areas. Numerous hyenas did their best to avoid the rarely seen kings, while gazelles, antelope, jackals and countless species of birds

---

[93] Mosley, Leonard. *Haile Selassie: The Conquering Lion.* Weidenfeld and Nicolson, 1964, p. 21.

[94] Ibid. Note that, in 1892, these animals were still hunted and tamed by the fearless youth of Harar.

time, is said to have advised the reporter to ask the women of Ethiopia questions of culture, saying that the women "know it all."[98]

THE SOLOMONIC BLOODLINE

Ras Makonnen was a nobleman with a historic bloodline. His family tree had many branches, including one of the world's most renown, though some outsiders dismissed his family history as myth. Nevertheless, none were able to disprove his tribe's claim to their famous ancestors.

Ras Makonnen, his cousin, Emperor Menelik II, and the other Rases of Shoa all traced their bloodline to Emperor Lebna Dengel, son of Emperor Zara Yacob, and to his ancestors before him, stretching back over three thousand years. These ancestors had never been conquered. They had never known the yoke of slavery by foreigners. Their DNA was that of Empress Makeda, otherwise known as the Queen of Sheba, or Queen of the South, the ancient queen of Ethiopia and Yemen. Although Empress Makeda was certainly an impressive ancestor, it was not this branch of the family tree that would become a source of controversy.

There was no controversy that Ras Makonnen's immediate and extended family, and by extension Ethiopia's Christian emperors, were known within Ethiopia and the wider region by various names. The Arabs called them *Habesh*. Within Ethiopia, different tribes and kingdoms claimed to carry the blood of the realm's ancient rulers, mainly the tribes and kingdoms of the

---

[98] Ibid.

Oromo, Amhara and Tigrayans. Most of the emperors of the realm were mixed due to intermarriage among the other tribes and kingdoms, including the Afar, Gurage and Agaw. This was common practice so that, in general, Ethiopia's tribal distinctions were more cultural than genetic.

As the fog of isolation cleared, and the reclusive realm reemerged in global consciousness, none of Ethiopia's internal tribal names would be the name used to describe Ethiopia's Emperor. The world's newspapers and radio stations would opt for a more well known tribe: The Tribe of Judah.

Christianity's conquest over the old gods of Europe meant that Europeans had reordered their entire conception of themselves around Hebrew traditions. As a result, the Hebrew monarchy and throne held a special place in European spiritual lore. Here now was a once isolated African nation living the story that the European elite had read about in the Bible. To say the least, it captured Europe's imagination and fascinated the entire Eurocentric world.

Ras Makonnen's baby boy would inherit the same legacy. He would grow up to continue the central claim of the Christian emperors – a direct, unbroken descent from the biblical King Solomon. For centuries, Ethiopia's emperors and church leaders had based the legitimacy of the Imperial throne on the very same claim.

SOLOMONIC DYNASTY IN EUROPE

Ethiopia's adversaries also made biblical claims. Europe's powerful Christian royal families shared Ethiopia's claim of descent from King Solomon and his father, King David. However, the Ethiopians considered that claim minor. Through the Kebra Nagast (or Kebra Negast) – literally, "the Glory of Kings" - they viewed European royals as descendants of the youngest son of King Solomon, while they themselves claimed descent from King Solomon's first born son. In addition, European royalty had intermarried with the Vikings and the Germanic tribes, making their claim that much weaker in the eyes of the Ethiopians.

The Jewish communities of Europe, despite persecution by Christian rulers there, had leaders who also claimed descent from the bloodline of King Solomon and his father, King David. However, they were a small scattered minority that had intermarried with Europeans and Arabs for hundreds of years. The French Rabbi Shlomo Itzhaki, born in 1040 CE in the city of Troyes, France, claimed descent from princes of Judah who were exiled in Iraq but there was no clear chain of descendants linking him to King Solomon or King David.[99] Likewise, the Jewish leadership of Spain traced their lineage to the sons of the last Davidic leader of Iraq's Jewish community, Hezekiah, who was killed in 1040 CE. These sons fled Baghdad after their father's death, moving to Spain where they intermarried with the Germanic tribes there before spreading into Portugal and France. They joined other fragmented Jewish communities in Iraq headed by families that claimed descent from King David. None of these communities had a king or a throne, nor did they control a realm.

The fact that an unconquered African empire could proudly make the claim, and possessed a king, a throne and a kingdom, rekindled the myth of Prester John while

---

[99] Epstein, Nadine. "King David's Genes." *Moment Magazine*, 2012 March-April, https://momentmag.com/king-davids-genes-2/.

simultaneously challenging the prevailing white supremacist conception of Africa in Europe. Slowly, Europeans began to travel to Ethiopia to see the mythical empire for themselves and they were in awe of what they found. In order to align the reality of Ethiopia with their worldview, they began to classify Ethiopians as "dark Caucasians." This solution allowed them to accept that dark-skinned people from Africa could unapologetically claim stewardship over the throne of King David and King Solomon.

At the onset of his time as Governor of Harar, Ras Makonnen did not care what the Europeans thought about his people. His concern was to protect Ethiopia and preserve his people's legacy in order to ensure a future for his heir, his newborn son.

threat to the monarchy, which Bismarck believed in with his whole, dark heart.

THE BISMARCK AND AFRICA

At first, Bismarck was not in favor of Germany taking African colonies. However, the wealth generated by European neighbors turned German popular opinion against his position. Forever the opportunist, he used his position as a premier statesman to convene a European conference in Berlin that would manage the division of the African continent.

Bismarck's sudden interest in Africa came as a surprise to even some close colleagues but the cunning 69-year-old chancellor had received word that Britain and France were planning to control the entire west coast of Africa and potentially impose custom duties on German traders.[104] Doing his due diligence, he discovered German traders on the ground advocating for German annexation of German-controlled ports before the other European powers, basing their request on the need to secure the "inexhaustible markets of the interior."[105] Bismarck would not allow Germany to be left out of the Scramble. On May 19, 1884, he sent secret orders for the German flag to be raised over Cameroon. Germany's men on the ground in Africa were also instructed to claim Togo and Namibia.[106]

---

[104] Pakenham, Thomas. *The Scramble for Africa: White Man's Conquest of the Dark Continent from 1876 to 1912.* 1992. Perennial, 2003, p. 204.

[105] Ibid., 206.

[106] Ibid., 201.

At the Berlin conference on November 15, 1884, Bismarck stated its goals: to spread "commerce, Christianity, and civilization." He went on to say that Europe would "promote civilization to the African natives by opening the interior of the continent to commerce..." Three major goals of the conference, according to him, were free trade for the Congo, free navigation on the Niger river and agreement on the formalities for future annexations of territory."[107]

The conference established how European countries would divide the mighty continent of Africa and Ethiopia was a slice of the cake. At the time of the conference, Ethiopia was unaware of the European treachery. In fact, the famed Ethiopian general, Ras Alula, was in the midst of war, honorably fulfilling Ethiopia's obligations under their treaty with the United Kingdom. Meanwhile, the United Kingdom was deciding the fate of Ethiopia and the rest of Africa in collusion with her European contemporaries. Thousands of kings, generals and tribal chiefs across the continent would find themselves in a similar position.

The Italians made good on their pledge at the conference by occupying the coastal port of Massawa in 1885. In January, the very same Ras Alula slaughtered an Italian battalion at Dogali. The ancient realm of Ethiopia would not be a pushover in the Scramble for Africa. Ras Alula would then go on to defeat an invading Mahdist army at the Battle of Kufit on September 23.

Meanwhile, Ras Alula's ruler, Emperor Yohannes IV, realized that Europeans were not to be trusted. Yet, he could have had no idea just how large in scope Europe's

---

[107] Ibid., 241.

plans were for his continent. Bismarck was merely one of the players positioning for Africa.

KING LEOPOLD II

The united Germany represented the pinnacle of European military and political power. However, not even the great Bismarck knew the full extent of how Europe's colonial powers were being moved by a shadowy figure not present at the conference. One of the great villains of modern history was the infamous King Leopold II, whose manipulations were crucial to the unfolding Scramble for Africa.

Leopold II was the son of Queen Victoria's dearest uncle and France's King Louis-Phillippe's oldest daughter. Belgium, his inherited kingdom, was made up of two warring tribes, the Flemish and the Wallon, and was further divided by religion as the people clung to either a liberal or catholic worldview.

Leopold II believed wholeheartedly in the power of colonialism. Having traveled to Egypt, India and China, he became assured in his desire for Belgium to have a colony, which he thought was the only way to ensure his country's wealth and prosperity.

It was a cruel twist of history when Leopold II ascended the Belgian throne due to the death of his father, King Leopold I, in 1865. That same year, the formal institution of slavery ended in the United States of America. While the world was beginning to feel shame for the subhuman bondage of Africans in slavery, Leopold II was getting ready to subjugate and kill millions of people in Africa. He saw a potential colony as not only a worthy monument for his fallen father, but also a way to enrich his royal coffers. He was not to be deterred by the fact that the Belgian government had no appetite for colonies due to the potentially enormous costs associated with maintaining them. Being one of the richest men in Europe – Leopold II increased his inherited wealth by investing in the Suez Canal - he decided to seek his own colony using his own resources. His travels served him well with global vision and his trips to Egypt opened his eyes to the future importance of the canal and the unlimited possibilities in Africa.

One thing that King Leopold II realized was that he could not demand a piece of the African cake outright and be taken seriously. Belgium did not have a military machine like that of Germany or other powers at the Berlin conference but Leopold II was a master manipulator. He would find a way to acquire territory by an appeal to all the powers. Soon, the International Association of the Congo was born and, using well paid proxies, Leopold II was able to get the support of the United States and France to back the Association as a protectorate over the Congo. The support of these respected powers would help to sway some of the other countries represented at the conference.

Bismarck did not trust Leopold II, describing him as follows:

> "...[h]is Majesty displays the pretensions and naïve selfishness of an Italian who considers that his charm and good looks will enable him to get away with anything."[108]

Realizing Bismarck's power and influence, Leopold II tried to win him over with a letter outlining his colonial ambitions. In addition to the Congo, he also made a claim

---

[108] Hochschild, Adam. *King Leopold's Ghost: A Story of Greed, Terror, and Heroism in Colonial Africa*. Houghton Mifflin, 1998, p. 83.

Stanley's meteoric rise as an explorer and "journalist" among European colonialists was inextricably linked to Ethiopia. Stanley cut his teeth in African exploration as an embedded correspondent during the British military expedition to Ethiopia in 1868. The expedition was escorted by the army of a young Ethiopian rebel claiming the Solomonic bloodline. That same young rebel would rise to become the King of Kings, Emperor Yohannes IV. At the time of the Berlin Conference, Emperor Yohannes IV was again working with the British to secure their interest against an Islamic uprising in their neighboring colony.

A young and impressionable Stanley did not know that the Ethiopians escorting the British forces would become the rulers of the realm or that his first assignment found him in the midst of a struggle of epic and historic proportions. The young prince that accompanied Stanley and company, 17 years before the conference, was seeking assistance to overthrow his predecessor, the first true Ethiopian King of Kings in hundreds of years. The Emperor that the young prince was trying to displace decided to show Europe his power by imprisoning some important British nationals. It was a decision that would change the fate of Ethiopia and Stanley would be given a front row seat.

The might of the British empire, including a regiment of East Indian war elephants, was brought to bear to retrieve her citizens. Stanley burst into global consciousness as the first person to report on Britain's adventure to mythical Ethiopia and the fall of Magdala, the Ethiopian emperor's legendary mountain stronghold. His flamboyant writing style made him a sensation in Europe.

In October or November of 1871, Stanley embarked on a journey that would cement his name. He led an expedition to recover the Scottish priest and explorer, Dr. David Livingstone. His words upon meeting Dr. Livingstone have been immortalized in history – "Dr. Livingstone, I presume." There is debate as to whether he ever uttered that statement but there is no debate that his writings on the expedition further catapulted him to fame throughout Europe.[110]

In 1873, Stanley traveled to the Ashanti region of Ghana to report on the wars there against the British. In 1874, he published his writings, *Coomassie and Magdala: The Story of Two British Campaigns in Africa*. After the death of Dr. Livingstone in 1873, Stanley saw an opportunity to continue his exploration and, with his maxim guns leading the way, found himself in the Congo. He had taken an epic journey into the heart of Africa, risking life and limb to travel from Tanzania on the east coast through the Congo to the Atlantic Ocean on the continent's west coast. Like Ethiopia, the Congo was of no interest to the British, so Stanley's dreams of a European protectorate there could not be immediately realized. That is, until he got a royal message from King Leopold II in 1878. Stanley accepted the invitation to meet him in Brussels.

By 1879, Leopold II had Stanley return to Congo under the auspices of his philanthropic association. By the time of the conference in Berlin, Stanley said the European nations reminded him of how his "black followers used to rush with gleaming knives for slaughtering game during our travels."[111] Despite the greed of his benefactors, Stanley was fully onboard. He gained renown for his inhumane,

---

[110] Jeal, Tim. *Stanley: The Impossible Life of Africa's Greatest Explorer.* Yale University Press, 2007.

[111] Hochschild, Adam. *King Leopold's Ghost: A Story of Greed, Terror, and Heroism in Colonial Africa.* Houghton Mifflin, 1998, p. 84.

bloodthirsty tactics for subduing rebellions that he encountered during his colonizing missions.

LEOPOLD II'S VISION

By May 29, 1885, King Leopold II issued a royal decree renaming his new territory the Congo Free State, but his ambitions did not end with the Congo. His vision was much larger. He dreamed to see the day when the two great rivers of Africa, the Nile and the Congo, could be linked by railway to provide smooth passage for goods and services from the east to the west coast. To this end, he sent expeditions in the early 1890s to Congo to make preparations. (One such expedition claimed an ancient copper mine of Bahr el Ghazal, Sudan as a part of Leopold II's personal possession.) About 540 Chinese workers were transported to Congo in 1892 to begin building the grand railway. Many lost their lives. in the attempt.[112] Their souls were joined by Africans brought from the Caribbean island of Barbados who, fooled into coming to the Congo, stirred up a short-lived rebellion when they learned of their destination and the reason for them being there. Two were murdered and several more injured, then the rest of them were taken to start work on the railway.

Leopold II had to endure delays before he could fully pursue his vision of controlling the trade between the Nile and the Congo rivers. For example, days before the birth of the baby boy in the highlands of Ejersa Goro, he received news in July 1892 that one of his expeditions had met with disaster. An African chief had risen up and inflicted key casualties on his team. More generally, he

---

[112] Ibid., 170.

knew he did not have the financial power or military muscle to challenge the British for Egypt – he wouldn't have known yet that Ethiopia was the source of the Nile itself.

Had King Leopold II known that Ethiopia was the source of the Nile, Ethiopia likely would have been counted among his targets but his manipulations to subdue Africans and the African continent were no match for the Almighty and the tide of history. In 1889, the young rebel who had accompanied Stanley and the British forces, before becoming a legendary outlaw (and subsequently becoming Emperor Yohannes IV), had recently died defending his nation against invaders. However, the Almighty and history would not leave Ethiopia without a ruler from the line of Solomon to defend her independence during the Scramble for Africa. In July of 1892, Ras Makonnen could rest assured that the throne was secure. Ras Makonnen did not know that the Lion of Judah was about to rise as never before on the world stage and to the center of global consciousness. Furthermore, Ras Makonnen had no knowledge that his baby boy would be responsible for lifting the symbol of the Lion of Judah to heights never before seen in modern times. Despite not having any knowledge of the future of his rightful heir, he could not stop thinking about the boy. As he rode his mule to his Harar residence he could not help but remember the birth of his son.

CHAPTER NINE

The Tribe of Judah in Africa

"The sceptre shall not depart from Judah, nor a lawgiver from between his feet, until Shiloh come; and unto him shall the gathering of the people be." – **Genesis 49:10**

Before the child was born, a steady stream of women had started arriving at the house with the conical, thatched roof in the Ejersa Goro mountains. They went to offer encouragement to the boy's mother, who was well loved. As the time grew closer, Ras Makonnen kept vigil outside the house and waited to hear news. He and his wife were not in Shoa, his homeland, but in an area that had only recently been brought under imperial rule. Although it was not appropriate for him to be by his wife's side at this time, he would still ensure that she was safe during this vulnerable moment.

As concerned as Ras Makonnen was about the health of his wife, and whether this child would survive, he had to hold his composure. All eyes not with his wife were on him, the newly appointed governor of Harar who was governing for less than three years. Ras Makonnen was a symbol of the crown and had to appear as such. As he waited, his silver sheathed sword contrasted brilliantly with his black bombazine tunic. His gun bearer stood behind him with his fine rifle (in its own scarlet cotton sheath), careful to hold it high enough as to not have the dust soil its shining handle. Fanned out in a semicircle on the hill were some of the greatest warriors in the realm. A large contingent of soldiers also waited in ceremonial dress, each holding his own loaded carbine.[113] Silently, they prayed with their leader, hoping he would have a legitimate heir at last.

Outside of the defensive perimeter of soldiers, clusters of poor farmers and tradespeople were on their knees in prayer. Ras Makonnen's fair rule and policies had won him supporters in Harar and there were few who did not know that his wife was expecting. Their prayers traveled into the house and the mother of the boy felt reassured.

The people prayed with Ras Makonnen and his soldiers, in part, for another reason as well. They believed that he was from the bloodline of King Solomon and, therefore, ruled in Harar with wisdom. Rumors of him being the emperor's chosen heir did not only live in the capital. The emperor had no male heir, so a healthy son born to Ras Makonnen would provide a pathway for a stable transition on the throne of Solomon.

The poor were keen observers of the politics of the realm because their very lives depended on it. Ras Makonnen's supporters recognized his level-headed leadership and believed in the power of the Lion of the Tribe of Judah, and the throne of Solomon and David to make their lives better.

---

[113] Beresford, Deena-Marie. *Gurage! Gurage! Gurage! The Story of a Wollo Princess: Woizero Yeshimabet Ali AbaJifar*. Yeshimabet's Books and Things, 2019, p. 50.

In 1892, Iraq and Jerusalem were both part of the Ottoman Empire. Ancient Judea was still called Palestine. Any remnants of the royal bloodline remaining in Iraq held no throne or power; and the same was true for Palestine. Similarly, the Jewish communities throughout Europe were not ruled by a king. The kings and queens of Europe claimed descent from King David and the Tribe of Judah when convenient but emphasized their European heritage.

Unsurprisingly, the ruling Catholic Church made no mention of Judah as it was not in its interest to preach about the throne of David while they claimed divine authority from the throne of Saint Peter.

In West Africa, the great Judah-influenced kingdoms had fallen and European powers had made the Africans their colonial subjects. The Judaean heritage of some of Africa's tribes remained with their griots, although reduced to a whisper and mainly spoken of in Western circles.

For Ethiopians, the developments of Judah in the wider world had no impact. As far as they were concerned, all other branches were dispersed, taken captive or subjugated long after King Solomon started the first legitimate branch with the Queen of Sheba. For Ethiopians, it was them alone who could claim legitimate descent of their throne from King David and King Solomon. This claim was made clear in all their correspondence with foreign powers.

Meanwhile, with the fall of the Greek, Roman and Persian empires, and then the rise of Islam and the Ottoman Empire, knowledge in the West of the Ethiopian claim to the Tribe of Judah faded into obscurity. Cut off from Jerusalem and the rest of the exiled or captive Judaeans in Iraq, Yemen, southern Europe, Egypt and the rest of Africa, the entire realm of Ethiopia was practically erased from global consciousness. In 1892, few Africans knew of the Judean connection with Ethiopia. Even fewer Africans among those born in the diaspora knew about the connection. To connect the dots, those Africans would require knowledge of the rise of the Axumite Empire during the first century CE.

THE KINGDOM OF AXUM

According to Ethiopian sources, Axum was founded by Noah's great grandson, Ityop'is, the son of Kush (or Cush), and it was also his burial place. Apparently, the early names of Axum's towns corresponded to the names of Ityop'is's children.[123]

James Bruce, a European explorer who famously visited Ethiopia in the 1770s, documented:

> "'...a tradition among the Abyssinians, which they say they have had since time immemorial', that in the days after the Deluge, Cush, the son of Ham, traveled with his family up the Nile until they reached the Atbara plain, then still uninhabited, from where they could see the Ethiopian table-land. There they ascended and built Axum, and sometime later returned to the lowland, building Meroë."[124]

It made perfect sense to the Ethiopians that their ancestors had sought out the highest region that they could

---

[123] Munro-Hay, Stuart. *Aksum: An African Civilisation of Late Antiquity*. Edinburgh University Press, 1991.

[124] Bruce, James. *Travels to Discover the Source of the Nile*. George Ramsay and Company, 1813, p. 376.

find after the biblical flood. That search led them to the holy mountains of the rift valley.

Ultimately, they founded the city-state of Axum, known as the "royal throne of the Kings of Zion, mother of all lands, pride of the entire universe and jewel of kings."[125] Axum's rulers were the first to be recorded as using the name *Ethiopia* to identify the region and bringing the term *King of Kings* into public consciousness.

The Ethiopians were not overly concerned about who didn't believe their claims of Solomonic descent. They could list all the King of Kings from the grandson of Kush to the Queen of Sheba, who was said to have reigned from Axum.[126]

THE LAND OF PUNT

Searching for historical sources outside the Bible, or Ethiopia's own oral and written traditions, for the origins of ancient Ethiopia or how Ethiopia and Judah became connected, leads only to Egyptian hieroglyphics. Pharaohs wrote about a land far to the south called Punt, now associated with Axum (Ethiopia) although some historians question this association. The first Egyptian expedition to Punt took place in approximately 2500 BCE,

---

[125] Munro-Hay, Stuart. *Aksum: An African Civilisation of Late Antiquity.* Edinburgh University Press, 1991.

[126] A complete list of Kings of Ethiopia was compiled by H.I.H. Tafari Makonnen and sent out on June 19, 1922. The list was published by Negro University Press in the book, *In the Country of The Blue Nile* by C.F. Rey, F.R.G.S., Commander of the Order of the Star of Ethiopia. See: http://rastaites.com/list-ethiopian-kings-haile-selassie-i-lineage/

at least 1500 years before the time of King David, the first king and patriarch of the tribe of Judah.

Punt was most famously mentioned during the reign of Queen Hatshephut in 1500 BCE. Sources state that Punt was an incredible source of frankincense, ivory, animal skins and exotic animals. Queen Hatshephut memorialized her famous expedition on a temple built in memory of her reign. Other hieroglyphs depict people of Punt arriving in Egypt on their own boats, showing that they did not rely solely on Egyptian naval technology for trade. One of the more convincing pieces of evidence is a hieroglyphic that speaks of a great deluge of rain in Punt that caused the Nile river to flood. Since time immemorial, heavy rains in the Ethiopian highlands have flooded the low lying Egyptian portion of the Nile.

The Persian King Darius is mentioned in biblical records as having been sent tribute from the people of Punt but it is not clear if Ethiopia's reigning sovereign at the time (circa 486 BCE), Emperor Safelya Sabakon, did indeed send tribute.[127] (Recall that many of the precious records of the early Ethiopian kings were lost during the wars of Imam Ahmad Gran.)

While it is unclear whether or not Punt was indeed Axum, it is clear that Axum was a powerful state that was actively engaged in international trade consistent with the type of trade that was identified in Punt. Scholars now place Punt as being located anywhere from southern Sudan to Somalia, further strengthening the argument that Punt could be Axum.[128]

---

[127] Munro-Hay, Stuart. *Aksum: An African Civilisation of Late Antiquity*. Edinburgh University Press, 1991.

[128] Zdziebłowski, Szymon. *"Polish Egyptologist Discovered... a Secretary Bird in the Temple of Hatshepsut." Science in Poland, 20 June 2018,*

D'MT CIVILIZATION

The fog of history has clouded the period between the fall of Punt and the rise of Axum. The former's disappearance gave way for another rift valley civilization to make its mark on the historical record. An advanced civilization called D'mt, founded on the Eritrean coast as early as the 8th century BCE, preceded the modern period of Axum.

No Judaic artifacts were found in D'mt and historians are not sure if it was connected to the claimed Solomonic legacy of Ethiopia, which was a realm of many kingdoms. Despite the use of iron tools, irrigation and plows, the D'mt culture disappeared in the 5th century BCE and made way for the emergence of the mighty Axumite empire.

THE WEALTH OF AXUM

A Persian religious leader in the 2nd century referred to Axum as one of the four most important cities in the world along with Rome, Persia and Sileos.[129] Indeed, so great was Axum's power and wealth that, next to Rome and Persia, it was one of the few ancient powers able to

---

http://scienceinpoland.pap.pl/en/news/news%2C29964%2Cpolish-egyptologist-discovered-secretary-bird-temple-hatshepsut.html.

[129] Munro-Hay, Stuart. *Aksum: An African Civilisation of Late Antiquity.* Edinburgh University Press, 1991. Sileos is thought to be located in China.

issue its own coinage. From as far back as 60 CE, a man of Greek heritage living in Egypt (while under Roman rule) wrote about Axum as an important market for ivory.[130] At the turn of the millennium, long before the importation of modern firearms, Axum's rulers generated legendary wealth from massive elephant herds whose prime habitat was the lush vegetation of the highlands and river valleys to the south. The Axumites also traded in exotic items such as turtle shells, animal hides and civet musk.[131] The accumulation of wealth allowed Axum to flourish as a kingdom of great renown, and to pursue arts and culture. Its leaders were said to be familiar with Greek literature.[132]

The Orthodox Church of Ethiopia identified Axum as originally being a Jewish state – the Queen of Sheba called it home and, according to tradition, it became the resting place of the holy Ark of the Covenant brought to Ethiopia during the time of King Solomon. Scholars, too, concede that Axum had significant Jewish influence despite the worship of the Afro-asiatic pagan god Ashtar (or Astar or Attar), a popular Arabian deity known as a god of war. For an expanding empire, the god of war may have been popular among the ruling elite.

Axum was the home and final resting place of the legendary King Bazen, also known as Balthazar. He was the Emperor who reigned during the time of the Christ. Some accounts say that he was one of the wise men who

---

[130] Ibid.

[131] Ibid.

[132] Schoff, Wilfred H., trans. and ed. *The Periplus of the Erythraean Sea: Travel and Trade in the Indian Ocean by a Merchant of the First Century*. London, Bombay & Calcutta, 1912.

visited Yeshua the Christ in Bethlehem.[133] According to oral tradition, it was he who brought frankincense to the baby Christ. Upon his return, it is said that he spread the news in Ethiopia about the birth of the Messiah. His tomb was a known landmark to the Church in Axum in 1892.[134]

THE FALL OF AXUM

The decline of Axum started sometime after the 7th century CE, following the rise of Islam. The second rise of the Persian empire in Arabia as well as internal factors forced Axum's rulers to move their capital into the interior. The loss of trading routes and Red Sea ports meant a consequent loss of wealth and power.

Meanwhile, a tide was sweeping the realm and there was no resting place to be found. In the end, Axum was toppled by a Jewish revival of sorts. The Ethiopian Jews, or Falasha, did not claim descent from the Solomonic dynasty for the most part, nor did they have any feelings of loyalty to the throne. Instead, their claimed heritage was from a much earlier period of Hebrew migration. Ethiopia's Jews looked to Moses' sons and the migrations sparked by the first destruction of the temple by Babylon (in 586 BCE) as critical parts of their origin story.

It is said that Queen Gudit, a rising monarch on a mission, proceeded to invade, plunder and weaken Axum. She took over the country and reigned for 40 years, amassing great power and prestige. The basis of her

---

[133] Munro-Hay, Stuart. *Aksum: An African Civilisation of Late Antiquity.* Edinburgh University Press, 1991.

[134] Ibid.

support was her promise to end the reign of Christian kings and return Ethiopia to the Hebrew foundations originally established by Queen Makeda.

QUEEN GUDIT

Before Ethiopia's Christian emperors would fight against Imam Ahmed Gran and his Islamic forces for the survival of their kingdom, they were made to contend with a powerful Judaic uprising led by the infamous Queen Gudit. Scholars dispute Queen Gudit's origins and whether she was, in fact, Jewish. Some think that she rose from Lasta, out of the Agaw people, and followed Hebrew traditions. The Agaw, also called Beta Israel, were Ethiopian Israelites who refused to convert to Christianity, even in the face of Axum's rulers and the powerful Ethiopian church. Others suppose that she likely came from the Sidama people, who had a matriarchal tradition.

What is not disputed is that she lived and that she exercised considerable power – neither did her movements go unnoticed outside of Ethiopia. An account has been written that the King of Abyssinia (likely the last King of Axum) or one of his descendants wrote to the King of Nubia. He was seeking a new Abuna from the Holy See of St. Mark in Alexandria,[135] and also spiritual reinforcements against the Queen's relentless onslaught. The impassioned letter detailed that a woman had risen up and was destroying churches, hunting Christians and

---

[135] *Abuna* is a title given to the Patriarch of the Ethiopian Orthodox Church.

devastating the countryside.[136] Some accounts blame her armies for toppling some of the large obelisks that stood as testimony to Axum's ancient glory. The famous monastery of Debra Damos was also said to have been burned by her forces.

Queen Gudit practiced international diplomacy once her domestic power was consolidated. There are accounts of the King of Yemen sending a zebra to the King of Iraq – it was originally gifted by the Queen of Ethiopia during this period.[137]

Unfortunately, her succession plan was interrupted when the Egyptian church heard the call of her daughter church and sent Abuna Dan'el to strengthen the remaining Christian community. The Abuna was determined to stop the tide of Judaic fervor and he spent much time among the Beta Israel in the Agaw kingdom. As a result of his efforts, many chose to embrace Yeshua the Christ as the risen Messiah. The work of the Abuna contributed to a Christian Agaw dynasty rising from the region of Lasta following the reign of Queen Gudit. Queen Gudit is sometimes credited as being the first monarch of this dynasty, which would become known as the Zagwe Dynasty. Already grounded in Judaic traditions, then becoming ardent Christians, the Zagwe Dynasty would leave an everlasting legacy in the realm of Ethiopia.

---

[136] Ullendorff, Edward. *The Ethiopians: An Introduction to Country and People*. 4th ed., Headstart Printing and Publishing Company, 1998, p. 58.

[137] Munro-Hay, Stuart. *Aksum: An African Civilisation of Late Antiquity*. Edinburgh University Press, 1991.

THE ZAGWE DYNASTY

The Solomonic descendants of the emperors of Axum did not completely disappear. Aside from writing to the church in Egypt, the final king of Axum, Emperor Dil Na'od, did all in his power to reclaim the throne of his ancestors from the powerful usurper queen. The Orthodox Church began spreading the idea that the Almighty was upset with the throne of David and was punishing the kings for their pagan ways. The remaining Christians, among both the nobility and the working class, were forced to examine their faith. Thus, the stage was set for a Christian revival.

One of Emperor Dil Na'od's generals, a young man named Mara Takla Haymanot (possibly a relative of Queen Gudit), rose up to provide the leadership necessary to reclaim the throne in Christ's name. With the arrival of Abuna Dan'el and the Christian revival that was taking place among the nobility, Mara Haymanot, a tested warrior of the Agaw people from Lasta, ambitiously sought to reign after Queen Gudit. To ensure the loyalty of the nobility and the remnant of King Dil Na'od's army and family, he married the King's daughter, Masoba Warq. This linked him to the Solomonic bloodline and gave some legitimacy to his claim for the throne of David.

Upon becoming emperor, Mara Takla Haymanot effectively began the Zagwe dynasty. While never fully accepted by the Orthodox Church, his descendants would rule for over one hundred years and leave an indelible mark on Ethiopia, proving to be ardent Christians and true defenders of the faith.[138] The Zagwe Dynasty was made famous by one of its last kings, Emperor Lalibela.

EMPEROR LALIBELA

Despite objections by religious leadership to the Zagwe dynasty, Emperor Lalibela is today recognized as a saint of the Ethiopian Orthodox Church. According to the legend of his life, Gebre Mesqel Lalibela was born in 1162 in the rugged country of Roha. Roha was under the jurisdiction of Lasta and was part of the Agaw-dominated region of Ethiopia that had been a base of power for Queen Gudit. It was said that a swarm of bees surrounded him at the time of his birth. This is the reason that he was given the name Lalibela, which means "the bees recognize his sovereignty" in ancient Agaw language. He was born into nobility and was the brother of the reigning king.

The miracle of the bees at his birth cast a shadow over his young life and he went into exile to escape persecution from his uncle and other family members who were concerned with keeping the throne in his brother's hands. Destiny could not be stopped though. Sometime around 1180, Lalibela ascended the throne of his ancestors.

The new emperor's queen, Masqal Kibra, exercised great power in her own right. She used it to insert her brother as a bishop and he would go on to wield considerable power within the church. When Lalibela temporarily abdicated the throne in favor of his nephew, Na'akueto La'ab, it was the Queen, according to some,

---

[138] Ullendorff, Edward. *The Ethiopians: An Introduction to Country and People*. 4th ed., Headstart Printing and Publishing Company, 1998, p. 62.

who was responsible for having him do so. Some scholars believe that La'ab seized power for himself.

Regardless, the internal intrigues of the Zagwe Dynasty did nothing to slow the spread of Islam throughout the surrounding country. In 1187, word reached Ethiopia that Muslims had captured Jerusalem. The fall of that ancient city would have been in line with the Ethiopian belief that Jerusalem had lost its divine blessing with the transfer of the Ark of the Covenant to Ethiopia during the time of King Solomon. Around the same time, Lalibela dreamt of building a new Jerusalem in Ethiopia.

CHURCHES IN THE ROCK

Some of Ethiopia's most remarkable features in 1892 were the rock-hewn churches of Lalibela – the town formerly known as Roha was renamed in honor of the emperor who had the 11 churches built. At the time, the construction of Egypt's pyramids was confounding even the brightest Western minds. The same could be said for Lalibela's churches, which boggled the mind with their precision, scope and magnificence, complete with rooms and windows carved out of the rocks. Partly a response to the Muslim takeover of Jerusalem, the most famous one of the churches was in the shape of a cross. Scholars are certain that the churches were built by teams of workers and that it took decades, if not centuries to complete. Local tradition, on the other hand, says that Lalibela was assisted by angels. As faith and science disagreed on the churches' origins, the Ethiopian people were on the side of faith.

Emperor Lalibela was succeeded by his son, Emperor Yetbarak, who undoubtedly reigned in his father's shadow and, unfortunately, would become the last Zagwe emperor. The Christian revival, sparked in response to the rise of Queen Gudit, had strengthened the Orthodox Church and there was a corresponding fervor among the scattered Axumite nobility. Their Judaean identity became a rallying point throughout the realm and the lack of direct male descent from the line of King Solomon soon became a liability to the Zagwe rulers.

SOLOMONIC RESTORATION

The stage was set for the return of the Axumite line of kings to power in Ethiopia. A legendary, Shoa-born saint – St. Tekle Haymanot – helped to make this a reality. Educated under the guidance of a famous monk, Iyasus Mo'a, whose lakeside monastery was known as Hayq Monastery, Haymanot's thirst for spiritual knowledge did not stop there. He traveled further north to Debra Damos monastery in Axum to study with Iyasus M'oa's teacher, Abbot Yohannes. As his knowledge increased, so did the number of his followers. Everywhere he went, he was surrounded by a loyal group of Ethiopians from all walks of life who were attracted to his light. His training complete, he returned to his native Shoa and established the monastery of Debra Libanos.

During Haymanot's time at Hayq, he encountered a young prince from the Axumite line who was willing to learn. His name was Yekuno Amlak and he absorbed knowledge from Haymanot as well as Mo'a, both of whom were of the mind that the reign of the Zagwe kings should be brought to an end.[139] The building of the rock churches

---

[139] Ibid.

in Lalibela could not excuse the Zagwes' lack of a male descendant from the Solomonic bloodline.

The news of these powerful monks and the young prince said to have descended from Emperor Dil N'od (the last emperor of Axum) spread to the then sitting emperor, Yetbarak, who had Yekuno Amlak imprisoned. Yekuno, not content to sit in prison, managed to escape with help from his growing followers. With his training and his endorsements from two legendary monks, he was able to rally the country and rise up an army against the Zagwe. Victorious, Yekuno Amlak ascended the throne as Emperor Tasfa Iyasus in August of 1270 CE. He would restore the glory of the Solomonic kings and the Tribe of Judah in Ethiopia.

Emperor Tasfa Iyasus made sure to reestablish strong connections with foreign powers. For instance, he sent the Byzantine Emperor Michael a gift of several giraffes to show the power of his kingdom. As a student of two legendary monks and a descendant of the last Emperor of Axum, he felt it was his duty to reestablish the throne as firmly Christian as well as firmly connected to the Solomonic legacy. His forefathers might have lost their glory by allowing paganism to creep into their administrations but this emperor would not make the same mistake. He would make it his mission to restore the international glory of Ethiopian kings.

THE KEBRA NAGAST

According to the Ethiopians, Judah's descendants remained intact and in command of their own destiny in only one place: the continent of Africa. The Kebra Nagast ('The Glory of Kings') memorializes Ethiopia's version of how the Tribe of Judah reached the highlands of East Africa. The version of the Kebra Nagast used in Ethiopia is at least 700 years old. It began to be widely disseminated during the rise of Yekuno Amlak and laid the spiritual foundations for his war against the Zagwe Dynasty. The Kebra Nagast is considered a repository of Ethiopian national and religious feeling.[140] It reveals their account of how the Judeo-Christian culture, which was incubated in Egypt and evolved in Jerusalem (ancient Northeast Africa), became inseparable with Ethiopian history and culture.

The history of Ethiopia up to 1892 could record no force that prevailed against the Tribe of Judah in Ethiopia. Imam Ahmad Gran of Harar and Queen Gudit came the closest and even they were ultimately defeated. Ethiopians were confident that the continued dominance of the Solomonic bloodline secured the God of Israel's covenant with his chosen people. According to the Kebra Nagast, while the princes of Judah were being taken in chains to Babylon by Nebuchadnezzar, their brothers by blood in Ethiopia were already spreading their faith and bloodline throughout an ancient civilization. The captive princes of Judah in what would become Iraq likely did not know that the mountain sanctuary of Ethiopia was the divine instrument that would preserve the throne of their forefathers as well as keep their bloodline and distinctive culture alive.

---

[140] Ibid., 75.

THE SOLOMONIC GOVERNOR

In 1892, Ras Makonnen did not have the luxury of treating his heritage as a myth. For him, the Kebra Nagast was a history book. It was not his concern what foreigners whispered behind closed doors about the authenticity of Ethiopian emperors' claims of sitting on the throne of David. The internal relationships of the realm were heavily dependent on the spread and preservation of royal Solomonic bloodlines. Wars were fought over these bloodlines. For Ras Makonnen, his ancestor Yekuno Amlak had rightfully reestablished the throne of Axum and confirmed the Solomonic bloodline to the world. In his travels to foreign countries, Ras Makonnen ensured he was addressed as a descendant of King Solomon and treated as such. He was a proud descendant of Yekuno Amlak and the kings of Axum and, as foreign minister of the realm, he proudly represented the land of the Lion of Judah in the civilized world.

CHAPTER TEN

The Hebrews' African Roots

"Princes shall come out of Egypt; Ethiopia shall soon stretch out her hands unto God." – **Psalms 68:31**

No expense had been spared to ensure Ras Makonnen's child would be born healthy. The physicians were nervous and hyper-aware of the many armed, disciplined men outside the house. The display of power was clear and the intensity of the moment could be felt by all present. Aside from the incessant sound of prayers pervading through the open windows and penetrating the walls of house, there were also priests inside the house clutching long prayer sticks.[141] Selected due to their reverence for the word of the Almighty, these priests kept their heads bowed and eyes averted so as not to cause offense to Ras Makonnen's wife. The doctors could feel the pressure to be successful in their endeavor but tried to remain relaxed as the mother-to-be entered her final stages of labor.

---

[141] Beresford, Deena-Marie. *Gurage! Gurage! Gurage! The Story of a Wollo Princess: Woizero Yeshimabet Ali AbaJifar.* Yeshimabet's Books and Things, 2019, p. 51.

Servants quietly filtered in and out of the room, fulfilling requests from the doctors and the woman herself, their hearts pumping with fear. One wrong move could cost them their lives. This was a delicate situation. The mother could be cursed. What if the child died? Would they be blamed? What would happen to them? The tension was almost unbearable as the mother was about to give birth.

The sound of prayer was interrupted by thunder. Everyone's hearts skipped a beat. Fear took hold of them, except for Ras Makonnen who showed none at the awesome display of the Almighty's power. The thunder was a sign. His eyes scanned the compound and saw the visible fright of all who gathered in the moment. Drowning in the sounds of thunder and prayer, the servants almost failed to hear the cries of the baby boy emerging from the womb, triumphant, his tiny body draped in his mother's red placenta lining and steaming in the cool mountain air.

There, in the highlands of Africa, the mother had successfully given birth to the baby boy from the house of King Solomon. Consistent with history, Africa had once again provided a safe space for the birth, protection, and provision of the Tribe of Judah.

AFRICA AND THE HEBREWS

Africa. Mama Africa. The mother of civilization. The continent that gave birth to mankind. Mainstream scholarship has not done justice in highlighting the role that Africa played in the development of the Hebrew faith. This is largely to conceal the proverbial elephant in the room: the fact that the original Hebrews, including Judah and his descendants, would have all been considered Black (or "Negro") by the racial standards existing in the world of 1892.

Africa's role as protector and preserver was only appropriate. The Hebrew patriarch, Abraham, was raised in the shadow of a mighty African civilization. He grew up in Ur, a suburb of the ancient city-state of Babylon, which, according to the book of Genesis, was established by Nimrod, the son of Kush.[142] Nimrod was the brother of the founder of Axum, Ityopis.[143] The name Ityopis does not appear in the Bible but three of Kush's sons, Seba, Sabtecah and and Sabtah are recorded in extra-biblical sources as having settled south of Mesopotamia, establishing kingdoms in the Nile Valley, Arabia and Yemen. According to the Ethiopians, one of them sailed up the Nile to Ethiopia. Kush's descendants – the Kushites – were the first major superpower recorded in the Bible and were credited with the first written language and the rise of civilization in Mesopotamia.

The pre-Semitic population of the Euphrates valley were known to their contemporaries as Sumerians – their civilization was known as Sumer. (The Bible records this civilization as Shinar, one of the cities ruled by Nimrod.) The people of Sumer referred to themselves as the "black-headed people."[144]

Contrary to the worldview of the attendees at the conference in Berlin, the Bible is an African story rather than a European one. Did the Hebrews not first grow into

---

[142] Genesis 10:8

[143] Munro-Hay, Stuart. *Aksum: An African Civilisation of Late Antiquity*. Edinburgh University Press, 1991.

[144] Hallo, William W. and Simpson, William Kelly. *The Ancient Near East: A History*. Harcourt Brace Jovanovich, 1971, p. 28.

a nation in Africa? Was it not an African who led them out of Egypt? Was it not true that the ten commandments of the law were given to the Almighty's chosen people while they wandered in Africa? Was the Ark of the Covenant, the dwelling place of the Hebrew Creator, not first built in Africa? The Hebrews were as African as any other African tribe, and their impact was felt throughout the continent.

There were three major dispersions of Hebrews from Northeast Africa (Palestine) into the interior of Africa. Aside from the Hebrew journey to settle in Ethiopia after the reign of King Solomon, there were waves of Hebrews that fled to Egypt during the Babylonian invasion. Thousands of Hebrews also fled to North Africa after Titus destroyed the second temple.[145]

While Judaeans were already present in West Africa, more were pushed south during the subsequent spread of Islam in North Africa. When the still powerful Moors returned to North Africa after their defeat by Queen Isabella in 1492, they conquered the region and led a campaign of conquest down the Niger river. They settled at Timbuktu and were in full control of it by 1591.[146] The waves of Muslim invasion made the Judaean colonies seek refuge rather than convert. As they scattered to the south, they intermarried with local tribes. Some would soon emerge on the world stage as the powerful Akan people. Judean descendants were also present in Liberia, Sierra Leone, Nigeria and Senegal. The presence of these communities were recorded in Arabic works such as the *Tarikh al-Fattash* and the *Tarikh al-Sudan*.

---

[145] Williams, Joseph J. *The Hebrewisms of West Africa: From Nile to Niger with the Jews.* Dial Press, 1930, p. 324.

[146] Ibid., 25.

AFRO-ASIATIC LANGUAGE GROUPS

The Hebrew language further uncovers the Tribe of Judah's African roots. Indeed, it is classified under one of the three major indigenous language groups of the African continent. These groups are: Afro-Asiatic; Nilo-Saharan; and Niger-Congo. The Semitic branch of the Afro-Asiatic group, which includes Hebrew, holds the distinction of being the only African language group that extends outside of continental Africa. Aside from the Semitic languages, the other Afro-Asiatic branches are Berber, Chadic, and Kushitic.

Early linguists tried to group Hebrew and the Semitic languages with the Indo-European languages. This theory, based in part on the philosophy of white supremacy, was later rejected by the majority of linguists. Despite efforts to distance it from its heritage, Hebrew (and other Semitic languages) is, at the root, an African language that shares far more in common with other African languages than with any of the languages of Europe or Asia.

SCIENTISTS, SCHOLARS AND THE ORIGIN OF THE HEBREWS

The Ethiopians had long depicted the Hebrews as Ethiopian in their iconography, sharply contrasting with European images made popular by the colonizing powers. By the time of the Berlin conference, the Italians were famous for their expertly painted depictions of Hebrews as Europeans, housed at the Vatican.

Italy's famous Sistine Chapel paintings, done in the 15th century, were not in line with accounts of the Roman Empire. Tacitus, the Roman historian, wrote in regard to the African origins of the Hebrews. He writes of the Jews that, "A few authorities hold that in the reign of Isis the surplus population of Egypt was evacuated to neighboring lands under the leadership of Hierosolymus and Judas. Many assure us that the Jews are descended from those Ethiopians who were driven by fear and hatred to emigrate from their home country when Cepheus was king."[147]

The Roman perception of Hebrews as descended from Ethiopians would not enter the modern era. In 1684, French scientist François Bernier published the first widely read classification of humans into distinct races, beginning a centuries-long academic campaign to dehumanize the African.[148]

During the Middle Ages, prior to Bernier's writings, it was widely believed in Europe, just as in Ethiopia, that all humans were the descendants of Noah. In contrast to Ethiopia's view that melanin-rich Africans were the original people, Europe's perspective was that the Black people of the world were the product of a curse given to Noah's grandson – the curse of Canaan. As the story goes, Noah's son, Ham, disgraced his father and his son, Canaan, became cursed.[149]

---

[147] Tacitus. *The Annals/The Histories.*

[148] Bernier, François. "A New Division of the Earth." from *Journal des Scavans*, 1684. Translated by T. Bendyshe in Memoirs Read Before the Anthropological Society of London, vol. 1, 1863-64, pp. 360–64. See: https://web.archive.org/web/20060524134126/http:/www.as.ua.edu/ant/bindon/ant275/reader/bernier.PDF

[149] Genesis 9:20-27

Ironically, this was also an admission by Europe that the original inhabitants of the "Middle East," the Canaanites, were dark-skinned people. Canaan, their founding ancestor, was Noah's grandson and the brother of Noah's other famous grandson, Kush. As the ancient Hebrew stories slipped through the ages, Kush became synonymous with Ethiopia. However, Canaan, morphed into a European as scholars and artists on that continent made efforts to minimize the African presence in the Bible as much as possible. On the contrary, in Ethiopia, Adam and Eve were considered Ethiopians and, thus, Noah and all his progeny were descended from Ethiopian stock.

As knowledge began to increase, Africa's massive imprint on the ancient world became more apparent. By 1892, learned scholars had traveled more and they began to accept that mankind originated in Africa and that advanced civilizations were not foreign to its peoples. French born historian and philosopher, Count Constantine de Volney, visited Ottoman controlled Egypt in 1782 and wrote:

> "All Egyptians have a bloated face, puffed-up eyes, flat nose, thick lips – in a word, the true face of the mulatto. I was tempted to attribute it to the climate, but when I visited the Sphinx, its appearance gave me the key to the riddle. On seeing that head, typically Negro in all its features, I remembered the remarkable passage where Herodotus says: 'As for me, I judge the Colchians to be a colony of the Egyptians because, like them, they are black with woolly hair...' When I visited the Sphinx, I could not help thinking that the figure of that monster furnished the true solution to the enigma (of how the modern Egyptians came to have their

'mulatto' appearance). In other words, the ancient Egyptians were true Negroes of the same type as all native-born Africans. That being so, we can see how their blood, mixed for several centuries with that of the Greeks and Romans, must have lost the intensity of its original color, while retaining nonetheless the imprint of its original mold."[150]

Scientists in 1892 had not yet championed the theory that white skin evolved in the northern latitudes of the planet within the last 6000 years, and that it was likely an adaptation for more efficient vitamin D synthesis due to lack of sunlight in those northern regions. Scientists also had not yet proven that the genetic Eve, the woman whose mitochondrial DNA inhabits all modern humans today, was a black African woman; or that Africa was the repository of the greatest genetic diversity. Nor did scientists know that the San people of Namibia have been found to have the most genetically distinct population, giving them the distinction of being considered the most ancient living population on Earth. In 1892, Ethiopians could not rely on foreign scientists to support their conception of the world. They had only their faith in their long-held conception of Adam and Eve, the original man and woman, as being Ethiopian.

Jewish historian, Flavius Josephus (37-100 CE), wrote about the Hebrew origin story in his famous work, *Antiquities of the Jews*. In it, he outlines the four rivers that "encompassed" the Garden of Eden, creating a picture of the garden as a massive territory between the Nile in Africa, the Ganges in India, and the Tigris and Euphrates

---

[150] Diop, Cheikh Anta. *The African Origin of Civilization: Myth or Reality*. Lawrence Hill & Co., 1974 p. 27.

rivers in the fertile crescent of Mesopotamia. Josephus's description pointed to regions where modern genetic research has proven that the indigenous peoples had melanated skin. The Hebrews have no oral history that speaks to a northern migration or northern sojourn or any great intermixing with northern populations as part of their story. A people born and evolved in lands dominated by the sun would have certainly possessed melanated skin. Interestingly, Ethiopians, at one time or another, also claimed to rule all the lands making up Josephus's conception of the Garden of Eden.

None of this information would have been known during the cold deliberations that took place in Berlin in 1884-85, or it would have been rejected if known. The Berlin conference attendees had benefited from the waves of non-melanated Europeans, hardened by Ice Age conditions, who had pushed south for thousands of years in search of greener pastures. In the process of conquest, they had promulgated the view that Africa had no civilization and that the Bible's major figures, with the exception of Ham and his offspring, were European in appearance. The presence of Jews in Europe – descendants of exiles in Iraq who had mixed for centuries with Europeans and therefore looked European – allowed Europe to dismiss any ties between the original Jews and Black Africa.

AFRICA, ETHIOPIA, MOSES AND THE BOOK OF GENESIS

As Europe rose and time passed, the African identity of the Hebrews faded among Europeans, existing only for those willing to look closely into the actual story of the Hebrews. Their connection to Africa was nowhere more apparent than in the life of one of the major figures in the Bible: Moses.

While there is still debate as to whether Moses was an actual historical figure, there is little debate on the historical impact of his story. Born and raised in Egypt, Northeast Africa over 4000 years ago, the highly educated Hebrew liberator and prophet, Moses, is credited with recording the oral history of the Hebrews on parchment scrolls.[151] The Book of Genesis was one of five books of the Bible credited to Moses and, while its historical accuracy is hotly debated, it provides important insight into the Hebrews' view of their own history as well as their thought process. Whether Moses was the author of Genesis is also widely disputed by scholars. However, given the fact that the Old Testament has been translated and transcribed through the ages, it is impossible to disprove that the original work was not based on the writings or oral tradition of an African man named Moses.

In the Kebra Nagast, Moses is described as a mighty prophet who foretold the coming of the Christ. It is said that he proclaimed, "A prophet like myself shall rise up from your brethren, and hearken ye unto him, and every soul that will not hearken unto that prophet ye shall root out from among the people."[152]

Moses was also said to have married a Kushite/Ethiopian woman and led successful military campaigns in Nubia/Kush. Josephus wrote about how Moses won the favor of the Egyptian Pharaoh and was given the rank of a general in the Egyptian army and then

---

[151] Later translated, edited and arranged in a collection known as *The Bible*.

[152] Brooks, Miguel F., comp., ed. and trans. *Kebra Nagast: The Glory of Kings*. 1995. Red Sea Press, 2002, p. 133.

sent to subdue Nubia. While Josephus wrote about Ethiopians, it is obvious that he was not talking about the Ethiopians of 1892 but of their brothers and sisters, the Kushites, in Sudan. However, it is a fact that during some periods Kush was controlled by rulers who dwelled in the region known as Ethiopia in 1892. Either way, Moses was clearly shaped by his experiences on the African continent. Josephus wrote:

> "...he came upon the Ethiopians before they expected him and, joining battle with them, he beat them, and deprived them of the hopes they had of success against the Egyptians, and went in overthrowing their cities and, indeed made a great slaughter of these Ethiopians. Now when the Egyptian army had once tasted of this prosperous success, by the means of Moses, they did not slacken their diligence, insomuch that the Ethiopians were in danger of being reduced to slavery and all sorts of destruction; and at length they retired to Saba, which was a royal city of Ethiopia, which Cambyses afterwards named Mero, after the name of his own sister...However, while Moses was uneasy at the army's lying idle, (for the enemies durst not come to a battle,) this accident happened: - Tharbis was the daughter of the king of the Ethiopians: she happened to see Moses as he led the army near the walls, and fought with great courage and admiring the subtlety of his undertakings, and believing him to be the author of the Egyptians success, when they had before despaired of recovering their liberty, and to be the occasion of the great

danger the Ethiopians were in, when they had before boasted of their great achievements, she fell deeply in love with him and upon the [prevalence] of that passion, sent to him the most faithful of all her servants to discourse with him about their marriage. He thereupon accepted to the offer on condition she would procure the delivering up of the city; and gave her assurance of an oath to take her to be his wife; and that when he had once taken possession of the city he would not break his oath to her. No sooner was the agreement made, but it took effect immediately and when Moses had cut off the Ethiopians, he gave thanks to God, and consummated his marriage, and led the Egyptians back to their own land."[153]

Moses was later criticized by his brother and sister for marrying another Kushite woman. The Book of Numbers, says, "And Miriam and Aaron spake against Moses because of the Ethiopian woman whom he had married: for he had married an Ethiopian woman."[154] This Kushite was not his wife from the Egyptian military campaign but a daughter of a Midianite priest. The Midianites were a branch of the Canaanites.

In an attempt to diminish the African roots of Moses's wife, some biblical scholars contend that it was not a Kushite woman but a woman from the Midianite tribe of Chushan. This theory does not address the fact that the Chushan were named for a prominent descendant of Kush,

---

[153] Whiston, William. *The Genuine Works of Flavius Josephus the Jewish Historian*. 1737.

[154] Numbers 12:1

Mesopotamian King Chushan-rishathaim, who enslaved Israel for eight years.[155] It also does not take into account Josephus's account of Moses's earlier marriage to a Kushite woman.

In the world of 1892, it is clear: Moses would have identified as a black man. Aside from marrying two Kushite women, Moses was also mistaken for an Egyptian by the Midianite family he eventually lived with after fleeing Egypt. It would seem, then, that the Hebrews were not easily distinguishable from the ancient Egyptians to the untrained eye. If he had looked European, Moses would have surely stood out to the Midianites as a Hebrew or as a Hebrew dressed as an Egyptian.[156] Notwithstanding what his racial identification would have been in 1892, it seemed as though the education Moses received growing up in the house of the Pharaoh compelled him to write down the oral history of his people.

Prior to the Hebrew sojourn in Egypt, the Hebrews were a seemingly loose confederation of nomadic shepherds and farmers. According to tradition, it was famine that sent their ancestors into the African superpower for refuge. Naturally, over the hundreds of years that they stayed in Egypt, they assimilated and adopted Egyptian culture. Moses represented the pinnacle of this assimilation by the time he produced what would become the first five books of the Bible – respectively, Genesis, Exodus, Leviticus, Numbers and Deuteronomy - collectively known as the Pentateuch.

Genesis records the genealogy of the African Moses and identifies Levi as his direct ancestor. Levi was a brother of Judah; both were sons of Jacob, who later

---

[155] Judges 3:8

[156] Exodus 2:19

became known by the name Israel. Genesis also records that Jacob was the son of Isaac, who was the son of Abraham. This same Abraham, it is written, was selected by the Almighty to restore the covenant of the first man, Adam. Given this incredible responsibility placed on Abraham, it should not be surprising that Abraham became the father of three of the world's major religions: Judaism, Christianity and Islam.

To those who are not familiar with Ethiopian popular culture and history, it may seem strange that Abraham, like Judah, could hold prominence in Ethiopian society, or even be connected to the baby boy born in Ethiopia's highlands. Given Abraham's role as the father of the three most popular world religions, and the impact of all three in shaping Ethiopia's history, it is difficult to do justice to any story about Ethiopia's history without a basic understanding of the historic role of the Hebrew patriarch himself. In the case of 1892 Ethiopia, it is necessary to know the story about the Ethiopian version of Abraham and his descendants.

Islam shaped the landscape of the baby boy's birthplace just outside of Muslim Harar, a landscape recently conquered in the name of a Judeo-Christian king. The coming together of the three faiths in Harar brought Abraham's legacy full circle.

ABRAHAM AND THE KUSHITE CONNECTION

In the Kebra Nagast, Abraham was a great man and spiritual pioneer. He grew up, thousands of years before Harar's existence, in a Mesopotamian city, Ur, founded by Africans. The father of the monothestic religions would have been intimately familiar with Kushite culture in which he was immersed.

While Kush's son, Ityopis, traveled south up the Nile to higher ground in Axum, his brother Nimrod went north and settled in between the mighty Tigris and Euphrates rivers. There he established Babylon, one of the most powerful nations on Earth, nourished by the bounty of the region, known as the fertile crescent.

Scholars debate whether Nimrod was an actual historical figure and attribute the founding of both Babylon and Ur to the Akkadians and Sumerians. Both of these peoples spoke Afro-Asiatic languages and were part of the fabric of the ancient Mesopotamian valley.

The biblical Kush and his sons spread and established Kushite culture and civilization from the banks of the Nile into the fertile crescent of Mesopotamia. To the Greeks, Kush and Ethiopia were one and the same. Melanated Africans inhabited the world's first superpowers 4000 years ago, when Europe was not yet significant in international relations.

It was in the land of Kush that Abraham's worldview was shaped. It was among the Kushites that Abraham made his living and formed his connection with the Almighty of his forefathers.

THE POWER OF EGYPT

In Abraham's time, the Kushites of Mesopotamia lived in the shadow of another African superpower: the mighty Egypt. Ethiopian Christians, Jews and Muslims alike, all viewed Egypt as being established by Noah's son (and Kush's brother), Miziram.[157] Scholars ascribe the founding of Egypt to King Menes, who is said to have united upper and lower Egypt in 3150 BCE.[158] Noah's flood took place anywhere from 2300 BCE to 3000 BCE, according to Bible scholars' estimates, which puts the flood after the reign of King Menes. Arab Muslim scholars assert that Egypt's pyramids were created by the wicked inhabitants of Earth before the flood.

Whether founded by Miziram or King Menes, so great was Egypt that its ruins still inspired awe in 1892. It was the center of trade in the ancient world and, though Babylon was a major power, Hebrew tradition has it that Egypt's crop surpluses made it the unquestioned superpower during the time of Abraham. To those with a biblical worldview, like the Ethiopians, it was to Egypt that Abraham traveled when the land of Ur was struck with a devastating famine.[159] While Mesopotamia could not sustain her peoples, Egypt was a refuge.

The influx of migrants would have only enriched the Pharaoh. It is said that the Pharaoh was so powerful that Abraham, a man with considerable resources, felt compelled to devise a plan to avoid himself being killed and his wife raped by the Egyptian God-King. Fearing for his own life due to the beauty of his wife, Abraham told the princes of Pharaoh that his wife, Sarah, was his sister. This decision would have unintended consequences. As Abraham anticipated, news of the beauty of his wife reached the ears of Pharaoh, who demanded that she be

---

[157] Windsor, Rudolph R. *From Babylon to Timbuktu: A History of Ancient Black Races Including the Black Hebrews.* 1969. Windsor Golden Series, 2003, p. 30.

[158] Ibid.

[159] Genesis 12:10

brought to his palace. In return for her, Abraham, thought to be her brother, was gifted with "sheep, oxen, male donkeys, male servants, female servants, female donkeys, and camels," thus greatly increasing his wealth. Soon, Abraham would witness the power of his newly discovered divine protector, one that he feared more than the Egyptian God-King. His new protector, according to the Kebra Nagast, was none other than the "Creator of the sun and the moon, Creator of the sea and the dry land, Maker of the majesty of the heavens and the earth:"[160] Yahweh!

It is written that, shortly after Sarah was taken captive, Pharaoh's house was hit with "great plagues" and he then found out that she was actually Abraham's wife. The wise Pharoah attributed the plagues in his house to the fact that he had taken a powerful man's wife. Fearing the power of such a man, the Pharaoh ordered Abraham to leave his kingdom. Not wanting to further anger the Creator of such a man, the God-King of Egypt allowed Abraham to leave with all his newly acquired possessions. Thus, Abraham survived an encounter and prevailed against the most powerful person in the ancient world, emerging as a more powerful leader by the power of his faith. According to tradition, following his stay in Egypt, Abraham prospered in all his works and grew to be respected and feared by all throughout the land.

THE FAITH OF ABRAHAM

Abraham's trust in one Almighty God was a new feature for a man from his polytheistic tribe in Ur. It was certainly unusual among the Afro-Asiatic language

---

[160] Brooks, Miguel F., comp., ed. and trans. *Kebra Nagast: The Glory of Kings*. 1995. Red Sea Press, 2002, pp. 11-12.

speakers who dwelled between the Nile and the Euphrates-Tigris regions where people worshipped many gods. It was the power of his faith that would propel him to becoming the central figure of the world's modern monotheistic traditions, and why Ethiopia's kings, princes and other nobles saw him as a spiritual pioneer. The Kebra Nagast speaks of Abraham's father, Terah, saying that he:

> "...begot a son and called him Abram, and when Abram was twelve years old his father Terah sent him to sell idols. And Abram said: 'These are not gods that can deliver us,' and he took away the idols to sell even as his father had commanded him. Then he said unto those unto whom he would sell them: 'Do you wish to buy gods that cannot make deliverance, things made of wood, stone, iron and brass, which the hand of the artificer made?' And they refused to buy idols from Abram because of himself had defamed the images of his father. And as he was returning, he stepped aside from the road and he set the images down, and looked at them, and said unto them: 'I wonder now if you are able to do what I ask you at this moment, and whether you are able to give me bread to eat and water to drink?' None of them answered him since they were pieces of wood and stone; and he abused them and heaped reviling upon them and they never spoke a word. Then he buffeted the face of one, kicked another with his feet, and a third one he knocked over and broke to pieces with stones, and he said unto them: 'if you are unable to deliver yourselves from him that buffeteth you, and

you cannot repay with injury him that injureth you, how can ye be called 'gods'? Those who worship you do so in vain, and as for myself I utterly despise you, and you shall not be my gods.' Then he turned his face to the east, stretched out his hands and said: 'Be Thou my God, O Lord, Creator of the heavens and the earth, Creator of the sun and the moon, Creator of the sea and the dry land, Maker of the majesty of the heavens and the earth, and of that which is visible and that which invisible; O Maker of the universe, be Thou my God. I place my trust in Thee, and from this day forth I will place my trust in no other save Thyself.'"[161]

The power of the innocence and truth in Abraham's search for divine guidance moved the "Creator of the sun and moon" to swear a covenant with Abraham, to establish a divine kingdom on Earth through Abraham's seed. To the Ethiopian kings of the Solomonic line – to Ras Makonnen as well – Abraham's example was pure inspiration.

ABRAHAM AND THE WAR OF KINGS

In Abraham's era, as in 1892 Ethiopia, there was no modern postal system but news traveled throughout the land. Although not many people were literate, many managed to stay up to date on important happenings. Merchants and other serial travelers were effective news carriers, bearing good and bad news alike in hard times

---

[161] Ibid.

when information could mean the difference between life and death. So, when word reached Abraham that war had broken out in his land, he had to take action.

Abraham was so powerful that he and his trained servants were able to slaughter the confederate armies of the Kushite Mesopotamian Kings.

As is written, the confederate armies of Mesopotamian kings who were serving the King Chedorlaomer of Elam (modern day Iran) started a rampage of conquest across Africa, Arabia and Mesopotamia. They included the armies of Amraphel (King of Shinar), Arioch (King of Ellasar) and Tidal (King of Nations), who made war with Bera (King of Sodom), Shinab (King of Admah), Shemeber (King of Zeboiim), Zoar (King of Bela) and Birsha (King of Gomorrah). It was a war of epic proportions.

The kings of Sodom and Gomorrah engaged King Chedorlaomer in battle to save their own kingdoms from being pillaged. The battle was pushed into an area filled with slime pits,[162] and both Bera and Birsha were forced to flee. King Chedorlaomer then pillaged their kingdoms and enslaved some of their people.[163] Unfortunately for him, one of his captives was Abraham's nephew, Lot. When the word got back to Abraham through the ancient grapevine, he decided to arm his trained servants and seek justice. To his mind, the pagan King Chedorlaomer was not acting in accordance with the Almighty's will.

---

[162] The slime pits were likely bitumen pits formed by crude oil seeping through fissures in the Earth's crust, evaporating into the air and leaving bitumen on the surface. Bitumen would ooze and bubble to the surface daily, trapping any animals that mistakenly made their way into the thick tar pits.

[163] Genesis 14:1-11

So powerful was Abraham and so great were his blessings from his Almighty that:

> "...when Abram heard that his brother was taken captive, he armed his trained servants, born in his own house, three hundred and eighteen, and pursued them unto Dan. And he divided himself against them, he and his servants, by night, and smote them, and pursued them unto Hobah, which is on the left hand of Damascus. And he brought back all the goods, and also brought again his brother Lot, and his goods, and the women also, and the people."[164]

Thus, Abraham and his 318 servants put an end to fourteen years of war. Only a man of great faith would even consider taking on one of the most powerful armies of the day, with only his servants to rely on, just to save a family member. The King of Sodom and his allies treated Abraham like a hero when they met him in the valley of Shaveh. His courage increased his legend among his contemporaries.

MELCHIZEDEK'S BLESSING OF ABRAHAM

After returning home from the great battle, Abraham was blessed by a priest called Melchizedek, who was known to early Christians and Hebrews as:

> "...king of Salem, priest of the most high God, who met Abraham returning from the slaughter of the kings, and blessed him; To

---

[164] Genesis 14:14-16

> whom also Abraham gave a tenth part of all;
> first being by interpretation King of
> righteousness, and after that also King of
> Salem, which is, King of peace; Without
> father, without mother, without descent,
> having neither beginning of days, nor end of
> life; but made like unto the Son of God;
> abideth a priest continually."[165]

For Ethiopians, Abraham's meeting with Melchizedek was no chance encounter, as shown in the Kebra Nagast:

> "Abraham had said: 'Wilt Thou in my days,
> O Lord, cast Thy word upon the ground?'
> And God said unto him: 'By no means. His
> time hath not yet come, but I will show thee
> a similitude of His coming. Get thee over the
> Jordan, dip thyself in the water as thou
> goest over, and arrive at the city of Salem
> where thou shalt meet Melchizedek, and I
> will command him to show thee the sign and
> similitude of Him.'

Abraham did this and he found Melchizedek and he gave him the mystery of bread and wine, that same which is celebrated in our Passover as a memorial of the sacrifice of our Lord Jesus Christ.

This was the desire and joy of Abraham as he went round the altar which Melchizedek had made, carrying branch and palm on the day of the Sabbath."[166]

The Book of Genesis says:

---

[165] Hebrews 7:1-3

[166] Brooks, Miguel F., comp., ed. and trans. *Kebra Nagast: The Glory of Kings*. 1995. Red Sea Press, 2002, p. 154.

> "And Melchizedek king of Salem brought forth bread and wine: and he was the priest of the most high God. And he blessed him, and said, Blessed be Abram of the most high God, possessor of heaven and earth: And blessed be the most high God, which hath delivered thine enemies into thy hand. And he gave him tithes of all."[167]

After meeting with Melchizedek, Abraham received the full extent of his covenant from his God, who promises, "Unto thy seed have I given this land, from the river of Egypt unto the great river, the river Euphrates."[168]

THE COVENANT OF ABRAHAM

Essentially, the God of the Hebrews promised Abraham the land from the Nile to the Euphrates. In other words, he would have dominion over the ancestral lands of Kush and Ham, the same lands geographically identified by Josephus as the Garden of Eden!

The Almighty goes on to outline the scope of his covenant:

> "And I will make thee exceeding fruitful, and I will make nations of thee, and kings shall come out of thee. And I will establish my covenant between me and thee and thy seed after thee in their generations for an everlasting covenant, to be a God unto thee, and to thy seed after thee. And I will give unto thee, and to thy seed after thee, the

---

[167] Genesis 14:18-20

[168] Genesis 15:18

land wherein thou art a stranger, all the land of Canaan, for an everlasting possession; and I will be their God."[169]

Ethiopian tradition taught that when Abraham encountered the Almighty:

"... there appeared unto him a chariot of fire which blazed, and Abram was afraid and fell on his face on the ground; and God said unto him: 'Fear thou not, stand upright.' And he removed the fear from him."

Ras Makonnen had seen that same look of fear when the thunder sounded before the birth of his baby boy. He and his fellow Ethiopians had learned for generations through the Kebra Nagast that:

"God held converse with Abram, and said unto him: 'Fear thou not. From this day thou art My servant, and I will establish My Covenant with thee and with thy seed after thee, and I will multiply thy seed, and I will magnify thy name exceedingly. And I will bring down the Tabernacle of My Covenant upon the earth seven generations after thee, and it shall go round about with thy seed, and shall be salvation unto thy race; and afterwards I will send My Word for the salvation of Adam and his sons forever. Those who are of thy nation are evil men, and My divinity which is true, they have rejected. As for thee, that day by day they may not seduce thee, come get thee forth out of this land, the land of thy fathers, unto the land which I will show thee, and I will give

---

[169] Genesis 17:6-8

it unto thy seed after thee,' and Abram made obeisance to God and was subject to his God. And God said unto him: 'Thy name shall be Abraham;' and He gave him the salutation of peace and went up into heaven."[170]

In the tradition of the Ethiopians, Abraham, after being called by God, forsook his pagan family and:

"...arrived in the city of Salem, and dwelt there and reigned in righteousness, and did not transgress the commandments of God. So God blessed him exceedingly, and at length he possessed three hundred and eighteen stalwart servants who were trained in war, and who stood before him and performed his will. They wore tunics richly embroidered in gold, and they had chains of gold about their necks, belts of gold round their loins and they had crowns of gold on their heads; and by means of these men Abraham vanquished his foes. He died in the glory of God, and was more gracious and excellent than those who were before him. He was gracious and held in honor and highly esteemed."[171]

While Abraham was a man of great faith and great wealth – he was also a warrior. Ethiopians, Ras Makonnen included, viewed Abraham as a king and Abraham would help set the mold of what a righteous man, and warrior king should be.

---

[170] Brooks, Miguel F., comp., ed. and trans. *Kebra Nagast: The Glory of Kings*. 1995. Red Sea Press, 2002, pp. 12-13.

[171] Ibid., 13.

Though promised that his seed would inherit the "promised land," Abraham was not blessed with any children until he was well past the prime of his life. His wife was so concerned with her inability to produce children that she convinced Abraham to sleep with her Egyptian maidservant, Hagar (an African), a union that produced Abraham's first son, Ishmael. Abraham was 86 years old.

Sarah, noticing that Hagar "despised" her, requested permission from Abraham to deal with the Egyptian according to her own will. Permission was granted and Sarah dealt with her so harshly that Hagar left the security of Abraham's house and fled to the wilderness.[172] There she is met by an "angel of the Lord," who tells her:

> "Return to thy mistress, and submit thyself under her hands. And the angel of the Lord said unto her, I will multiply thy seed exceedingly, that it shall not be numbered for multitude. And the angel of the Lord said unto her, Behold, thou art with child and shalt bear a son, and shalt call his name Ishmael; because the Lord hath heard thy affliction. And he will be a wild man; his hand will be against every man, and every man's hand against him; and he shall dwell in the presence of all his brethren."[173]

Ishmael, the son of a father from the African diaspora and a born African for a mother, would be seen by the followers of Islam as the fulfillment of a biblical

---

[172] Genesis 16:1-6

[173] Genesis 16:7-12

promise. Muslim tradition places Ishmael as an ancestor of the Prophet Mohammed and, therefore, Ishmael would have been an important figure within the walled city of Harar.

Adherents to the Hebrew scriptures (including Ethiopia's Christians), viewed Abraham's biblical covenant differently from their Islamic brothers. For them it is Abraham's second son that would fulfill prophecy. Abraham did not lose faith in Sarah and continued to make love to his wife. At the age of 99, he received a vision of his God saying to him:

> "...I am the Almighty God; walk before me, and be thou perfect. And I will make my covenant between me and thee, and will multiply thee exceedingly... Neither shall thy name any more be called Abram, but thy name shall be Abraham; for a father of many nations have I made thee. And I will make thee exceeding fruitful, and I will make nations of thee, and kings shall come out of thee..."[174]

The Creator goes on to promise him that his wife, who should be called Sarah and no longer Sarai, would have a child and be blessed to be "a mother of nations" and that "kings of people shall be of her."[175] Despite the solemnity of the blessing, Abraham actually laughed at the thought his wife having a child at the age of 90. Demonstrating his balance between spiritual and material interests, and being the father that he was, Abraham pleaded that Ishmael be found worthy but there was no change in the prophecy:

---

[174] Genesis 17:1-8

[175] Genesis 17:15-16

> "Sarah thy wife shall bear thee a son indeed; and thou shalt call his name Isaac: and I will establish my covenant with him for an everlasting covenant, and with his seed after him."[176]

Still, the Almighty did not neglect Abraham's appeal for his first born son. He tells Abraham:

> "...as for Ishmael, I have heard thee: Behold, I have blessed him, and will make him fruitful, and will multiply him exceedingly; twelve princes shall he beget, and I will make him a great nation."[177]

Ishmael was the chosen son of Abraham in places like Harar. However, Ethiopia was not ruled by Muslims. It was Abraham's second son - his first and only son from his first wife, Sarah – who was the chosen son for the rulers of those highlands.

Ras Makonnen could identify with Abraham. His first born son from a common law marriage, Yilma, was not his lawful heir as he was not born within an Orthodox marriage. A marriage endorsed and carrying the formal blessing of the church was necessary for the heirs of nobility. With the birth of the baby boy born to his lawful wife, he now had an heir that could inherit his legacy.

THE BLESSINGS FOR ABRAHAM'S CHILDREN

When Abraham died, the promised blessing passed to Isaac. The Kebra Nagast says, "Isaac his son became

---

[176] Genesis 17:19

[177] Genesis 17:20

King and did not transgress the commandments of God; he was pure in his soul and in his body, and he died in honor."[178]

The Bible does not record Isaac as being a king. However, with Abraham's wealth, trained men and infrastructure, he was likely a de facto king in the region he inhabited. When Isaac died, the promise passed to his second child, Jacob, who would take on a new name during the course of his life, and that name would ring out through the annals of time. That name was Israel.

While many disregard the stories of Jacob as myth, variations of these stories pervaded the ancient world until they began to be transcribed onto physical scrolls. Ethiopians, who could claim to have the most ancient and complete version of the Bible in the world, were united under a distinct cultural identity. They had access to Jacob's legend in ways not included in the Western versions of the Bible, especially via information found in the Book of Jubilees (in the Ethiopian Bible) and the Kebra Nagast.

Like his father, Jacob received the divine blessing over his older brother, Esau, whose birthright he took with the help of his mother, Rebecca. (The cunning that secured him a covenant with the Almighty – seemingly, the Almighty preferred intelligence over brute strength – was a quality exemplified in many of the Solomonic kings of Ethiopia over time.) Jacob may not have been aware that he was part of a pattern and that history would repeat itself in short order. His own firstborn son would also be denied his birthright. According to the Ethiopian version of the story:

---

[178] Brooks, Miguel F., comp., ed. and trans. *Kebra Nagast: The Glory of Kings*. 1995. Red Sea Press, 2002, p. 12.

"After him, Jacob's first born transgressed the commandments of God and the kingdom departed from him and from his seed, because he had defiled his father's wife, and his father cursed him, and God was angry with him. He became the least among his brethren, and his children became leprous and scabby. Although he was the firstborn son of Jacob, the kingdom was rent from him. Then his younger brother reigned and was called Judah because of this; his seed was blessed, and his kingdom flourished."

Before his death, Jacob passed the promise prophetically to a younger male child. According to his prophecy, his son Judah was destined to father the line that would protect his Creator's promise to Abraham ("kings shall come out of thee") and maintain divine governance over the Almighty's chosen people. Jacob gathered all his sons, saying:

"Judah, thou art he whom thy brethren shall praise: thy hand shall be in the neck of thine enemies; thy father's children shall bow down before thee."[179]

He went on to utter words that would echo throughout the annals of human history, and have particular significance in the highlands of Ethiopia as well as the small, distant island of Jamaica:

"The sceptre shall not depart from Judah, nor a lawgiver from between his feet, until

---

[179] Genesis 49:8

Shiloh come; and unto him shall the gathering of the people be..."[180]

---

[180] Genesis 49:10

CHAPTER ELEVEN

The Glory of the Kings

"Behold, the days come, saith the Lord, that I will raise unto David a righteous Branch, and a King shall reign and prosper, and shall execute judgment and justice in the earth. In his days Judah shall be saved, and Israel shall dwell safely: and this is his name whereby he shall be called, The Lord Our Righteousness."

– Jeremiah 23:5-6

At the high altitude of Ejersa Goro, the air was thin and clean and it was further purified by the falling rain. As the physicians and their attendants surrounded the new mother, ensuring that she was feeling well, the baby boy's strong cries brought joy to the hearts of everyone present. After he was removed from the mother, servants diligently washed and anointed him with the finest oils.[181]

Outside, word of the birth reached the soldiers encamped at the compound. Ras Makonnen had started in Harar with a garrison of 3,000 of the realm's best soldiers.[182] He had gradually added Oromo and Somali

---

[181] Beresford, Deena-Marie. *Gurage! Gurage! Gurage! The Story of a Wollo Princess: Woizero Yeshimabet Ali AbaJifar*. Yeshimabet's Books and Things, 2019, p. 51.

[182] Marcus, Harold G. *The Life and Times of Menelik II: Ethiopia 1844-1913*. Red Sea Press, 1995, p. 93.

horsemen to his army to create a blended force of Muslims and Christians. His army was one of the most powerful in the realm, and his work ethic and skills on his own horse won him the respect of his men. At the news of the birth of his son, they immediately raised their firearms and squeezed the triggers. The servants' ears rang as the gunfire echoed in the distance, announcing the birth throughout the countryside. Bullets were expensive and uncommon in the realm but this was a special occasion.

Ras Makonnen and the new Christian inhabitants of Harar rejoiced. The baby boy was highly anticipated among the noble class. He was the newborn son of the great Ras Makonnen, a relative of the King of Kings. He carried the bloodline of Yekuno Amlak and the kings of Axum and, by extension, King Solomon and his father, King David, the first King of Israel from the line of Judah.

JUDAH

Fittingly, for the Hebrews, the man whose name would become synonymous with the throne of the Almighty on Earth was given a name meaning *to praise* or *to thank*. Born as the fourth son of Jacob, it was Judah who convinced his brothers not to kill their brother, Joseph. Instead, Judah suggested selling him to a Midianite merchant, who in turn sold Joseph into bondage in Egypt. Joseph was blessed and soon went from being a slave to being a high official in Egypt.

When famine ravaged their land, Joseph's brothers were forced to travel to Egypt for relief, just like their ancestor, Abraham. They encountered Joseph there but did not recognize him because he now had the appearance of an Egyptian. (It is worth noting a similarity here with Moses, giving further credence to the theory that the Hebrews were indistinguishable from the Egyptians aside from their culture.) Joseph, on the other hand, recognized his brothers and decided to test them by arranging to have his youngest brother, Benjamin, separated from them to remain in Egypt. Again, it was Judah who pleaded for another brother. So impassioned was his plea that Joseph decided to reveal his identity to his brothers.[183]

Such was the honorable character of Judah, whose descendants produced one of Israel's greatest personalities, a man instrumental to Ethiopian church life and cultural ethos – the great King David.

THE GREAT KING DAVID

True to Jacob's prophecy, Judah had many legendary offspring prior to 1892. So great have been the progeny of Judah that their names have cast a shadow even over that of their larger-than-life ancestor, Abraham. The Tribe of Judah includes names that ring out through history and are embedded in global consciousness: King David, King Solomon, Daniel, Joseph and, the most famous of all, Yeshua (Jesus) the Christ.

All the above personalities have contributed significantly to the enduring legacy of Judah in their own right. Yet, David, youngest son of Jesse, carried particular weight in establishing the first and only true, royal dynasty of Israel, ten generations after Judah. In the Book of Revelation, the final book of the Bible, the ultimate

---

[183] Genesis 45

redemption of Israel is foretold through the line of King David. Chapter 5, verse 5 reads:

> "And one of the elders saith unto me, Weep not: behold, the Lion of the tribe of Judah, the Root of David, hath prevailed to open the book, and to loose the seven seals thereof."

For the faithful, King David was the descendant of Judah who confirmed the prophecy of Abraham and Jacob for all time. The Kebra Nagast agrees that the salvation of the children of Adam rested with King David:

> "...And unto David will I give seed in her, and upon the earth one who shall become king, and in the heavens one from his seed shall reign in the flesh upon the throne of the Godhead. As for his enemies, they shall be gathered together under his footstool, and they shall be sealed with his seal."[184]

David was a famed warrior in his younger days. He made his name by slaying a giant man called Goliath from the tribe of the Philistines, the descendants of Kush's brother, Canaan. He was also known for being one of the chief musicians of the realm. He was a man after the Almighty's *own heart* and was anointed by the powerful dreadlocked high priest, Samuel.[185]

It was King David who established a permanent home for Israel in Jerusalem. He also saved resources to build one of the wonders of the ancient world before passing his crown to his offspring and chosen heir, King

---

[184] Brooks, Miguel F., comp., ed. and trans. *Kebra Nagast: The Glory of Kings*. 1995. Red Sea Press, 2002, p. 15.

[185] 1 Samuel 13:14

Solomon. King Solomon was also legendary for proving himself wiser than all of Israel's kings.

In 1892, King David held an important place in the hearts of all Ethiopia's monotheists. It was King David's grandson (King Solomon's son) who established the throne of the God of Abraham in the highlands of Ethiopia and championed the worship of one Almighty. For Muslims in particular, King David was a faithful servant and prophet of Allah. King David's psalms were integral to the rituals of the Orthodox Church – then governed by its mother church in Alexandria (Egypt), the Church of St. Mark – and were likely among the many prayers being chanted at the birth of the baby boy in Ejersa Goro.

THE EARLY YEARS OF DAVID

King David had humble beginnings as a boy and led a life that was not far removed from that of an Ethiopian shepherd in 1892. Though he only led sheep, he was foreseen as a great leader by the dreadlocked Nazarene prophet, Samuel, who revealed him as the future King of Israel.

David came to prominence due to his cunning akin to that of his ancestor, Jacob. He slew Goliath by using a slingshot, demonstrating that a wise mind could overcome brute force. He would go on to join the army of King Saul, the first King of Israel, and was soon put in charge of Saul's entire army. As a gifted musician, David also calmed the emotional King and eased his nightmares.

Around 1000 BCE, one of the great prophets of Israel and a trusted spiritual advisor to King David, Nathan, received a vision from the God of the Hebrews:

"Go and tell my servant David... I will set up thy seed after thee, which shall proceed out of thy bowels, and I will establish his kingdom. He shall build an house for my name, and I will stablish the throne of his kingdom for ever."[186]

King David would spend much of his reign accumulating materials to build a temple to honor his Creator. It was later completed by his son, King Solomon, and became known as the Temple of Solomon. King David also used his music (his psalms) to glorify God and his fame grew even greater. Another of his gifts was that of prophecy and, as such, he revealed that "Ethiopia shall soon stretch out her hands unto God."[187] King David's exposure to Ethiopia during his life was limited, yet those words became well known in the Ethiopian highlands, not to mention that his psalms would form the backbone of Ethiopian Church ritual.

The reigns of both David and Solomon were during the pinnacle of the Hebrew people's time as an independent and relatively stable kingdom. Jerusalem was the capital and the Hebrews had subdued the Canaanites for control of the rest of Palestine. While David was a priestly warrior king, Solomon was a priestly scholar king whose reign was characterized by an era of peace and love, attributed to his divine wisdom. So great was his wisdom that it inspired the Kebra Nagast. He also inspired one of the greatest overland journeys of a monarch recorded in ancient time. No one can be sure if King David knew that Ethiopia would start stretching out her hands so soon after his declaration but, not long after his death, Ethiopia's

---

[186] 2 Samuel 7:5-13

[187] Psalms 68:31

Queen of Sheba visited his capital city, Jerusalem. She went to see the famed Solomon and, as it turned out, ignited one of the greatest love stories in human history.

KING SOLOMON AND EMPRESS MAKEDA

Though the intimate details were not recorded, the Ethiopians were well acquainted with one of Judeo-Christianity's iconic love stories. The Bible states that "when the queen of Sheba heard of the fame of Solomon concerning the name of the Lord, she came to prove him with hard questions."

It goes on to say:

> "And Solomon told her all her questions: there was not any thing hid from the king, which he told her not. And when the queen of Sheba had seen all Solomon's wisdom, and the house that he had built, And the meat of his table, and the sitting of his servants, and the attendance of his ministers, and their apparel, and his cupbearers, and his ascent by which he went up unto the house of the Lord; there was no more spirit in her."[188]

The wisest queen of the ancient world had found a man who made her weak in the knees! The flames of love were kindled between them and Solomon discovered his first and only true love. (According to the Kebra Nagast, one of his wives, the royal Princess of Egypt, was to be part of his ultimate downfall.) Solomon was so taken with the Ethiopian queen that he "gave unto the queen of Sheba all

---

[188] 1 Kings 10:1-5

her desire, whatsoever she asked, beside that which Solomon gave her of his royal bounty." The Biblical encounter ends abruptly and after having been showered with all of Solomon's love and attention, the Queen of Sheba "turned and went to her own country, she and her servants."[189]

While the Hebrew chroniclers of the King omitted many details, the Ethiopian chroniclers recorded and maintained a much more detailed account of the events. The Kebra Nagast records that, one fateful night, Solomon invited the Queen to dinner in the royal palace. After the servants retired for the evening, he approached her and said, "Take thine ease for love's sake until daybreak." Filled with passion for the King but being a virtuous woman, the Queen replied, "Swear to me by thy God, the God of Israel, that thou wilt not take me by force. For if I, who according to the law of men am a virgin, be seduced, I would then travel on my journey back in sorrow, affliction and tribulation."[190] Solomon wasn't worried by her demand. After all he was known as the wisest man on Earth and maintained a household with over 300 wives and hundreds of concubines.

Before the dinner had even begun, Solomon had concocted a plan to make love to the Queen. While eating dinner, he gave her "meats which would make her thirsty and drinks that were mingled with vinegar, and fish and dishes made with pepper;" with the knowledge that she would again become thirsty soon after eating. Having made sure that she had no water to drink, he answered her request. "I swear unto thee that I will not take thee by

---

[189] 1 Kings 10:13

[190] Brooks, Miguel F., comp., ed. and trans. *Kebra Nagast: The Glory of Kings*. 1995. Red Sea Press, 2002, p. 30.

force, but also swear unto me that thou will not take by force anything in my house."

During the time she spent in Jerusalem, the Queen had grown close to King Solomon, so close that they slept in the same room. After swearing her oath, she went to sleep only to rise shortly afterwards with an extremely dry mouth. Thinking King Solomon was asleep, she rose without a sound to get a drink of water. Before a drop could touch her lips, King Solomon grabbed her hand and said, "Is there anything that thou hast seen under the heavens that is more precious than water?"[191] The Queen knew she had been outsmarted. The King wasted no time. He looked in her eyes and asked if he was "free from the oath which thou hast made me swear?" The Queen replied, "Be free from thy oath, only let me drink water."[192]

Ethiopia would never be the same.

DESTRUCTION OF JUDAH IN JERUSALEM

King Solomon's connection with his soulmate was short lived and as he drifted to sleep after obtaining "biblical" knowledge of the Queen, he had a dream. The Kebra Nagast records it as follows:

> "…there appeared unto King Solomon in a dream a brilliant sun, and it came down from heaven and shed exceedingly great splendor over Israel. And when it had tarried there for a time it suddenly withdrew itself, and it flew away to the country of

---

[191] Ibid.

[192] Ibid., 30-31.

Ethiopia, and it shone there with exceedingly great brightness forever, for it desired to dwell there. And the King said: 'I waited to see if it would come back to Israel, but it did not return. And again while I waited a light rose up in the heavens, and a sun emerged from the tribe of Judah, and it sent forth light which was very much brighter than before.' And Israel, because of the brightness of that sun treated that sun with cruelty and would not walk in the light thereof. And that sun paid no heed to Israel, and the Israelites hated Him, and it became impossible that peace should exist between them and the sun."[193]

True to King Solomon's vision, the blessings of the Almighty seemed to fade from Israel after his death. Jerusalem descended into war and discord. His son, Rehoboam – not as wise as him – allowed his friends to lead Jerusalem against the surrounding provinces and thereby lead his people down the path of civil war. The infighting weakened the descendants of Jacob to the point that foreign conquerors who set their sights on Jerusalem had little trouble completing their conquest.

According to the Book of Jeremiah, the Tribe of Judah's rule in Jerusalem ended with the invasion of Nebuchadnezzar of Babylon in 586 BCE. The land of the Almighty's covenant was invaded, Solomon's Temple was destroyed and the princes of Judah were all taken captive. Though the temple was rebuilt in 516 BCE and some of the descendants of Judah returned to Jerusalem, the throne of David was never reestablished there. Had the Almighty

---

[193] Ibid., 31-32.

abandoned his covenant to Abraham, Isaac and Jacob? Was the hope of the great King David lost?

In the realm of Ethiopia, the Almighty's covenant to David was not seen as a casual promise. The prophet Nathan revealed to David that the Almighty had decreed:

> "If [one of your sons] commit iniquity, I will chasten him with the rod of men, and with the stripes of the children of men: But my mercy shall not depart away from [the throne of David], as I took it from Saul, whom I put away before thee. And thine house and thy kingdom shall be established for ever."[194]

The Ethiopians viewed the Almighty as being always light years ahead of the will of man. Accordingly, their account of history records that the Almighty had already put in motion a plan to preserve King David's bloodline and throne, long before Nebuchadnezzar's armies closed in on the gates of Jerusalem. The true love between Solomon and the Queen of Sheba was the vehicle that the Almighty used to transport his covenant to the place where mankind was created and first walked the Earth.

INTO THE KEBRA NAGAST

For Ethiopians, the reason why the God of Israel had sent their mightiest and wisest empress to commune with the reigning King of Israel in Jerusalem was clear. Ethiopia was viewed as the Almighty's peculiar treasure, a land more ancient than recorded history, a land that the

---

[194] 2 Samuel 7:14-16

Almighty would give to no one but his chosen to have dominion over. This sentiment pervaded the cultures of coastal and highland Ethiopia alike, and was best expressed in the Kebra Nagast.

The true purpose of Ethiopia's sacred book was to explain one of Ethiopia's most closely guarded secrets: how Empress Makeda and King Solomon's love produced a son, Menelik I. The Kebra Nagast further illustrates how Menelik I brought the Ark of the Covenant (the Almighty's seat on Earth) to Ethiopia and established the throne of David there.

For Ethiopians of faith in 1892, Ethiopia was Zion – the home of both King David's throne and the Ark of the Covenant!

As Ethiopians maintained that Menelik I began the Solomonic line of kings in their homeland, the biblical record of how Judah's offspring reached those highlands was well known among world historians, albeit the subject of much discussion and debate. Even at the time of the Christ, it was accepted that the sons of King Solomon reigned in the distant realm of Ethiopia. The Axumite Empire, ruled by the sons of Menelik I, dominated the northern coast of Ethiopia during this period and was an important trading partner of the ancient world during the time when the Christ walked the earth. This empire would have been well known to the inhabitants of Jerusalem at the dawn of the millennium. In fact, Ethiopian Jews were recorded to have made the pilgrimage to Jerusalem to pray in the temple there.[195]

---

[195] Book of Acts 8:26-27. "And the angel of the Lord spake unto Philip, saying, Arise, and go toward the south unto the way that goeth down from Jerusalem unto Gaza, which is desert. And he arose and went: and, behold, a man of Ethiopia, an eunuch of great authority under

Supported by the knowledge of their Solomonic heritage, and aware of their unique status as heirs to the legacy and throne of King David, Ethiopia's kings managed to rally the country to face invaders throughout the centuries and maintain Ethiopia's independence throughout recorded history.

FROM THE LINE OF SOLOMON

The legacy of the baby boy born in the highlands surrounding Harar started with the son of King Solomon and Empress Makeda – Bayna-Lehkem, otherwise known as Menelik I or, sometimes, David II. He was the first Ethiopian king from the Solomonic line and an esteemed ancestor to the baby boy.

The boy's Solomonic ancestry meant that he was born into a position of power. That power was represented in a real way by the presence of his father, Ras Makonnen, and his troops at his birth. That power was also represented by the many priests and physicians who were in attendance. The poor farmers of Ethiopia, who were the backbone of the realm, could not afford such luxury. Only those who could claim descent from the Solomonic line could receive such benefits. With the support of Ethiopia's most powerful institution, the Orthodox Church, the Solomonic kings were a symbol of power and unity, and they were living reminders of the Almighty's divine covenant with Abraham, Jacob and King David. Their displays of wealth, consistent with the wealth of the

---

Candace queen of the Ethiopians, who had the charge of all her treasure, and had come to Jerusalem for to worship."

Solomonic kings mentioned in the Bible, were viewed as the results of that covenant.

The sitting emperor in 1892, Emperor Menelik II, was named after the first King of Kings who confirmed Ethiopia as the land where the Almighty would fulfill the promise made to Abraham.

CHAPTER TWELVE

The African Christ

"Behold, my father David hath renewed his youth and hath risen from the dead...Ye said unto me, he resembleth thee but this is not my stature, but the stature of David my father in the days of his early manhood, and he is handsomer than I am."

– Kebra Nagast[196]

Gunshots rang out through the countryside and the noise brought joy to Ras Makonnen's heart. After all, the shots signalled a new life. He allowed himself, only for a moment, to forget that those arms could one day be needed to defend against the Europeans who now controlled Ethiopia's access to the Red Sea. Guns were a necessary evil and constant companions for an Ethiopian noble in 1892. Since Ras Makonnen took over Harar, it had become the center of the gun trade in Ethiopia.[197] However, without control over the coast, Ethiopia was forced to deal with middlemen and tariffs to bring in the arms that would be necessary for the realm's defense. It

---

[196] Brooks, Miguel F., comp., ed. and trans. *Kebra Nagast: The Glory of Kings*. 1995. Red Sea Press, 2002, p. 40.

[197] Marcus, Harold G. *The Life and Times of Menelik II: Ethiopia 1844-1913*. Red Sea Press, 1995, p. 93.

was the Red Sea access as well as control over the interior that made ancient Axum a world power.

On August 1, 1891, Ras Makonnen had reached out to the French in Djibouti to arrange Ethiopian access to the ports. The Italians were in control of most of Ethiopia's coastline and Ras Makonnen was trying to maintain Ethiopia's options. The French signalled that they were not in support of Ethiopia falling within the Italian sphere of influence, but they were careful not to offend Italy while they kept communication channels open with Ethiopia.[198]

While the French were protecting their interest in Djibouti, Ras Makonnen was securing the interest of Ethiopia. On July 21, 1891, he had overseen the loading of a caravan leaving from Harar. The caravan carried eight camel loads of ivory and musk as well as 3,000 ounces of gold. The goods were sold to the French and the proceeds were used to pay down an Italian loan.[199] Ras Makonnen did not want to owe any foreigner anything and he was only too happy to lessen Ethiopia's burden. Ethiopia was reeling from the drought and famine of the Kifu Ken and Emperor Menelik II did not want to risk open war with the Italians who occupied the coast. Ras Makonnen, like many nobles of the day, dreamed of restoring Ethiopia to its ancient borders with access to the sea. He had read about the glory of Ethiopia's ancient kings since he was a boy, and he believed that Ethiopia's current emperor would indeed restore the kingdom to the status of his namesake.

---

[198] Ibid., 140.

[199] Ibid., 141.

MENELIK I

Emperor Menelik II was named for the man said to have transferred the Solomonic dynasty to Ethiopia. That man was Menelik I. An ancestor to both Emperor Menelik II and Ras Makonnen.

Dismissed as myth by many, the oral and written tradition concerning Menelik I and his impact on Ethiopian life cannot be denied. (Ras Makonnen was a living testament to that impact.) This great ancestor to the royal Ethiopian bloodline was said to be born nine months and five days after King Solomon consummated his relationship with Queen Makeda.[200] Plagued with and a longing for the beauty and people of her mother country, his mother left Jerusalem and the intrigues of the royal house of Israel. Queen Makeda headed home to the highlands of Ethiopia where she gave birth to Menelik I.

Also referred to as David II, Menelik I would later visit his father in Jerusalem as a grown man. The Kebra Nagast records that when Solomon saw his son, he said, "Behold, my father David hath renewed his youth and hath risen from the dead."[201] He then remarked to his attendants, who had told him that the visitor from the south strongly resembled him, "Ye said unto me, 'He resembleth thee,' but this is not my stature, but the stature of David my father in the days of his early manhood, and he is handsomer than I am."[202]

---

[200] Ibid., 33.

[201] Ibid., 40.

[202] Ibid.

The reason for Menelik I's journey was to receive his father's blessing to establish in righteousness the throne of David in Ethiopia. The Queen had sent word to Solomon:

> "Take this young man, anoint him, consecrate and bless him, and make him King over our country, and give him the command that a woman shall never again reign in Ethiopia, and send him back in peace."[203]

Solomon, however, had other plans. He told the Ethiopian delegation his thoughts:

> "Besides travailing with him and suckling him, what else hath a woman to do with a son? A daughter belongeth to the mother, and a boy to the father. God curse Eve, saying: 'Bring forth children in anguish and with sorrow of heart, and after thy bringing forth, shall take place thy return to thy husband.' As for this son of mine, I will not give him to the Queen, but I will make him king over Israel. For this is my firstborn, the first of my race whom God have given me."[204]

Menelik I, focused on his mission and raised to value the spiritual over the material, told his father:

> "Gold and silver and rich apparel are not wanting in our country, But I came hither in order to hear thy wisdom, to see thy face, to salute thee and to pay homage to thy

---

[203] Ibid.

[204] Ibid.

kingdom, and to make obeisance to thee, and then I intended thee to send me away to my mother and my own country."

Menelik I continued:

"...thou hast a son who is better than I am, namely Rehoboam who was born of thy wife lawfully, whilst my mother is not thy wife according to the law."[205]

Solomon was also a famous judge in matters of the law, renown for his wisdom. He was quick to refute his son's assertions of not being worthy or legitimate to rule in Jerusalem, pointing out that he, himself, was:

"...not the [lawful] son of my father David, for he took the wife of another man whom he caused to be slain in battle, and he begot me by her, but God is compassionate and He hath, forgiven him. Who is wickeder and more foolish than men? And who is as compassionate and wise as God? God hath made me of my father, and thee hath He made of me, according to His will."[206]

He went on to explain:

"My son Rehoboam is a boy six years old, and thou art my first born son. Thou hast come to reign and to lift up the spear of him that begot thee. Behold, I have been reigning for twenty-nine years and thy

---

[205] Ibid., 42.

[206] Ibid., 43.

mother came to me in the seventh year of my kingdom;"[207]

After much discussion, Solomon finally conceded his son's wish to return to his own country. However, he would give him as much assistance as possible, so he assembled his chief counselors, officers and elders of his kingdom and told them:

> "I am not able to make my son consent to dwell here. And now, hearken ye unto me and to what I shall say unto you. Let us make him king of the country Ethiopia, together with your children; ye sit on my right hand and on my left hand, and in like manner the eldest of your children shall sit on his right hand and on his left hand. Ye councilors and officers, let us give him your firstborn children and we shall have two kingdoms; I will rule here with you, and our children shall rule there."[208]

THE ARK OF THE COVENANT LEAVES JERUSALEM

It is on this trip that the Ark of the Covenant is said to have left Jerusalem with Menelik I and ended up in Ethiopia, thus signaling the divine sanction of the Ethiopian royal family and starting the Ethiopian Davidic line of kings. According to Ethiopian tradition in 1892, the Ark rested in Axum.

---

[207] Ibid.

[208] Ibid., 44.

It is written that Azariah, one of the sons of King Solomon's priest, accompanied Menelik I on the journey. He had a vision where an angel appeared and stated:

> "Stand up, be strong and rouse up Elmeyas and Abis and Makri, and take the pieces of wood and I will open for thee the doors of the sanctuary. And take thou the Tabernacle of the Law of God, and thou shalt carry it without trouble and discomfort. And as I have been commanded by God to be with it forever, I will be thy guide when thou shalt carry it away."[209]

The Kebra Nagast assures its reader, "Had it not been that God willed it, Zion could not have been taken away."[210]

Upon reaching Ethiopia, Azariah stated:

> "'Bring hither the jubilee trumpets and let us go to Zion, and there we will make new the kingdom of our lord, David.' And he took the oil of sovereignty and filled and horn and he anointed [David II] with the unguent, with the oil of sovereignty."[211]

The Kebra Nagast goes on to say:

> "And they blew horns and pipes and trumpets, and beat drums, and sounded all kinds of musical instruments, and there was singing, dancing, games and displays with horses and all the men and women of the country of Ethiopia were present, small and

---

[209] Ibid., 62.

[210] Ibid., 63.

[211] Ibid., 124.

great, and the pygmies, six thousand in number..."

The mention of a delegation of pygmies is significant as the pygmies were also recorded in ancient Egypt, which suggests that ancient Ethiopia's borders were far beyond those of 1892 Ethiopia. Indeed, the Kebra Nagast describes the borders of the kingdom as follows:

"Thus the eastern boundary of the kingdom of the King of Ethiopia is the beginning of the city of Gaza in the land of Judah and Jerusalem, and its boundary is the Lake of Jericho passing by the coast of its sea to Leba and Saba, bound by Bisis and Asnet...Its other boundary is the Sea of the Black and Naked Men, going up to Mount Kebereneyon into the Sea of Darkness, that is, the place where the sun setteth, extending to Feneel and Lasifala, and its borders are the lands near the Garden of Paradise where there is plenty of food and abundance of cattle; this boundary extendeth as far as Zawel and passeth on to the Sea of India with its boundary as far as the Sea of Tarsis. In its remote part lieth the Sea of Medyam, until it cometh to the country of Gaza."[212]

Some modern scholars have called it myth but the history and legacy of the Solomonic dynasty in Ethiopia has been defended with real blood against all challengers, foreign and domestic. All who went to conquer were defeated, preserving the bloodline of Solomon and the tradition of Zion in those highlands.

---

[212] Ibid., 125.

Ethiopia did not limit itself to the Pentateuch. Another offspring of Solomon, Rehoboam, gave rise to another branch of his bloodline that would produce the most renown member of the Tribe of Judah, one who would have the most impact on Ethiopia – Yeshua Ben Yosef, also known as Iyesus Kristos to the Orthodox world and Jesus Christ in the West. The revelation of the Christ swept from Northeast Africa through the rift valley into the highlands. In fact, the Kebra Nagast infuses the prophecy of Yeshua throughout the Old Testament and ascribes prophetic statements about his coming to many of the early prophets.

YESHUA BEN YOSEF

Born in 4 BCE in the village of Bethlehem, the same town as his ancestor, King David, Yeshua would forever change the course of human history. As with the other biblical patriarchs, there remains scholarly dispute as to whether he was an actual historical figure. However, there is no dispute about the impact of Yeshua Ben Yosef, otherwise known as Jesus the Christ. The very measurement of global time was altered to acknowledge his birth.

Yeshua's birth was a divine miracle. He was born of a virgin, Mariam, although acknowledged as the son of an earthly father, Joseph. Joseph's genealogy is detailed in the Book of Matthew in the New Testament and was traced back to King David and King Solomon, through Solomon's second son, Rehoboam. It is unclear what tribe Mariam claimed descent from but it is thought that she was also a descendant of Judah. Joseph did not consummate his union with Mariam and his faith was tested when her pregnancy was revealed. It is written that he chose to remain with his wife after receiving the counsel of an angel.[213]

For the Christian faithful, Yeshua was the anointed one foretold in the Hebrew scriptures. In Ethiopia, the Kebra Nagast makes considerable effort to connect Yeshua to the Old Testament prophets and the Ark of the Covenant. The Kebra Nagast explains:

> "[The Creator] made Adam in his own image and likeness, so that He might remove Satan because of his pride, together with his host, and might establish Adam, His own plant, together with the righteous, His children, for His praises. For the plan of God was decided upon and decreed in that He said: 'I will become man, and I will be in everything which I have created, I will abide in flesh.' And in the days that came after, by His good pleasure there was born in the flesh of the Second Zion the Second Adam, who was our Saviour Christ. This is our Glory and our faith, our hope and our life, the Second Zion."[214]

It is written that the *Magi*, or wise men, were drawn to his birth by signs in the stars. Some Ethiopian traditions state that an Ethiopian king was one of the wise men. He was King Bazen, who reigned since around 10 BCE. He is thought to have been the first to bring news of the Christ's birth to Ethiopia. The tomb of King Bazen was a prominent landmark in Axum in 1892. Others assert that all the wise men were Ethiopians, based on the fact that, at

---

[213] Matthew 1:18-25

[214] Brooks, Miguel F., comp., ed. and trans. *Kebra Nagast: The Glory of Kings*. 1995. Red Sea Press, 2002, p. 5.

the time of Christ's birth, only Judea and Ethiopia carried a large number of people versed in the Hebrew prophecies. Proponents of this theory point to the fact that Yeshua was given gold, myrrh and frankincense, all of which were common items in Ethiopia. As for the stars that attracted the Magi, detailed descriptions of the celestial placement of these are found in the *Mahl'ete ts'ge*, an ancient Ethiopian text written in Ge'ez.

As with many Ethiopian traditions, these theories did not carry much weight outside of Ethiopia. Western traditions identify the three wise men as coming from India, Persia and Babylon. It has also been said that they were three Persian astrologers, as the word *Magi* was associated with Zoroastrianism and its priestly magos class.

The visit of the three wise men was said to have triggered one of the most horrific events in biblical history. The book of Matthew records:

> "...when [the Magi] were departed, behold, the angel of the Lord appeareth to Joseph in a dream, saying, Arise, and take the young child and his mother, and flee into Egypt, and be thou there until I bring thee word: for Herod will seek the young child to destroy him. When he arose, he took the young child and his mother by night, and departed into Egypt: And was there until the death of Herod: that it might be fulfilled which was spoken of the Lord by the prophet, saying, Out of Egypt have I called my son. Then Herod, when he saw that he was mocked of [the Magi], was exceeding wroth, and sent forth, and slew all the children that were in Bethlehem, and in all

the coasts thereof, from two years old and under, according to the time which he had diligently inquired of [the Magi]. Then was fulfilled that which was spoken by Jeremiah the prophet, saying, In Rama was there a voice heard, lamentation, and weeping, and great mourning, Rachel weeping for her children, and would not be comforted, because they are not."[215]

Yeshua's flight from Northeast Africa deeper into Africa would have made sense for a poor family escaping persecution from the Roman-controlled powers in Judea. Yeshua's family would have been aiming to blend in among the poor of Egypt. (Yet again, their actions were consistent with the many Hebrew accounts of Hebrews being mistaken for Egyptians.) For the faithful, it fulfilled the prophecy of Hosea: "When Israel was a child, I loved him, and out of Egypt I called my son."[216] The poor of Egypt in Yeshua's time, as in 1892, would have been the indigenous, melanated Nile Valley inhabitants who were being colonized by powerful Roman invaders.

The Romans who ruled Judea were not the first invaders to exert influence on the once mighty Egypt. Greece had also managed to conquer the mighty African nation. At the time of Yeshua, Egypt had just witnessed the last of the Ptolemaic pharaohs with the death of the famous Cleopatra in 30 BCE. That line of pharaohs descended from Macedonian/Greek King Alexander's general, Ptolemy. Their fall to the Romans is well documented in history.

---

[215] Matthew 2:13-18

[216] Hosea 11:1

Herod, the ruler referenced in the New Testament, had been installed by the Romans to keep what was left of the Tribe of Judah under the foot of Rome. The Roman Empire, led by general Pompey the Great, had conquered Judea in 63 BCE. Herod took control of Jerusalem by displacing the ruling Hasmonean Dynasty in 36 BCE. He was granted the title of King of Judea by the Roman Senate and ruled during Cleopatra's time. Despite his power and many achievements, Herod would not be successful in his legendary quest to kill a child destined to change the world.

The events that shaped Yeshua after coming out of Egypt are not clear. Although details about his early life are wanting, it is written that he spent time in Galilee and Nazareth, and that he was trained as a Carpenter. Judging by his utterances, he was a highly literate man of considerable knowledge for the time. Extra-biblical sources state that he traveled widely, including to Ethiopia and India.

Yeshua's utterances electrified his oppressed people, not to mention the pages of history. He was clear that his mission was Hebrew redemption and an end to Roman aggression, and he stood firmly in the traditions of his forefathers, saying, "Think not that I am come to destroy the law, or the prophets: I am not come to destroy, but to fulfill."[217]

He preached the power of each individual and not overdependence on the organized church, a radical message for its time:

> "...verily I say unto you, If ye have faith as a grain of mustard seed, ye shall say unto this mountain, Remove hence to yonder place;

---

[217] Matthew 5:17

and it shall remove; and nothing shall be impossible unto you."[218]

Yeshua began to awaken the divine potential in his people, spending his time among the poor, working class as opposed to the religious elites of his day. When challenged by the highly educated, Roman-controlled Hebrew scribes and Pharisees, he would reply:

> "They that are whole need not a physician; but they that are sick. I came not to call the righteous, but sinners to repentance."[219]

His message of leadership through service was needed by a people under the heel of Roman oppressors. He would preach:

> "And whosoever of you will be the chiefest, shall be servant of all. For even the Son of man came not to be ministered unto, but to minister, and to give his life a ransom for many."[220]

The expectation of the oppressed in Jerusalem and Judea was that Yeshua was going to reestablish the throne of David in Jerusalem. The Book of Luke records Mariam being visited by an angel who prophesied:

> "He shall be great, and shall be called the Son of the Highest: and the Lord God shall give unto him the throne of his father David: And he shall reign over the house of Jacob

---

[218] Matthew 17:20

[219] Luke 5:31-32

[220] Mark 10:44-45

for ever; and of his kingdom there shall be no end."[221]

It is also said that, when Yeshua made the decision to enter Jerusalem, the masses waved palm trees and shouted, "Hosanna to the Son of David!"[222] When he was asked directly by his followers whether he would inhabit the throne, he responded, "It is not for you to know the times or the seasons, which the Father hath put in his own power."[223]

Yeshua also had vivid and prophetic utterances:

> "...the stars shall fall from heaven, and the powers of the heavens shall be shaken: And then shall appear the sign of the Son of man in heaven: and then shall all the tribes of the earth mourn, and they shall see the Son of man coming in the clouds of heaven with power and great glory. And he shall send his angels with a great sound of a trumpet, and they shall gather together his elect from the four winds, from one end of heaven to the other."[224]

Yeshua never attempted to establish the throne of David. He would go on to be captured by the Romans, crucified, and then resurrected. He then mysteriously disappeared and left his trusted followers to spread his message. Through his faithful followers, Yeshua's words caused millions to leave their ancient traditions and turn all

---

[221] Luke 1:32-33

[222] Matthew 21:9

[223] Acts 1:7

[224] Matthew 24:29-31

their praise and adoration towards him and the Hebrew traditions.

YESHUA AND ETHIOPIA

Yeshua, who spent some of his formative years in Egypt, clearly had knowledge of Ethiopia. He is recorded in the New Testament as saying:

> "The Queen of the South will rise at the judgment with this generation and condemn it; for she came from the ends of the earth to listen to Solomon's wisdom, and now something greater than Solomon is here."

Aside from demonstrating Yeshua's knowledge of Ethiopia, this highlights the important place Queen Makeda's visit to King Solomon held in Hebrew culture at the turn of the millennium. Perhaps, knowing about the throne of his ancestors in Ethiopia, he felt free to not focus on reclaiming the physical throne of David.

The Book of Revelation describes Yeshua as having hairs "white like wool, as white as snow; and his eyes were as a flame of fire; And his feet like unto fine brass, as if they burned in a furnace."[225] This description is consistent with the prophecy of Daniel, which says, "I beheld till the thrones were cast down, and the Ancient of days did sit, whose garment was white as snow, and the hair of his head like the pure wool."[226] These descriptions correlate to that of Greek historian Herodotus's description of Black Egyptians with woolly hair, as well as other descriptions of Ethiopians with woolly hair. It is the brown-skinned,

---

[225] Revelation 1:14-15

[226] Daniel 7:9

woolly-haired Yeshua who first appears in Ethiopian iconography.

Ethiopians also hold that St. Matthew, apostle of Yeshua and author of the first book in the New Testament, traveled to Ethiopia to share the good news of Yeshua's resurrection with the people there. Matthew was said to have been in Ethiopia during the rule of either Queen Garsemot Kandake, 48-58 CE, or Hatazo Bhar Aseged, 56-86 CE. (The exact dates of their reigns are disputed as there are variations in the records of Ethiopia's rulers at the time.) Queen Garsemot was said to be the queen whose administrator, an Ethiopian eunuch, traveled to Jerusalem and was baptized by the apostle Philip. That baptism is said to have begun the spread of Christianity in Ethiopia.

YESHUA AND HISTORY

Secular accounts of Yeshua were not non-existent. Jewish historian Flavius Josephus wrote about him around 93 CE, saying:

> "About this time there lived Jesus, a wise man, if indeed one ought to call him a man. For he was one who performed surprising deeds and was a teacher of such people as accept the truth gladly. He won over many Jews and many of the Greeks. He was the Messiah. And when, upon the accusation of the principal men among us, Pilate had condemned him to a cross, those who had first come to love him did not cease. He appeared to them spending a third day restored to life, for the prophets of God had foretold these things and a thousand

other marvels about him. And the tribe of the Christians, so called after him, has still to this day not disappeared."[227]

In the second century CE, Roman historian Tacitus wrote:

"But not all the relief that could come from man, not all the Bounties that the prince could bestow, nor all the atonements Which could be presented to the gods, availed to relieve Nero from the infamy of being believed to have ordered the Conflagration, the fire of Rome. Hence to suppress the rumor, he Falsely charged with the guilt, and punished Christians, who were Hated for their enormities. Christus, the founder of the name, was Put to death by Pontius Pilate, procurator of Judea in the reign Of Tiberius: but the pernicious superstition, repressed for a time Broke out again, not only through Judea, where the mischief Originated, but through the city of Rome also, where all things Hideous and shameful from every part of the world find their Center and become popular. Accordingly, an arrest was first Made of all who pleaded guilty; then, upon their information, an Immense multitude was convicted, not so much of the crime of Firing the city, as of hatred against mankind.[228]

Although both historians gave us these two well known, non-biblical accounts that provide evidence for

---

[227] Josephus, Flavius. *The Antiquities of the Jews.*

[228] Tacitus. *The Annals.*

Yeshua as a historical figure, their accounts were irrelevant to the Ethiopians. Their faith in the word of Christ was unshakable.

THE NATURE OF YESHUA THE CHRIST

Once Christianity was established in Ethiopia, there arose serious disputes about the nature of this extraordinary man. Among three schools of thought regarding what Yeshua represented, the first and most powerful was the Tewahedo sect.

THE TEWAHEDO

The Tewahedo hold that Yeshua the Christ was the product of two births – one birth from the Almighty and one from the virgin Mariam. These two births represented the two natures of Christ, making him part human and part divine.

The authority of the Tewahedo rested in Egypt and the Tewahedo faithful could boast that they were protectors of the true Alexandrine doctrine. The church in Alexandria was founded by St. Mark, the author of the oldest book written in the New Testament. The Book of Mark was written in 70 CE and was the first account of the miracles, prophecy and powerful words of Yeshua. Like Matthew, Mark traveled south further into Africa to spread the good news about the life and teachings of Yeshua, and his teachings spread rapidly among the native Egyptians who had been oppressed for centuries by Greeks and Romans.

196

THE QIBAT

The adherents of the Qibat sect believed that the Christ was anointed in the womb of Mariam, where his flesh became divine. It was only at that point in time that Yeshua was elevated to the Son of God and, thus, made into a divine being. The Qibat followers' stronghold was Gojjam and one of its main proponents was Ras Alula Qubi, who controlled much of central and northern Ethiopia during the time of the Zemene Mesafint. He supported the doctrine as espoused by the Ewostatian monks who were named after Ewostatewos, a 12th century Ethiopian saint. Ewostatewos established monasteries that remained faithful to Judaic observances long after they were no longer practiced by the Christian Emperors. With the rise of the priestly warrior kings after the Zemene Mesafint, the Qibat faded into obscurity.

SOST LIDET (THREE BIRTHS)

The followers of the Sost Lidet believed that the Christ was first birthed by the Almighty, then by the womb of Mariam, and then experienced a third birth at the time of his baptism by John the Baptist. This view had considerable support in Shoa as well as parts of Gondar.

The Shoan adherence to the Sost lidet was particularly worrisome to the leadership of the Tewahedo church as Shoa had emerged as one of the more powerful branches of the Solomonic bloodline and its influence was growing rapidly in the realm. The rise of Shoa culminated in the 1889 coronation of Emperor Menelik II, the reigning emperor in Ethiopia in 1892. In his younger days, he was partial to the Sost Lidet philosophy but, by the time he ascended the highest throne in the realm, Emperor Menelik II had fully embraced the Tewahedo doctrine. His former ward, Ras Makonnen, was also firm in his faith in the Tewahedo doctrine.

It was from this rich Solomonic heritage that the newly appointed governor of Muslim Harar forged his identity. On July 23, 1892, as the rain fell on the parched land and he listened to the combination of thunder and rifle fire and women raising their voices in praise around his lawful wife's bedside, Ras Makonnen knew that the Lion of Judah had once again prevailed. His greatest prayer had been answered.

CHAPTER THIRTEEN

The Ras Named Makonnen

"A wise man is strong; yea, a man of knowledge increaseth strength." – **Proverbs 24:5**

Ras Makonnen's chaplains and astrologers were certain: a baby boy would be born and he would have an heir. They had carefully studied the pathways of both Neptune and Pluto, and they were confident that the intersection of the planets would coincide with the moment of the child's birth. The stage would then be set for a special soul to enter into the realm of the living and Ethiopia would be delivered!

The two planets had been steadily moving together since they last intersected in the year 1399.[229] Similar to

---

[229] Jenkins, Palden. "Astrological Cycles in History." http://cura.free.fr/xx/20palden.html. Astrologist Palden Jenkins explains astrological cycles and history: "We're looking at historical trends, undercurrents and threads. Trends take at least decades, if not centuries, to unfold. Therefore, there can often, but not always, be a time-delay between an astrological and an historical event. Also, as astrologers, we're privy to understanding the underlying tides of human thought and feeling. In other words, we're looking at humanity's 'psychosphere' - its body of collective psychological motion and the way it oozes, leaks and expresses itself into the world. This

Ethiopia in 1892, the year 1399 was one of instability for the Eurasian continent. A half a century earlier, the bubonic plague (popularly called the Black Death) had ravaged Europe. Just like the Evil Days in Ethiopia, one third of Eurasia's population died during the years-long plague. In the wake of the largest tragedy in Europe's history, the energy from the celestial alignment descended on a beleaguered continent and fueled the seeds that were quietly being sown for that continent's renaissance. The Moors were still ruling in Spain and the plague helped loosen the grip of the Roman church on Europe. The aftermath of the plague weakened the status quo enough to allow Moorish culture and ideas to spread quicker.

The celestial energy of 1399 also was marked by royal births. In China, the Xuande Emperor was born in 1399. The Xuande Emperor was known not only for his powerful armies with garrisons as far as Vietnam, but also for being a lover of literature and an accomplished painter. In the same year, China would see rebellion as the Prince of Yan, Zhu Di rose against the prevailing power structure.

Over in West Africa, the Songhai dynasty still reigned in 1399. The rulers of the Songhai and other powerful African dynasties had no idea that Prince Henry of Portugal had just started another world-changing development: a mariners college with the purpose of embarking on African and Atlantic explorations. The college would provide the training necessary to

---

means we can (theoretically, at least) detect the points at which historical thought-processes begin, change and go through their modulations. It also means there can be a time-delay between inner process and noticed event. However, this said, there are exceptions." While Jenkins explains the significance of the intersection of Pluto and Neptune during 1891-1892, his studies do not mention events in Ethiopia.

that he maintained a relationship with the former woman since two years later he had his first child, Lij Yilma Makonnen.[234] The latter woman was still very young at the time of their union and it is likely that the marriage was not immediately consummated.

That princess from Wollo was named Woizero Yeshimebet.[235] She was from a royal family and noted for her beauty and charm.[236] Her marriage to Makonnen was not by chance. Yeshimebet's mother, Woizero Wolete Ihata Giyorgis Yimeru, was once married to Menelik II's uncle, Ras Darge Sahle Selassie. Thus, her family had already been tied to the Solomonic bloodline. To cement the union for all time, Makonnen and Yeshimebet were married in a Christian ceremony according to Ethiopian Orthodox custom and they established a home in the province in Shoa.

Ras Makonnen did not have long to honeymoon with his new wife. Ethiopia had entered a period of rapid change and upheaval, and war was the order of the day. As a skilled warrior, he was called to conduct military expeditions on behalf of his leader and older cousin, Menilik II, and he chose to leave his wife at home in Shoa.

A French Monk, Monseigneur Jarosseau, who lived for many years in Harar, wrote:

---

[234] Beresford, Deena-Marie. *Gurage! Gurage! Gurage! The Story of a Wollo Princess: Woizero Yeshimabet Ali AbaJifar.* Yeshimabet's Books and Things, 2019, p. 40.

[235] Selassie, Haile, I. *My Life and Ethiopia's Progress: The Autobiography of Emperor Haile Sellassie I, King of Kings, Lord of Lords, Conquering Lion of Judah*, vol. 1. Frontline Distribution International, 1999, p. 14.

[236] Beresford, Deena-Marie. *Gurage! Gurage! Gurage! The Story of a Wollo Princess: Woizero Yeshimabet Ali AbaJifar.* Yeshimabet's Books and Things, 2019, p. 40.

> "Makonnen, justly admired as the greatest military leader that Abyssinia has perhaps ever known...respected on all sides for his high intelligence and his uprightness, was also beloved for his justice and goodness, and his spiritual character."[237]

He was described by the Europeans as being:

> "... a small dark man with delicate hands, large expressive eyes, a small black beard and moustache, and a most intelligent cast of countenance. His voice is very gentle and his manners extremely dignified and quiet. What he said was little but to the point, and he gave us then and thereafter the impression of a man who wielded a good deal of power in a quiet way."[238]

Ras Makonnen did wield a good deal of power, indeed. It was he who Emperor Menelik II trusted like a firstborn son or brother, and who was sent out on the most important missions for the empire. Ras Makonnen was the one making diplomatic contact with the European powers that were increasingly encroaching on Ethiopian territory – he visited Italy in 1888. He would also visit France and England in order to secure Ethiopia's borders against European incursion and forge alliances to help protect his homeland from future invasion.

---

[237] Sandford, Christine. *The Lion of Judah Hath Prevailed*. 1954. Research Associates School Times Publications, 1998, p. 15.

[238] Ibid.

THE CONQUEST OF HARAR

In 1887, Makonnen helped his cousin, then King Menelik II, to subdue and bring Harar under the imperial rule and administration of the Lion of Judah, King of Kings, Emperor Yohannes IV. The addition of Harar to the Ethiopian empire was so important that Menelik II himself moved on the city-state along with Makonnen and 40,000 cavalry and foot soldiers.

Previous Christian invasions had been no match for the expert troops of the Emir, Abdullahi Harari, who took over the reins of power following the British withdrawal of Egyptian soldiers. The Emir, who was a descendant of the noble family that controlled Harar before the Egyptian takeover, still maintained cordial relations with the British and received a few hundred well trained soldiers, between 300 and 400 rifles, some cannon and other munitions from them.[239] In addition to Harar's troops, the Emir also had the support of the surrounding Oromo confederation.

By 1887, Harar was a bustling trading destination and one of the principal routes through which King Menelik II received shipments of weapons from French and Italian traders. Possibly concerned by King Menelik II's increasingly bold military campaigns, the Emir of Harar took the step of cutting off arms shipments to Shoa. The stage was set for war.

The conquest of Harar was a long-held goal of Menelik II as he wanted to control this important transshipment point between the coast and the interior of

---

[239] Marcus, Harold G. *The Life and Times of Menelik II: Ethiopia 1844-1913*. Red Sea Press, 1995, p. 89.

Ethiopia. Its importance had only increased under Egyptian occupation and, as early as 1885 (following the withdrawal of the Egyptians), Menelik II had communicated with his Italian contacts that he intended to control Harar.[240] Fortunately, the Emir was not a skilled leader and made several moves that alienated the local population.

A fear of the ever expanding Shoan empire caused the Emir to put restrictions on Harar's European population. They became prisoners in their homes or shops, and many decided to leave the walled city. When the Emir decided to change the local currency, it was widely rejected and the economy collapsed.[241] Soon, Oromo and Somali traders were nowhere to be found in Harar's markets.

The shadow of King Menelik II haunted the Emir and he remained on high alert. He ordered the slaughter of an Italian expedition in the Ogaden, fearing that they were coming to aid Menelik II in the conquest of Harar.[242] He may have felt that the honor of Muslim Harar was on his shoulders and he was prepared to do anything to prevent the city-state from falling into Christian hands on his watch.

The Emir won an early victory against an advance force, which King Menelik II ordered to camp near Harar to send a clear message to the Emir that his reign was coming to an end. The Emir's Turkish general launched fireworks and pushed forward with an assault that resulted in Menelik II's force breaking ranks and fleeing for their lives. Fireworks were new to them, plus the general's

---

[240] Ibid., 90.

[241] Ibid., 91.

[242] Ibid.

modern weapons overwhelmed the already weakened advance force.

News of the defeat alarmed Menelik II. To salvage the situation, he marched his forces to Harar and camped outside the city at Chilanqo.

BATTLE OF CHILANQO

Part of the reason that King Menelik II camped at Chilanqo was that Christmas was approaching. The birth of Yeshua the Christ was cause for celebration across Ethiopia and, as a devout Christian, he would try to avoid war on the occasion. In the spirit of Christ, Menelik II sent a letter to the Emir of Harar requesting his peaceful surrender and promising that he would be allowed to maintain his rule as long as he remained subservient to King Menelik II.[243]

According to imperial government chroniclers, King Menelik II stated:

> "I have come to bring your country under subjection, but not to ruin it. If you submit, if you become my vassal, I shall not refuse you the government of the country. Reflect upon this so that you will not be sorry about it later."[244]

The Emir, a proud Muslim, was in no mood to bow to a Christian, especially not when his Turkish general had won him an early advantage against Menelik II's advance force. He reportedly responded by sending MenelikII a

---

[243] Ibid.

[244] Ibid.

turban and a prayer rug, and telling him that his life would not be spared unless he converted to Islam.

Both men were firm in their faiths. Neither would shift his position. The tension mounted and war was imminent. Knowing that starvation was a real possibility, given the absence of traders and goods within city walls – his own fault – the Emir decided to make the initial move. Thinking it better to strike first than to allow a siege on Harar (and a slow, painful and dishonorable death), the Emir thought to strike when the Christians could be caught unaware: on Christmas day.

Surely, the Emir thought he would come out the victor after assaulting his opponents while they were celebrating and drinking. This was a mistake. King Menelik II had traveled to Harar for war, not to party. Harar was a jewel too important to his centralization plan to let up his guard, so his camp was alert and under strict orders. When the Emir's army charged into the camp at 11:00am, they met a well-trained, disciplined fighting force. Confident in the victory, King Menelik II decided against the use of the traditional Liqa Maqas (officers who deceive the enemy by impersonating a king) and engaged the enemy at the head of his army.

The battle was over in 15 minutes.[245]

When the dust cleared, over 1,000 of the Emir's soldiers were dead. The Emir himself fled east into the Somali region with his wives and children. Before his escape, he left a message pleading Menelik II not to destroy the city. The Emir's uncle and other leading personalities of Harar visited the victorious King to plead for mercy. Menelik II learned tolerance from the mistakes of his *jegna* (teacher), the former Emperor Tewodros II,

---

[245] Ibid., 92.

duty to use the power given to him to secure resources to protect the greater good of the realm. With his whole heart, he believed in Emperor Menelik II's vision of a united Ethiopia. Unfortunately for the tribes south of Harar in the Ogaden, their traditional practices were not in line with the centralization mission and they paid the price in blood and treasure.

In October 1891, the Ugase of Gadabursi and the Ugase of Ogaden arrived in Harar to present tribute in recognition of Ras Makonnen's total control of the area.[254] Menelik II's armies controlled the Haud by mid-1892.[255] The Haud represented all the thorn bush and grasslands east of Harar, stretching to the Somali borders. Somali herdsmen had grazed their cattle on those dependable lands for generations.[256] They now had to recognize the rule of the Solomonic dynasty.

Harar was seen as a key asset in the realm and its conquest was viewed as reclaiming an ancient part of the empire. During the many military campaigns, Ras Makonnen left his wife behind in Shoa but when the war was over and the countryside was relatively safe, he sent for her to join him in Harar, which became his permanent base of operation.

---

[254] Ibid.

[255] Ibid., 138.

[256] Deblauwe, Vincent, et al. (2012). "Determinants and Dynamics of Banded Vegetation Pattern Migration in Arid Climates." *Ecological Monographs*, 2012, vol. 82, no. 1, pp. 3–21.

WINNING HEARTS AND MINDS IN HARAR

Naturally, after the conquest of their lands, the proud Oromo and Somali tribes were not pleased. However, due to the mismanagement of Harar's former rulers and a series of wise moves by Ras Makonnen, Harar's inhabitants gradually grew to tolerate and then admire Makonnen.[257] He did not waste a lot of time. Quickly, he placed his trusted officers in key positions throughout the city and province, ensuring that he had a core group of loyal men to carry out his plans. Not relying on them alone, he also invited Muslims into both his newly formed civil administration and his army.[258] He utilized the natural skill of his Oromo brothers in a new cavalry. They would etch their names into history in the coming years.

Ras Makonnen also helped stimulate the market for khat, a native plant that serves to keep its consumer awake, similar to coffee. Ras Makonnen knew from experience that effective administration required economic resources. As a cash crop, khat provided some needed revenue to keep his administration running effectively.

Ras Makonnen also made plans to provide for the spiritual needs of the local population. He encouraged the Oromo to build a new mosque, even as he also built a Coptic Tewahedo Church for his soldiers and administrative scribes. He was careful to allow the mullahs to resolve disputes among Harar's Muslim citizens,

---

[257] Mosley, Leonard. *Haile Selassie: The Conquering Lion.* Weidenfeld and Nicolson, 1964, p. 25

[258] Ibid., 26.

according to Islamic law. Such attention to the spiritual integrity of Harar helped endear him to the people.

Despite his consistent efforts to build bridges, Ras Makonnen's success was by no means assured. Ethiopia was surrounded by nations hostile to her ancient, peculiar Christian faith. It was said that Ethiopia was an island of Christianity in a sea of Islam. At various times, such as in the era of Imam Ahmed Gran, the high tide from the Islamic sea crashed into Christian Ethiopia. Ras Makonnen lived in such a time. One year after the conquest of Harar, Jihadists from Sudan invaded the realm. It was while battling them heroically in 1889 (in the midst of the Kifu Ken) that Emperor Yohannes IV had died. Emperor Yohannes IV had successfully stopped the rising tide of Islam in Ethiopia two times prior. His third attempt, though also successful, was to be his last.

In 1892, the Jihadist invasion was fresh in the minds of Ethiopians. Emperor Yohannes IV was not universally loved during his time but his heroic death in defense of the realm's borders and Christian identity cemented him as a legend. Emperor Yohannes IV was lionized as a champion against Islamic aggression. As one of the few Christian residents in Muslim Harar, Ras Makonnen knew this all too well. His job now was to ensure that the Muslim sea did not overflow its banks and flood Christian Ethiopia, especially from the city that was once Imam Ahmad Gran's base of operations.

MUSLIM HARAR

In terms of importance, Harar was long considered by Muslims to be behind only Mecca, Medina and Jerusalem. This meant that, before the Christian takeover of Harar, it was effectively controlled by Islamic powers outside of Ethiopia. There was concern that the conquest would reignite the Sudanese Jihadists, enrage the wider Muslim world and bring down the wrath of Ethiopia's other Muslim neighbors. Surely, it helped lead to the invasion that resulted in the death of Emperor Yohannes IV. In his eyes, as well as his successor, Emperor Menelik II's, the risks that came with conquering Harar were outweighed by a greater concern: that allowing Harar to remain under the influence of foreign governments was a threat to Ethiopia's jealously guarded independence.

Ethiopia's future was, in part, riding on how events unfolded in Harar. This was precisely why Emperor Menelik II entrusted the task to his own family member, one who shared his Solomonic bloodline. At the time he was appointed governor of Harar, Makonnen was not yet a Ras. When he became one in 1889, he was already facing the Kifu Ken. Then, years into those Evil Days, he had a baby on the way.

Now, the baby boy was here and Ras Makonnen would need his strength, his intelligence and his faith to make things work in Harar while helping his cousin and emperor navigate trying times for Ethiopia. His Christian faith – based on the life and teachings of the fully human, fully divine Yeshua – would be tested.

CHAPTER FOURTEEN

Christianity Comes to Zion

"And the angel of the Lord spake unto Philip, saying, Arise, and go toward the south unto the way that goeth down from Jerusalem unto Gaza, which is desert. And he arose and went: and, behold, a man of Ethiopia, an eunuch of great authority under Candace queen of the Ethiopians, who had the charge of all her treasure, and had come to Jerusalem for to worship, Was returning, and sitting in his chariot read Esaias the prophet." **– Acts 8:26-28**

Ras Makonnen was part of a proud Christian tradition. Indeed, the ruling elite that governed and protected the Ethiopian realm from foreign invasion credited Yeshua for their success. On that fateful and thunderous night in Ejersa Goro, as his soldiers and servants celebrated, Ras Makonnen was well aware of the legacy he would bequeath to his newborn son. It was one of Christian ancestors who had reigned for centuries in isolation from the Western World.

THE ETHIOPIAN EUNUCH

Orthodox Christianity was established as Ethiopia's state religion in 330 CE. Prior to that, the Book of Acts in the Bible records that an Ethiopian eunuch traveled to Jerusalem on official business and encountered one of Yeshua's apostles.[259] Scholars do not agree on whether he was from within the borders of modern Ethiopia or Sudan as all dark-skinned Africans were commonly referred to as Ethiopians. The argument that the eunuch was Ethiopian is strengthened by Ethiopia's own account as well as the fact that the Axumite empire also controlled areas in Sudan at different times during its reign.

According to oral tradition, the Ethiopian Jew was already very familiar with the prophet Isaiah. The fact that he was a eunuch speaks to the fact that he was likely born into slavery and then converted to Judaism. Birth circumstances aside, it was that Ethiopian Jew who first brought the good news about Yeshua the Christ south of Egypt to the highlands of Ethiopia. The faith spread fast in a land that had been a home for Judaism for close to a thousand years.

Ethiopian tradition has it that the eunuch's name was Jen Daraba, and that he was a servant of a queen named Garsemat Kandake. The fascinating Ethiopian account recalls that, as a favorite of the Queen, he was permitted to make the pilgrimage to Jerusalem. Upon his return, Jen Daraba became a great teacher of the gospel in Ethiopia.

---

[259] Acts 8:26-39

SAINT MATTHEW IN ETHIOPIA

Jen Daraba was soon joined by Saint Matthew, according to tradition, and the two men set about spreading the teachings and life example of Yeshua.[260] It was Jen Daraba who provided sanctuary for St. Matthew upon his arrival in Ethiopia.

Legend says that St. Matthew outsmarted two magicians and, through the power of the Christ, subdued and chased their pet dragons "that belched forth a sulphurous fire from their mouths and nostrils, and slew all within reach."[261] St. Matthew's continued demonstration of power had a great impact on the kingdom and he managed to convert the King (Fulvian[262] or Egippus[263] or Hatosza Bahr Asaged,[264] depending on the account) and the ruling court to followers of Christ. Among the miracles ascribed to St. Matthew were being unscathed by fire and raising the King's son from the grave. He is also credited with building the first Christian church in Ethiopia.

Surviving works about St. Matthew's Ethiopian sojourn agree that he was martyred there. Tradition holds

---

[260] Voragine, Jacobus. *The Golden Legend of Jacobus de Voragine*. Translated and adapted by Ryan, Granger and Ripperger, Helmut. Arno Press: Longmans, Green & Co., 1941, pp. 561-566.

[261] Ibid.

[262] This is the name that is used in the Greek Orthodox Synaxaria.

[263] Voragine, Jacobus. *The Golden Legend of Jacobus de Voragine*. Translated and adapted by Ryan, Granger and Ripperger, Helmut. Arno Press: Longmans, Green & Co., 1941, pp. 561-566.

[264] See: http://rastaites.com/list-ethiopian-kings-haile-selassie-i-lineage/

that King Hirtacus, who ascended the throne to replace his dead brother, wanted to marry a royal virgin who had caught his eye.[265] After St. Matthew refused to perform the marriage, Hirtacus's men stabbed the saint in the back.

The actual history of St. Matthew's time in Ethiopia is unclear but, whatever the case, it is clear that Christians inhabited Ethiopia shortly after the crucifixion and disappearance of Yeshua. Yet, it is also clear that Ethiopia's rulers were no longer Christian by the time Emperor Ezana ascended the throne in Axum in 330 CE.

EMPEROR EZANA

During the lifetime of Yeshua the Christ, Ethiopia was being ruled by the powerful Axumite kingdom. In the centuries following Yeshua's crucifixion and St. Matthew's reported ministry in the holy mountains, Ethiopian emperors and empresses (with a few exceptions) provided sanctuary for Christians escaping persecution in Rome, Greece and Europe-dominated North Africa. For many of those refugees, it could not have been easy journeying through the Rift Valley by land – hard terrain, harsh weather and hundreds of miles of pristine wilderness full of dangerous animals awaited them. Fortunately, Axum was also a trading empire on the Red Sea.

The Axumite kingdom reached its pinnacle under the rule of Emperor Ezana. There was stability and accumulated wealth commensurate with the kingdom's control over southern Red Sea travel. Axum's economy

---

[265] Voragine, Jacobus. *The Golden Legend of Jacobus de Voragine.* Translated and adapted by Ryan, Granger and Ripperger, Helmut. Arno Press: Longmans, Green & Co., 1941, pp. 561-566.

benefited greatly from the incense and spice trades, and was home to some of the greatest architects and engineers of the time. A 100-foot obelisk stood in Emperor Ezana's capital as a testament to the skill and creativity of these great builders.

As was common in the ancient world, prosperity translated into wars of conquest. Ezana waged war against the smaller surrounding kingdoms, expanding into the highlands and to the banks of the Nile river. He even extended his rule deep into Sudan and exercised effective control over the ancient Kushite capital of Meroe. In the opposite direction, he waged war against Yemen and Arabia and was able to extend Axum's power to the eastern shores of the Red Sea.

While his prowess as an emperor was well regarded in the ancient world, Emperor Ezana is most remembered for officially converting the Ethiopian realm to Christianity. This conversion was not due to the small but growing Christian community that certainly existed in Ethiopia at the time. Instead, it was instigated by outsiders whose destiny put them on a collision course with the ancient realm.

THE RISE OF FRUMENTIUS, THE FIRST BISHOP OF AXUM

Before the time of Emperor Ezana (during the reign of his father, Ousanas, also known as Emperor Ella Allada), two children of Phoenician sailors traveled to Ethiopia on a trade mission with their uncle. They were brothers named Frumentius and Edesius. Unfortunately for them, Ethiopian emperors were very suspicious of ships coming from foreign ports. So, after the long journey, the ship was boarded by local authorities and all adults aboard were slaughtered. The children were spared and brought to the emperor as a gift.

After Ezana was born, his mother, the Queen, charged Frumentius to become the boy's tutor. Frumentius became a member of the royal court. Edesius was allowed to return to Tyre once Ezana came of age. Back in his homeland, Edesius was ordained as a bishop and remained there for the rest of his life. Frumentius, on the other hand, did not share his brother's desire to return home. He stopped in Egypt to speak with the Coptic Archbishop, intending to persuade the Archbishop to become the head of the Christian church in Ethiopia. He had likely heard the legends of St. Matthew and witnessed the potential of Ethiopia's budding Christian community. The Archbishop was so impressed with Frumentius's appeal that he consecrated him as the Bishop of Ethiopia. With this blessing, Frumentius returned to Ethiopia, baptized the new Emperor Ezana and embarked on his mission to spread Christianity throughout the realm.

Frumentius built many churches in Ethiopia and encouraged the Christians already living there to practice their faith more openly. He was soon given the title of *Abuna* and was referred to by the Christian community as *Kesate Birhan* (Revealer of Light) and *Abba Salama* (Father of Peace). Following the conversion of the royal court, Christianity spread throughout the realm and Ethiopia became the world's first Christian State.[266]

---

[266] Armenia also makes this claim. However, it has been challenged as not being supported by history.

CHAPTER FIFTEEN

The Christ in Ethiopia

"And the fourth kingdom shall be strong as iron: forasmuch as iron breaketh in pieces and subdueth all things: and as iron that breaketh all these, shall it break in pieces and bruise."
– Daniel 2:40

Ras Makonnen was a devout Christian. He served a Christian Emperor in a Christian realm. He, as his forefathers before him, would raise his baby boy as an Orthodox Christian. Despite governing in the fourth holiest city in Islam, Ras Makonnen would hold fast to his Christian faith. Ethiopia had embraced Christianity before Rome and, therefore, before the Europeans, and it was important to Ras Makonnen to preserve his realm's ancient way of worship of Yeshua the Christ.

Ethiopia's coast was now controlled by vassals of the Catholic Church – Italy and France. Catholic ideology was firmly rejected in Ethiopia, and Ras Makonnen made sure that the Catholics in Harar were closely monitored within the city's walls. He and his countrymen were not naive. They saw the European missionaries as a necessary evil, as they possessed valuable secular knowledge. Ras Makonnen invited the French mission, under the leadership of Monseigneur Taurin, to add educational and medical projects to their mission.[267] As for matters of the faith, Ras Makonnen was confident in Ethiopia's ancient cultures and traditions.

YESHUA THE CHRIST RISING

An embrace of Yeshua the Christ as messiah had swept the world. People all over began proclaiming that there was one Almighty creator, and that he had manifested on Earth in his son, and that his son died and resurrected to atone for the sins of man. The good news proved to be infectious. Pagan tribes everywhere abandoned or disregarded their old gods in favor of this new faith. The faith was even a unifying factor for previously warring tribes. They now came together under the banner of Christ.

The world was changing politically as well. Kingdoms were falling as the nation state emerged. The art of war had been revolutionized by the invention of the gun, and then the machine gun, and many of the Earth's ancient empires had been destroyed by younger, more technically advanced ones.

The empires of Europe were at the forefront of the new technological revolution. They, too, embraced Christianity but that did nothing to moderate their philosophy of white supremacy. The Romans popularized the name Jesus and, at the same time, depicted him as a Roman. Yeshua's Afro-asiatic Hebrew roots were

---

[267] Mosley, Leonard. *Haile Selassie: The Conquering Lion.* Weidenfeld and Nicolson, 1964.

downplayed and eventually erased. It did not take long for all the Hebrew patriarchs and prophets to be depicted with European features. Egypt, Ethiopia and other pockets of Christianity were not seen as sibling nations in the faith but as strategic outposts in the European thrust for power and resources.

In 1892, Christian Europe was closing in on the world of the baby boy in Harar. For the time being, God and history had entrusted the baby boy's and Ethiopia's security and fate to his father's cousin, the reigning King of Kings, Emperor Menelik II, who was very familiar with European ways. In 1868, he had witnessed firsthand how they could shift the balance of power between the kingdoms of Ethiopia. His failure to read the situation then resulted in his rival benefiting from European technology and, thus, gaining the upper hand. It was impossible for Menelik II to ignore or underestimate the European threat.

As the reigning King of Kings, Menelik II carried with him lessons of monarchy learned firsthand from a previous, visionary leader. His own vision and leadership would become legendary, yes, but he himself would have acknowledged that he was building on the foundation set by a man considered to be Ethiopia's first modernizing leader. Just as any legend worth a grain of salt, this man's story starts with controversy: he was a contender for the throne who was not from the main Solomonic bloodlines. He was a man of the people, a man who robbed from the rich and gave to the poor. He was a man whose military prowess was unmatched on the battlefield and he managed to emerge victorious from a special period of Ethiopian history known as the Zemene Mesafint, or age of princes.

During the Zemene Mesafint, the proud emperors of the Solomonic line were reduced to mere figureheads.

They were controlled by powerful Rases who held power through the might of their private armies. In fact, some of these Rases were the Oromo benefactors of the power vacuum left after Imam Gran had devastated the country.

The man who would bring these powerful players to heel was Kassa Hailu. In the process, he would conquer Shoa and take a young Menelik II captive to be educated along with other captive princes and become part of a new, united Ethiopia. Despite his lack of royal bloodline, Kassa Hailu would etch his name into the pages of history as Emperor Tewodros II, the emperor who brought Ethiopia out of myth and into the public consciousness of the Western World.

Future Emperor Menelik II would find great inspiration in this predecessor, not only because he began to forge the modern outline of an Ethiopia united under Yeshua the Christ, not only because he managed to lead a renaissance in Ethiopian Amharic literature and culture, but also because his reign provided the first glimpses at how European powers could shift the balance of power for Ethiopia's monarchs.

CHAPTER SIXTEEN

The Rise of Emperor Tewodros II

"I know their game. First the traders and the missionaries: then the ambassadors: then the cannon. It's better to go straight to the cannon." – **Emperor Tewodros II**[268]

Ras Makonnen knew that the celebratory rifle fire echoing throughout the countryside would send a message. Bullets were not cheap or common. Firing them in the air could be helpful – a strategic display of power letting all who did not support Emperor Menelik II (as well as bandits) know that his governor in Harar had ample resources to defend his post. Harar was one of the last great independent kingdoms to be incorporated into the realm and Ras Makonnen knew that kindness could be mistaken for weakness. His cousin had taught him about the days of the Zemene Mesafint, when the kingdoms were at perpetual war.

---

[268] Davidson, Basil. *Africa in Modern History: The Search for a New Society.* Allen Lane, 1978.

Ras Makonnen was ready to continue the work of unification necessary to survive the encroachment of the modern world. It could take generations, but the birth of his legitimate heir was a good sign and he was feeling positive about the future. Ethiopia could not be permitted to return to the tribal chaos of the Era of Princes – the Zemene Mesafint. Ras Makonnen was confident his wise cousin had learned the lessons, both good and bad, of his greatest teacher, Emperor Tewodros II, Ethiopia's first priestly warrior king of the modern era.

EMPEROR TEWODROS II

The ascendance of Emperor Tewodros II, who was from the Agaw Kingdom, harkened back to the time when the Agaw ruled supreme in the Ethiopian highlands, especially the time of Emperor Lalibela. The Agaw were an ancient people, thought by some scholars to be the original culture of the northern highlands.[269]

Emperor Tewodros II was born Kassa Hailu in 1818. He was the son of Ato Hailu and Emmett Atitegeb.[270] Kassa was not blessed to grow up under the protection and influence of his father, Ato Hailu, who died early on in his life. He and his mother were forced to live the life of landless peasants and she sold the traditional healing medicine, kosso, to keep them both alive. Kassa's humble

---

[269] Ullendorff, Edward. *The Ethiopians: An Introduction to Country and People.* 4th ed., Headstart Printing and Publishing Company, 1998, p. 37.

[270] Araia, Ghelawdewos. "The Great Unifier: Emperor Tewodros II of Ethiopia." *Institute of Development and Education for Africa (IDEA),* 2006. https://www.africanidea.org/emperor_tewdros.pdf.

beginnings ignited his passion and drive and ability to bond with the working class. Kassa's lofty ambitions made him unique among his working class peers. Notwithstanding his humble beginnings, he did have some advantage due to his family ties. The story of his rise to power has its foundations in his family's ancestral land, far from the action of the age of princes.

Kassa was raised in Qwara, near the border with Sudan,[271] which was part of the land holdings of his distant relative, Dejazmatch Maru of Dambya.[272] Dejazmatch Maru was a known figure in Ethiopia during the 1820s and was himself related to the powerful Yejju dynasty and the dynasty of Semen. He did not take notice of Kassa and his mother's plight but another relative did. Kassa's uncle, Dejazmatch Kenfu observed his potential and convinced his mother to allow Kassa to be sent to a monastery to be educated.[273]

That monastery, Mahbere-Selassie, would become where Kassa learned the history of his kingdom and where his passionate love for Yeshua the Christ was ignited. There he learned about Abraham, Israel, Judah and the songs of King David. The monastery education, like most traditional, formal education at the time, was based on the Ethiopian Bible and Kebra Nagast. Young Kassa would have learned about the many saints of Ethiopia who worked miracles and spread the good news of Yeshua to the far corners of the empire.

---

[271] Zewde, Bahru. *A History of Modern Ethiopia 1855-1991*. 2nd ed., Addis Ababa University Press, 2001, p. 27.

[272] Ibid.

[273] Araia, Ghelawdewos. "The Great Unifier: Emperor Tewodros II of Ethiopia." *Institute of Development and Education for Africa (IDEA)*, 2006. https://www.africanidea.org/emperor_tewdros.pdf.

The Zemene Mesafint was characterized by intense power struggle. It was not a good time for nobles and some would die at the hands of even their relatives. Kassa's education was interrupted when the monastery was attacked by Dejazmatch Maru, who was said to be avenging his father who he felt had been disrespected and abused by members of the region's aristocracy. Dejazmatch Maru, as with many of the princes of the Zemene Mesafint, had aspirations of becoming a king. Killing the students of Mahbere-Selassie, some of whom would have been the children of prominent nobility, sent a powerful message of his intent. A born survivor, Kassa escaped the slaughter of innocents and returned to Qwara. His time at the monastery, though interrupted, had already shaped him with a passion for learning. A priestly zeal for Yeshua was forever planted in his heart.

Dejazmatch Maru's vicious act against the children of Mahbere-Selassie stirred the angel of death into action and, in October of 1827, Dejazmatch Maru himself died fighting against his noble relatives at the Battle of Koso Bar.[274] Upon his death, Empress Manan Liban (the real power behind the Solomonic throne) granted his lands to another son of Dambya, Dejazmatch Kenfu Hailu, and gave it the name *Ya Maru Qammas* ("what has been tasted by Maru").[275] Qwara would become an important center of activity within Ya Maru Qammas. Shortly after the Battle of Koso Bar, a young Kassa Hailu would move there to live with his uncle Kenfu.

Qwara's proximity to the Sudanese border meant that the Ethiopian identity of its inhabitants would have been strong. Sudan was controlled by the Ottoman Empire

---

[274] Zewde, Bahru. *A History of Modern Ethiopia 1855-1991*. 2nd ed., Addis Ababa University Press, 2001, p. 27.

[275] Ibid.

and their Egyptian subjects, who were looking to expand their area of control into Ethiopia. Dejazmatch Kenfu would soon forge a reputation as a great defender of the Ethiopian border. In 1837, he defeated an Egyptian fighting force deep within Sudan.

Dejazmatch Kenfu was fighting to preserve Ya Maru Qammas for his sons. Though he was fond of Kassa, he was uneasy with his growing popularity and charisma. Some called him Kassa Maru and some even said that he looked like one of Ethiopia's greatest rulers, Amda Tsion.[276] These comparisons did not sit well with Dejazmatch Kenfu. After all, he was fighting to preserve lands for his own legacy, not for Kassa who was not his son. Sadly, he would not live to see his sons inherit his possessions as he died in 1839 and Empress Manan decided that Ya Maru Qammas would not be given to them.

Empress Manan Liban also had no plans to give the land to Kassa Hailu either. Therefore, in the warlike atmosphere of the Zemene Mesafint, without a chance to inherit any land by legitimate means, and without the protection of the family of Dejazmatch Kenfu, Kassa Hailu decided to become an outlaw. To the local power structure he was simply a *shefta*, or bandit.

THE OUTLAW KASSA

His days as an outlaw helped to establish his legend and cement his control over his brothers-in-arms. Kassa's leadership was distinguished by his discipline and the fact

---

[276] Gabre-Sellassie, Zewde. *Yohannes IV of Ethiopia: A Political Biography*. 1975. The Red Sea Press, 2014, p. 57.

that he lived as his fellow bandits. No matter how much power he gained or how many battles he won, he never forgot the value of hard work. He could be found ploughing fields and distributing stolen goods and money to peasants to buy farming equipment.[277] He also never forgot his spiritual and intellectual roots from his time at the monastery. (Later, during his reign, he would assemble a formidable library at his eventual mountain fortress at Magdala.)

Kassa's fame as an outlaw began to spread throughout the land, eventually leading to conflict with the Ottoman Empire in the form of the Egyptians. They handed Kassa his first military defeat, humbling his outlaw brigade with their disciplined soldiers and modern artillery.

Despite losing to the Egyptians, Kassa managed to win control of Qwara. Thus, the powers of the Zemene Mesafint could no longer ignore the growing threat at the Sudanese border. Empress Manan's son, Ras Ali, the instrument of Empress Manan and the true power of the era, decided to marry his own daughter to the outlaw with the hopes of bringing him under control. However, Kassa was not content to be a quiet family member and fade into the background. He had a larger vision for Ethiopia and for the Christian world. He would first bring Ethiopia under control and then he would launch a war to liberate Jerusalem from the Ottoman Empire, which he referred to as the Turks.

By the time it became apparent to the princes of the Zemene Mesafint that Kassa could not be controlled, it was too late to forcefully remove him from his power base.

---

[277] Zewde, Bahru. *A History of Modern Ethiopia 1855-1991*. 2nd ed., Addis Ababa University Press, 2001, p.27.

The outlaw from humble beginnings could not be defeated on the battlefield. He had ignited imaginations and the people of the countryside rallied to his cause. His band of outlaws were now a disciplined army and, one by one, the armies of the powerful Rases fell to Kassa's growing number of seasoned fighters. He was able to outmaneuver the major players of his time: Ras Ali of Begemder, Ras Goshu of Gojjam, Ras Ubye of Tigray, Dejazmatch Webe of Gondar and King Haile Melekot of Shoa. All of them felt the force of Kassa's iron fist.

THE END OF THE ERA OF PRINCES

Kassa was destined to put an end to the era of princes, the Zemene Mesafint, and restore the power of Ethiopia's emperor. His awesome victories against the Yejju Oromo shifted the balance of power and made the emperor the realm's central authority again. Conquering with a vision, Kassa took his defeated opponents' sons captive, so as to be educated in line with his envisioned future Ethiopia.

Empress Manan was following Kassa's achievements carefully and, after he defeated one of her trusted generals, she decided to take action. The wise and shrewd Empress stepped out of the shadows to demonstrate her power, mobilizing an army of 20,000 men and mounting her horse to march into battle.[278] She was ready to put a stop to the legend of Kassa. Indeed, her victory seemed assured as her confident forces swarmed those of Kassa. Unfortunately for the Empress, she was

---

[278] Araia, Ghelawdewos. "The Great Unifier: Emperor Tewodros II of Ethiopia." *Institute of Development and Education for Africa (IDEA)*, 2006. https://www.africanidea.org/emperor_tewdros.pdf.

about to become another character in his legend. Just as all seemed lost for Kassa, one of his disciplined men managed to strike the Empress herself, knocking her off her horse. She was quickly captured and brought to Kassa and her massive army was forced to cease fighting. Kassa, knowing that only the Almighty could have bestowed this victory on him, was careful not to mistreat Empress Manan. She was given the respect and honor befitting her title. Empress Manan's husband, Emperor Yohannes III – a puppet emperor on the throne only because of his bloodline – was also captured.[279]

Like wildfire, the news spread throughout the realm. Ras Ali quickly negotiated his mother's freedom in exchange for land and titles for Kassa. No longer would he be called an outlaw. He was now known as Dejazmatch Kassa, governor of Dembya and Qwara. He was unmatched militarily with a well-oiled war machine. He killed Ras Goshu of Gojjam at the Battle of Gur Amba in 1852 and he slowly gained control of the Ethiopian highlands.[280]

DEJAZMATCH KASSA

Kassa's time as Dejazmatch was characterized by putting the finishing touches on the era of princes. Ras Ali raised a massive army of 100,000 men to stop the enterprising Kassa but it was too late. In 1853, Kassa and

[279] Gabre-Sellassie, Zewde. *Yohannes IV of Ethiopia: A Political Biography*. 1975. The Red Sea Press, 2014, p. 61.

[280] Ullendorff, Edward. *The Ethiopians: An Introduction to Country and People*. 4th ed., Headstart Printing and Publishing Company, 1998, p. 80.

his disciplined forces defeated Ras Ali in battle, compelling him to retire from political life.

The final pillar of the Zemene Mesafint crumbled when Kassa defeated Dejazmatch Webe at the Battle of Derasge on February 8, 1855. The death of his son, Eshete, on the battlefield was too much for Dejazmatch Webe and he surrendered. The battle was bloody, and the angel of death was pleased with his bounty at the end of hostilities.

After defeating his rivals, Kassa was crowned in a church constructed by an Egyptian bishop brought to Ethiopia by Dejazmatch Webe. He also took the opportunity to display his knowledge of Ethiopian spiritual life by choosing a name that was tied to an Ethiopian prophecy. It was foretold that a man would arise with that name to unify Ethiopia and restore the realm to its ancient glory.[281] Proudly claiming the titles of Lion of Judah and the King of Kings in 1855, he was known from then on as Emperor Tewodros II.

EMPEROR TEWODROS II

Emperor Tewodros II began his reign as a man of the people. He walked tall, proud and barefooted. He slept in a tent with his soldiers and avoided excess. In one of his first actions, he attempted to ban slavery in Ethiopia.[282] This long entrenched institution was not the same as the chattel slavery of the West but it was unacceptable to an emperor building a nation united in Christ.

As history shows, Tewodros II did indeed unite the fractured Ethiopian nation and, in doing so, set the

---

[281] Ibid., 81.

[282] Ibid., 82.

foundation that succeeding emperors would build upon, including future Emperor Menelik II. In 1856, the newly crowned emperor marched his massive army into the interior mountains of Shoa and crushed the forces of Menelik II's father, King Haile Melekot. He took the young prince Menelik II captive and would leave a lasting impression on him in time to come.

Tewodros II's monastery education was never forgotten. He carefully collected and commissioned works documenting Ethiopia's great history, then assembled them at his mountain palace in Magdala. The Magdala palace would serve as a stable base of governance in contrast to the royal tents that characterized his living quarters while he kept the rebellions of the realm at bay. As powerful as he was, the emperor had one major problem, a lingering controversy that casted a shadow over his reign. He was a man of humble beginnings and the branches of the Solomonic dynasty in Ethiopia did not recognize his claim to the throne. His chroniclers would later emphasize his genealogical links to the Solomonic line. However, others would never overlook his Agaw roots. He was viewed as a usurper and was commonly and insultingly referred to as "the koso vendor's son."[283] Still, he would not be defined by his detractors. He had dreamt of a united Ethiopia, from the Red Sea to the river Nile and beyond. His military force was unbeatable and all the realm's kings and sultans fell before him.

Even so, Tewodros II's lack of a solid noble family base led to multiple revolts throughout the realm. These revolts were often led or supported by Rases who claimed Solomonic descent.

---

[283] Zewde, Bahru. *A History of Modern Ethiopia 1855-1991*. 2nd ed., Addis Ababa University Press, 2001, p. 29.

EMPEROR TEWODROS II AND THE EUROPEANS

With his vision to unite the realm under Christ, Emperor Tewodros II proclaimed himself the husband of Ethiopia and the fiancée of Jerusalem.[284] The Almighty had called him, blessed him and anointed him to change the world. His task was clear!

His response to his internal problems was to seek outside assistance from some of the Christian superpowers of the day. Through his education, he was aware that this strategy had worked for Emperor Lebna Dengel with the Portuguese. Perhaps, it could work for him. He also knew the tales of Imam Ahmad Gran and the advantage that foreign assistance and modern weapons provided. Tewodros II spent considerable time and resources seeking to acquire armaments and technicians. He sent correspondences to Russia, Prussia, France and Great Britain.

The answer that he received was silence.[285]

The Europeans were engaged in their own internal wars and had no time to consider the requests of a distant African king. The Crimean War had broken out in 1853 and lasted until 1856. The Russians fought against an alliance of the Ottoman Empire, Britain, France and Sardinia (Italy). The Prussians stayed neutral during the

---

[284] Araia, Ghelawdewos. "The Great Unifier: Emperor Tewodros II of Ethiopia." *Institute of Development and Education for Africa (IDEA),* 2006. https://www.africanidea.org/emperor_tewdros.pdf.

[285] Moorehead, Alan. *The Blue Nile.* Hamish Hamilton, 1922. The French were the only government to respond.

war and were preparing for future wars by building their railway system to facilitate rapid movement of armaments and troops. Bismarck, as always, was using the chaos in Europe to strengthen Prussia and advance his plan to unite the German tribes.

Having no details of what was happening in Europe, Emperor Tewodros II was outraged. He was determined to show the Europeans that he was not to be taken lightly. He came across Henry Stern, a British missionary who had written a book on Tewodros II. In it, he spoke of "the eventful and romantic history of the man, who, from a poor boy, in a reed built convent became... the conqueror of numerous provinces, and the Sovereign of a great and extensive realm." His narrative did not sit well with Tewodros II, who was desperately trying to establish his Solomonic bloodline, so Stern became the embodiment of the British Empire and was taken hostage. The British counsel, Charles Duncan Cameron, tried to intercede and was also taken hostage. Unsure who to trust, Tewodros II then ordered all Europeans in the imperial court to be put in chains. Thus, the stage was set for one of the most dangerous colonial missions in all of history.

THE NAPIER EXPEDITION

Due to the situation in Ethiopia, Queen Victoria decided to take action on August 21, 1867. She summoned famed General Napier out of India to lead the mission to restore the honor of the British crown. No expense was spared for the £9,000,000 mission.[286] A massive military force consisting of 44 war elephants, 5,735 camels, 17,943

---

[286] Marcus, Harold G. *The Life and Times of Menelik II: Ethiopia 1844-1913*. Red Sea Press, 1995, p. 31.

mules and ponies, 8,075 bullocks and 2,538 horses was shipped to the horn of Africa.[287] The fighting force consisted of approximately 13,088 British troops. Consistent with the imperial wars of the Scramble, the majority of soldiers were non-white troops from Britian's colonial possessions. About 9,050 of those sent to potentially die in the Ethiopian highlands for the Queen were Indian. Only 4,038 were British.[288] Racial considerations aside, the United Kingdom mobilized a massive force for the time in order to bring justice for the Queen.

In order to face Emperor Tewodros II's army, it took them more than 3 months of marching over 400 kilometers into the highlands but fortune was on their side. In his quest to unite Ethiopia, Emperor Tewodros II had become paranoid and crushed any dissent without mercy. As a result, the realm no longer supported Tewodros II and were likely happy that a force had arrived to do what no internal army had been able to accomplish. The British met with rebels, including one of the royal sons of the Solomonic line of Tigray, Dejazmatch Kassa Mercha. In exchange for non-interference, supplies and guidance, they were able to secure clear passage to Tewodros II's mountain stronghold.

Had the Ethiopians been united, they would not have cooperated with General Napier and the British expedition would have surely ended in defeat, if not disaster. By the time of the Napier expedition, Tewodros II's army had dwindled considerably. He no longer had the 40,000 strong fighting force that previously brought Shoa

---

[287] Sharf, Frederic A., et al. *Abyssinia, 1867-1878, Artists on Campaign: Watercolors and Drawings from the British Expedition Under Sir Robert Napier*. Tsehai Publishers, 2003, p. 26.

[288] Ibid.

under control. Now, there were no more than an estimated 10,000 men. When the final battle took place outside the mountain fortress of Magdala, it resulted in heavy Ethiopian casualties. The infamous Napier expedition ended with Emperor Tewodros II taking his own life while foreign troops penetrated deep into Ethiopian territory.

General Napier gave his troops permission to loot Magdala. Many manuscripts and precious jewels, including gold and silver processional crosses, were stolen and taken back to England. The amount of works that found their way into private collections via the black market would never be recorded. Ultimately, the great effort of Emperor Tewodros II in collecting works of Ethiopian history and culture was in vain.

It was the modern British weapons used during the expedition that most shifted the internal balance of power. They effectively gave Dejazmatch Kassa Mercha – Tewodros II's former captive, ally, then newly sworn enemy – the power to be crowned as the next emperor. Inspired, in part, by Tewodros II, Kassa Mercha began to build a legacy of his own and sought to continue his teacher's centralizing mission. (The same British guns would later contribute to Kassa Mercha's ability to defend Ethiopia from the Egyptians and the ever encroaching Europeans.)

RAS MAKONNEN'S LESSON

Emperor Menelik II had learned a valuable lesson from that first successful foreign intervention in Ethiopia. He also had been in communication with the British and had stayed out of their way when they came for his beloved teacher. The weapons given to Kassa Mercha ensured that there was no way Menelik II could defeat him on the battlefield.

In turn, Ras Makonnen had learned the same lesson from his cousin and teacher. The lesson was simple: strategic foreign relationships could swing the balance of power in Ethiopia.

As Ras Makonnen's warriors fired volleys of gunfire throughout the countryside on that fateful night in 1892, he gave thanks for the feeling of relief at the birth of his son but he also recalled a time, not too long before, when it was not Emperor Menelik II who controlled the bulk of realm's firepower. He still vividly remembered the reign of the second priestly warrior king in Ethiopia's modern era, Emperor Yohannes IV

CHAPTER SEVENTEEN

The Rise of Emperor Yohannes IV

"Thus hath God made for the King of Ethiopia more glory, grace and majesty than for all the other kings of the earth because of the greatness of Zion, the Tabernacle of the Law of God, the heavenly Zion." – **Kebra Nagast**[289]

The nervous physicians and attendants prepared the child for inspection – he was anointed with oils and a small amount of butter was placed on his lips. At first sight, Ras Makonnen had the words of all his advisors, astrologists, priests and elders swirling in his mind. Would this boy be an asset to Ethiopia? Would he live to become a true heir? Ras Makonnen hid his emotions as sporadic gunfire still went off around the countryside.

Like many children born in his era, the child was the embodiment of the many peoples of Ethiopia. He was Amhara, Tigray, Gurage and Oromo. The baby boy was born in Ethiopia and Ethiopia was born in the baby boy.

---

[289] Brooks, Miguel F., comp., ed. and trans. *Kebra Nagast: The Glory of Kings*. 1995. Red Sea Press, 2002, p. 173.

Ras Makonnen could easily recall a time before his cousin's reign, when the power of the realm rested in the north, in Tigray. It was their guns that gave them an edge over Shoa. Ras Makonnen was connected to Tigray too, by way of his paternal grandfather, Ato Wolde Melekot Yemane Kristos.[290] Originally from Tembien, Ato Wolde was a member of the Tigrayan nobility who had moved to Shoa and married into the Shoan nobility. His son would marry the daughter of King Sahle Selassie.

At the moment, relations with Tigray were tense since the Tigrayan heir of the last emperor was not permitted by Emperor Menelik II to claim his father's throne. Menelik II's predecessor had died suddenly and he had quickly filled the void, feeling like destiny had called him to rule. No one in Ethiopia was surprised by his move. In fact, his seizure of the reigns of power was no different than that of his predecessor, the great Emperor Yohannes IV. Although both men were bitter rivals, they had deep respect for one another, maybe because of their shared history.

Ras Makonnen had nothing but respect for the legendary Emperor Yohannes IV. It was Emperor Yohannes IV who had ordered the conquest of Harar and generally set a high bar for ruling Ethiopia in the modern age. Ras Makonnen would be sure to teach his son about the lessons of his reign.

---

[290] Beresford, Deena-Marie. *Gurage! Gurage! Gurage! The Story of a Wollo Princess: Woizero Yeshimabet Ali AbaJifar.* Yeshimabet's Books and Things, 2019, p. 37.

EMPEROR YOHANNES IV

A power vacuum had opened in the realm immediately following the death of Tewodros II. All the usual contenders for the throne were either killed or imprisoned by him, and the powers of the Zemene Mesafint had their wings clipped. Yet, the aura of Tewodros II's leadership had left an imprint on the people and started a new chapter in the story of Ethiopia. Even his death by suicide – not allowing foreigners the privilege of capturing him – ignited widespread imagination. Thus, the power vacuum did not last long as great men began emerging to claim the central power that Tewodros II had renewed in the throne.

Three powerful leaders were soon set to battle for the throne of David: Kassa Mercha of Tigray, Menelik II of Shoa and Wagshum Gobaze of Lasta. It was Wagshum Gobaze who made the first major move by quickly having himself crowned as King of Kings, Emperor Tekle Giyorgis II. Meanwhile, Menelik II had assumed the title of King of Kings since his escape from Tewodros II's fortress in 1865. Kassa Mercha prepared for war.

EARLY DAYS OF KASSA MERCHA

Kassa Mercha was born Kassa Abba Babbez in 1831, the son of Shum Temben Mercha and Woizero Silas.[291] He was taken captive during the military campaigns of Tewodros II along with his brothers, Gugsa

---

[291] Gabre-Sellassie, Zewde. *Yohannes IV of Ethiopia: A Political Biography*. 1975. The Red Sea Press, 2014, p. 67.

Mercha and Maru Mercha, and lived in Tewodros II's court with the other captured princes of the realm. It was here that he would meet his future rival, Menelik II. Once Tewodros II felt confident that Kassa Mercha and his brothers would help him to carry out his vision for Ethiopia, they were granted titles and governorships over regions in their native Tigray. Kassa shared Tewodros II's zeal for Christ and the church, and was given the title of Balambaras.[292]

Kassa Mercha's good fortune in achieving freedom from Tewodros II, and being elevated to the title of Balambaras, was followed by a period of hardship that was necessary to mold him into his legendary future self. While in Axum for the celebration of St. Mary of Zion, Kassa Mercha had a brief encounter with the angel of death, appearing in the form of a terrible illness. Knocking at death's door, he prayed and death did not open it. He survived. Confident of the Almighty's hand in his victory over death, Kassa Mercha devoted his life to Christ and entered a monastery. Whether or not this was inspired by Tewodros II's time in the monastery cannot be known but, as with Tewodros II, the experience laid a priestly foundation in his heart and cultivated a lifelong focus on matters of the church. Kassa Mercha was convinced by respected men that a monastic life would not be the best use of his gifts, Instead, he made a vow not to take vengeance on his enemies or horde the wealth of his beloved nation for his personal gain.[293]

At first, Kassa Mercha carried out his duties in Tigray as expected by Tewodros II. However, he decided to rebel when the emperor turned on the church and

---

[292] Ibid.

[293] Ibid.

imprisoned the Abuna – Kassa Mercha and other nobles received correspondence from Abuna Salama himself. The church was, for the most part, historically immune from any fighting among the nobility, so the Abuna's imprisonment was unacceptable. Emperor Tewodros II was now violating his oath to be a defender of the Orthodox faith. As a man of principle, Kassa Mercha now felt free to follow his former captor's precedent. He became an outlaw.

Like Tewodros II, Kassa Mercha went on a military campaign in the land of his family, winning acclaim and followers battle by battle. After defeating Dejazmatch Gabre Mikael in 1865, he took to himself the title of Dejazmatch. True to his pledge, and in contrast to the cruelty then being demonstrated by Tewodros II, he did not hold vengeance against those who still followed the emperor. He granted amnesty to those that agreed to follow him.

The angel of death that had previously spared Kassa Mercha showed no mercy to the armies of three of Tewodros II's competent, war-hardened generals. Dejazmatch Tekle Giorgis, Dejazmatch Deres and Dejazmatch Sahlu were sent to crush the upstart but, instead, watched their faithful warriors fall to a dreadful epidemic as they marched on Dejazmatch Kassa Mercha's position.[294] Dejazmatch Tekle Giorgis would lose his own life. Kassa Mercha's faith was strengthened by this seeming act of divine intervention as his fighting force also grew in strength.

Emperor Tewodros II must have seen the similarities between his own rise and that of his namesake – the King of Kings was once called Kassa, too. He grew

---

[294] Ibid., 68.

even more determined to put an end to this Tigrayan uprising. However, uprisings were erupting all over his empire. To make matters worse, a second attempt to march on Tigray met the same fate as the first. The epidemic again ravaged his armies as they marched on Dejazmatch Kassa Mercha.[295]

Kassa Mercha and his army marched through the north unmatched. By the time the British Napier expedition was ready to rescue their countrymen, he was in control of practically all the regions leading to Tewodros II's Magdala fortress. The British were forced to cut a deal with him or risk all out war from their initial landing in Ethiopia. To win Dejazmatch Kassa Mercha's confidence, a proclamation was shared, stating, "When the time shall arise for the march of a British army through your country, bear in mind, People of Abyssinia, that the Queen of England has no unfriendly feelings against your country or your liberty."[296] After he received assurances that the British had no plans to stay, he agreed to provide guides and provisions for the British army while they were in Ethiopia. After all, they would be doing his work for him. Emperor Tewodros II was in his way and needed to be removed.

As a result of the assistance he granted the British during the Napier expedition, Dejazmatch Kassa Mercha was destined to be crowned the victor in the war of two King of Kings and one Dejazmatch. He was in no rush to crown himself as anything, despite requests by his countrymen, and proved that divine protection and determination triumphed over titles and ambition. After crushing the forces of Tekle Giyorgis II, Kassa Mercha

---

[295] Ibid.

[296] Ibid., 69.

was crowned in Axum as Emperor Yohannes IV. He was a legend in Tigray and his respect now extended to the far reaches of the Ethiopian realm. He would gain even further renown for defeating the armies of the ever troublesome Egyptians, who continued to represent the interests of the Ottoman Empire and were determined to control the source of the Nile.

EMPEROR YOHANNES IV AND THE EGYPTIANS

The Ottoman Empire had conquered Egypt and, using its Egyptian soldiers, made an aggressive move to control Massawa and the kingdoms north of the Mareb River in Ethiopia. The Muslim Ottomans determined that having a zealous Christian king in power was not good for their interest on the Red Sea coast. Emperor Yohannes IV's domestic policy of forcibly converting Muslims to Christianity certainly did not improve his relations with his Muslim neighbors.

The Muslim Egyptians thought that Menelik II was a better option. Since Shoa was in the highlands, they felt that he could be contained and not interfere with their activities on the coast. It is likely that their long-term plan was to control Ethiopia as a vassal state. At a minimum, they would control large portions of Ethiopia and have a local, sympathetic ruler control the realm's day-to-day administration. After all, control of Ethiopia would mean control over the source of the Nile river, the very lifeblood of Egypt.

In 1875, when their armies marched inland from the coast into Tigray, the Egyptians also sent a fighting force to take control of the Muslim holy city of Harar.

German commercial relations with Egypt, which are quite important. Therefore, it is not advisable to answer Yohannes letter, leaving aside our doubts about its form and the person presenting it."[299]

Britain and France also did not want to risk relations with Egypt for Ethiopia. Queen Victoria responded to Emperor Yohannes IV's request for a neutral observer, saying that she had been assured Egypt had no ill intent and was merely acting to defend against bandits.[300]

When the Egyptian troops entered Ethiopian territory with 2500 men armed with Remington rifles, two six-gun batteries of mountain artillery and six rocket stands, Emperor Yohannes IV was sent the clear message that their actions were not defensive. The Egyptians were hoping that their brazen move would encourage rival kingdoms to revolt but the plan failed. The legend of Emperor Yohannes IV had begun to take root and he had established himself as a force to be reckoned with. None of the great kingdoms wanted to openly oppose him.

The Egyptian general, Arendrup, received instructions to move his troops to Adwa and set up camp as if they intended to occupy the region permanently. He was also instructed to send messages to Yohannes IV's rivals to encourage them to fight for the Egyptian cause with promises of protection and aid.[301] Despite being such a powerful adversary, the well-equipped Egyptian army was surrounded and annihilated by the emperor's forces at

---

[299] Gabre-Sellassie, Zewde. *Yohannes IV of Ethiopia: A Political Biography*. 1975. The Red Sea Press, 2014, p. 86.

[300] Ibid., 88.

[301] Ibid., 101.

the Battle of Gundet on November 16, 1875. General Arendrup was killed in the battle.

THE BATTLE OF GURA

The Ottoman Empire was embarrassed by their defeat in Ethiopia. Preparations for revenge were planned in Cairo. The very next year, the stage was set for another battle of epic proportions: the Battle of Gura. Emperor Yohannes IV repeated his victory, destroying between 15,000 and 20,000 Egyptian soldiers at the 3-day Battle of Gura between March 7-9, 1876.[302] The Egyptians came well equipped and their military contingent even had American Civil War veterans – 2 colonels and 6 officers from the U.S. were part of the force. Overall, there were 18 senior officers, 12,000 soldiers, 1058 horses and 1204 mules.[303]

The appearance of such a large, well armed force to remove Emperor Yohannes IV gave some of his rival's courage. The governor of Yejju (the former seat of power during the Zemene Mesafint), the governor of Sokota and the governor of Gondar made their intentions known to Egypt. Wolde Mikael, the governor of Hamasien who had been imprisoned by the emperor, tried to play both sides but was rumored to favor the Egyptians.

Emperor Yohannes IV was confident that the Creator and the north of Ethiopia was on his side. He rode through the north with arms and money to awaken the

---

[302] Pankhurst, Richard. *The Ethiopians: A History*. Blackwell Publishing, 1998, p. 166.

[303] Gabre-Sellassie, Zewde. *Yohannes IV of Ethiopia: A Political Biography*. 1975. The Red Sea Press, 2014, p. 104.

national pride of his people. He was a legend in Tigray and he used this to his advantage. Despite not having the support of the major kingdoms, his army was estimated to be 72,000 Ethiopians, including 3,000 cavalry and 6,000 barefoot warriors carrying guns. As a result of his earlier conquests, he was also in possession of 18 artillery pieces.[304] The north had indeed rallied to protect the honor of their champion, the King of Kings, the King of Zion. The offspring of Solomon would not face the foreign threat without the strength of the north.

Meanwhile, Wolde Mikael finally chose a side. He soon arrived in the Egyptian camp with news of Yohannes IV's troop movements. This helped boost morale somewhat; however, the Egyptian general estimated that 22 Rases had remained loyal to Emperor Yohannes IV.[305]

To make matters worse, all was not well in the Egyptian camp on the eve of battle as the Americans and the Egyptians were not on the same page. The Americans were concerned that a loss would damage their reputation, while the Egyptian commander, Rateb Pasha, was offended that one of the greatest Egyptian fighting forces assembled on foreign soil was split between his command and that of the Americans. Having brought the latest in military techniques and warfare science, the Americans were so valuable that General Loring was given the title of Chief of Staff and second-in-command.

Confusion between the American and Egyptian strategies meant that their forces were separated when the Ethiopians finally attacked. Inspired by their legendary emperor, the northern warriors rushed into battle and would not be stopped by modern weaponry. American

---

[304] Ibid., 105.

[305] Ibid., 107.

Colonel Dye wrote passionately about the battle and described the onslaught:

> "While fusiliers [a soldier armed with a fusil/light flintlock musket], spearsmen, and men with knobbed clubs, from bush, ravines and rock, on our front and against our right, rushed madly on. Shot after shot now pealed from our battery, intermingling with angry rockets, the fire of our few cavalry and of infantry. But still the Abyssinians continued their advance."[306]

So furious was the Ethiopian assault that Rateb Pasha estimated their forces at around 250,000 soldiers.[307] When the dust cleared after the first day of fighting, the Egyptians had lost 7 battalions and 19 cannons. The Egyptians also found themselves surrounded as Emperor Yohannes IV watched from the hills and waited for them to make their next move. Since the Egyptians were hurt and did not move, the Ethiopians assaulted their fort with captured artillery pieces. The following day, the Egyptians returned fire with their Krupp cannon, causing Emperor Yohannes IV to move his camp when a shell fell near his tent.

With the Egyptians firmly in their fort the battle had reached a stalemate but the damage had been done. Colonel Dye recorded that, of the 12,000 Egyptians who had landed in Ethiopia, Rateb Pasha led 5,200 soldiers into battle. Of that number, 400 returned to the fort uninjured and 1600 with injuries. About 1,000 men lost their lives in the Ethiopian assault, while 2,200 were captured. The Ethiopians slaughtered 1000 of the captives and 230 more

---

306 Ibid., 108-109.

307 Ibid., 109.

died of their wounds in captivity. The Ethiopians allowed 130 of their captives to return to the Egyptian fort. Historical figures vary but, even according to Egyptian accounting, 3,657 Egyptians were dead or missing.[308]

The Egyptians did their best to conceal their losses but the damage was done and the battle was lost. The Ethiopians also sustained heavy losses – about 5,000 warriors – in addition to those who abandoned the war effort once they had plundered the fallen Egyptians on the battlefield. Knowing the weakness of his forces and the superior arms of the Egyptians, Emperor Yohannes IV demonstrated wisdom and restraint. He did not try to go after the Egyptians in the fort or march on their base at Massawa. Instead, he wrote to Egypt to negotiate terms for peace. Again, true to his vow, the emperor did not seek vengeance on the Egyptians for their invasion.

Ultimately, while his forces were not at full strength, Emperor Yohannes IV did gain more modern armaments. Thus, he strengthened his position against his internal rivals, Menelik II of Shoa in particular. In fact, one of the reasons why Yohannes IV did not pursue running the Egyptians completely out of Ethiopia (and reclaiming ancient territory of Massawa) was that Menelik II was gaining strength.

THE SUBMISSION OF MENELIK II

Menelik II had conquered Wollo and was importing foreign arms of his own. Therefore, Yohannes IV, making sure he had sufficient strength to deal with this threat, began to turn his attention south and started his war

---

[308] Ibid., 111.

march. Mohammed Ali, the strongest of Wollo's leaders and formally Menelik II's ally, had smartly switched allegiance to the emperor rather than risk combat with the legend of Tigray. By January of 1878, he reached the borders of Shoa.

Menelik II ordered the drums of war to be activated and Shoa's warriors answered the call but, after some initial clashes, Menelik II retreated to Leche due to the emperor's battle-tested and hardened fighting force with modern armaments. Shoa's elders and wise men counseled Menelik II, advising that peace would be the best option.

So great was Emperor Yohannes IV that, upon marching into the province on March 20, 1878, Menelik II met him with a stone on his shoulder as a sign of penitence and withdrew his claim to the imperial throne.[309] The agreement came to be known as the Leche Agreement. Menelik II agreed to pay tribute, supply the royal army whenever it passed through Shoa, and renounce the title of King of Kings, which he had been fighting to claim for ten years prior.[310] Ras Adal was there as a witness, along with a court minstrel whose sole purpose was to sing songs chiding Menelik II for his foolish ambition.

In return for Menelik II's submission, Emperor Yohannes IV officially recognized Menelik II as the King of Shoa.[311] In a sign of strength, the emperor declared to Menelik II:

> "You are accordingly king and master of a
> land conquered by your forebears; I shall

---

[309] Marcus, Harold G. *The Life and Times of Menelik II: Ethiopia 1844-1913*. Red Sea Press, 1995, p. 166.

[310] Ibid., 168.

[311] Ibid.

respect your sovereignty if you will be faithful to the agreement decided between us. Whoever strikes your kingdom, strikes me, and whoever makes war on you, make it on me. You are accordingly my eldest son."[312]

Having previously and proudly claimed the title of King of Kings prior to his submission, it was now clear to Menelik II and to all in the realm, Shoa in particular, that there was only room for one King of Kings in Ethiopia. Tewodros II's legacy was sustained – a King of Kings who ruled not just in name but with actual power – and the legend of Emperor Yohannes IV reached its zenith.

THE FALL OF A LEGEND

Emperor Yohannes IV was killed in battle while fighting against the armies of the legendary Mahdi of Sudan at Matamma in 1889. Like his ancestor, King David, and other Ethiopian kings before him, he was wounded in the battle while leading his troops. Yohannes IV led his troops from the center and managed to break through the enemy lines but, in the chaos of war, he was shot through his left hand and the bullet landed in his chest.[313] Death by bullet in 1889 was often not an immediate affair. With his final breath he called together his inner circle and declared Dejazmatch Mengesha his natural son born by his brother's wife.[314] The child's paternity was in question and the declaration was meant to

---

[312] Ibid., 56.

[313] Ibid., 111.

[314] Ibid.

dispel any lingering doubts. He died shortly afterward.[315]
He was the last head of state to die on the battlefield.[316]

The news of Emperor Yohannes IV's death broke the spirit of the Ethiopian fighting force. Many of the soldiers deserted. The inner circle tried their best to hide his death from the larger army but the smell of the body under the African sun soon confirmed to the camp the gravity of the situation. Word soon reached the Mahdists who swept into the camp and satisfied the angel of death's appetite for blood. The emperor's body was captured and his head was removed from it, put on a spike and sent to the Khalifa at Omdurman, who displayed it as a symbol of Muslim power – the powerful King of Kings, who had forced Muslims into Christianity, had fallen by the power of Allah. Emperor Yohannes IV's head was taken by camel throughout northern Sudan as a recruitment tool and symbol of the power of the Mahdist state.[317]

The power of the Mahdist state was still no match for Ethiopia. King Menelik II would quickly fill the void left by the death of Emperor Yohannes IV, just as the latter had filled the void after Emperor Tewodros II before him. The age of priestly warrior kings was secure and would continue.

---

[315] Gabre-Sellassie, Zewde. *Yohannes IV of Ethiopia: A Political Biography*. 1975. The Red Sea Press, 2014, p. 300.

[316] This distinction has been left out of the history books.

[317] Marcus, Harold G. *The Life and Times of Menelik II: Ethiopia 1844-1913*. Red Sea Press, 1995, p. 112.

CHAPTER EIGHTEEN

General of Generals

"For a day in thy courts is better than a thousand. I had rather be a doorkeeper in the house of my God, than to dwell in the tents of wickedness." — **Psalms 84:10**

As Ras Makonnen inspected his baby boy, he was keenly aware of the presence of his gun bearer and, moreover, the role that loyal soldiers played in maintaining the Ethiopian realm. He, a great man in his own right, had been serving Emperor Menelik II faithfully for as long as he could remember. A man of honor forced to engage in war, and arguably one of the greatest generals of his generation, Ras Makonnen was a great part of why his cousin had been so successful. He loved Menelik II dearly and worked day and night to ensure his reign was successful.

Ras Makonnen also respected Emperor Yohannes IV's legacy and was aware that his story was not yet complete. Similarly, he respected the fallen emperor's most loyal general, Ras Alula, who was a legend in his own right. Ras Alula did not die with Yohannes IV. He was still active in Tigray and spent considerable time on Ras Makonnen's mind.

Ras Alula was supporting Yohannes IV's son, Ras Mengesha, a living heir of the former emperor, which meant there would be potential challenges to the throne of Emperor Menelik II. Ras Makonnen would have to be vigilant to ensure the success of Emperor Menelik II's reign. If there was anything that gave Ras Makonnen concern for the future of his baby boy in 1892 as much as (or even more than) the Europeans, it was the shadow of this great man of Tigray, Ras Alula.

RAS ALULA

The throne of David and Solomon in Ethiopia was not sustained by one person. The realm's history is a testament to the truth that success is a collective effort. Accordingly, Emperor Yohannes IV had owed a lot of his military success to his trusted general, Ras Alula, a man of humble origins and an excellent example of Ethiopia's merit-based military system. He would rise from a lowly position to become the head of one of the most powerful armies in Ethiopian history.

Ras Alula grew up in the domain of Tigrayan ruler, Ras Araya Demsu, one of the captives of Emperor Tewodros II who gained his freedom following that emperor's fall. Ras Alula began his career as a servant of Ras Araya, who assisted Alula to become *elfegn kalkay*, a chamberlain and door keeper for Dejazmatch Kassa. Diligent in his duties, he was soon elevated to the rank of Agafari, responsible for organizing meals in the court as well as being the head of Dejazmatch Kassa's personal security forces.

Ras Alula proved himself in battle against one of Dejazmatch Kassa's rivals, Emperor Tekle Giyorgis II, at the famous battle where a Dejazmatch faced a King of

Kings and won. The fearless Alula was in command of battle-hardened, disciplined warriors armed with modern armaments received from the British following the Napier expedition. Tekle Giyorigis II was no match. Post battle, Alula's fame began to rise within the realm and, according to oral tradition, it was he who captured the emperor on the battlefield. As a reward, he was raised to the imperial rank of Shalaqa (commander of a thousand troops).

As his leader gained supreme power in the land, Alula's role continued to grow in importance. Being of humble origins, he had no support among the nobility of Tigray outside of Emperor Yohannes IV. Therefore, he could be trusted to be loyal and not seek personal ambition to the detriment of the emperor.

Alula's fame only increased when he decimated the powerful Ottoman army. Confidently, he told the Egyptians that "Ethiopia goes up to the sea; Egypt begins there."[318] He was named the Lion of Gura after outmaneuvering the Egyptian forces at the final Battle of Gura.[319] By 1877, he was head of an army with over 10,000 Remingtons.

Despite his lack of formal education, Alula grew into a seasoned leader and statesman who truly believed in Ethiopia. As Emperor Yohannes IV's greatest general, he was given a title that reflected his special status within the realm. It was said by a royal biographer, who lived in the time of Alula, that Emperor Yohannes IV stated:

> "'With what name shall I magnify him, and with what name shall I honour him for this

---

[318] Erlich, Haggai. *Ras Alula and the Scramble for Africa, A Political Biography: Ethiopia & Eritrea 1875-1897*. The Red Sea Press, 1996, p. 17.

[319] Ibid., 12.

man [Alula] is faithful, after my own heart, and he does all my wishes, and he does not hold back from doing my commands...' He [Yohannes IV] called his father and his counselor, the great chief of the priests Echage [Tewoflos]...whose sea of knowledge is not depleted...The king and Echägē met a second time, in private, not in public, and it was said: Behold, we have found an honourable name and a high rank which is fitting for the elect and blessed Ras Alula, and saying this they named him Turk Basha, saying 'There is nothing which is greater than this name, and there is nothing which is better than this rank' and they closed the matter with this counsel."[320]

The title of Turk Basha was associated with the introduction of modern weapons. It likely referenced the modern armaments wielded by the armies of Imam Ahmad Gran whose Jihad was supported by the Ottoman Turks and remained fresh in the minds of Ethiopia's nobility. Before the Era of Princes, it carried weight as modern firearms often helped change the balance of power within the realm. However, as the power and influence of the emperors themselves diminished, this title had also lost its importance. Ras Alula's new additional title was significant because it was synonymous with the power of Emperor Yohannes IV.

It is said that the Emperor "adorned [Alula] with all adornments...He did nothing like this for the other officers. When Yohannes, King of Kings, completed the ceremony of appointment for Ras, he said to him: '...Let your_authority be under me. Do all that you wish, and

---

[320] Ibid., 19.

there will not be found one of the princes or officers who will be honoured more than you. And for me, there is nothing with which I could make you greater, except only the throne of my kingdom.'"[321]

When the powerful Menelik II of Shoa had finally submitted to Yohannes IV with the traditional stone on his shoulder, it was said that Ras Alula was given the honor of removing the stone.[322] A biographer of Ras Alula chronicled his impact on Shoa as follows:

> "When the king and rulers of the country of Shoa and all the creatures from man to the animals, heard the news, they trembled and were afraid, and melted like wax, all those who were living there. The land trembled, and the whole of the country of Shoa was troubled because of the majesty of the coming of Yohannes, king of kings, and because of the strength of the power of Ras Alula, chief of princes, for they greatly feared Ras Alula...Ras Alula did in that land great deeds which...cannot all be written or told. If all the deeds which were done in the land of Shoa were written down singly, the matter would be too much for us. And it would seem false to the hearers."[323]

Following the submission of King Menelik II, Ras Alula was given the government of the province of Adwa, a place whose name would soon ring out through the ages.

---

[321] Ibid.

[322] Ibid., 20.

[323] Ibid.

Despite the legend of Emperor Yohannes IV in the north, once he turned his attention to the rest of Ethiopia and began to travel to seek tribute, northern Ethiopia once again became deeply divided. Rebels, each hoping to create their own legend, openly challenged the authority of the central government. In the highlands of the Mareb Melash, a province beyond the Mareb River (north of Tigray), Ras Walda Mikael rose as a main contender. To challenge the military might of Emperor Yohannes IV, he attempted to follow his blueprint and strike a deal with a foreign power. Egypt still controlled large areas of northern Ethiopia and supported rebel activity. Ras Alula was the principal representative of Emperor Yohannes IV in the north and he used his well-trained army as a means of containing Egyptian power. It became known that it was Ras Alula who gave teeth to the legend of Emperor Yohannes IV. Few wanted to face his military mastery on the battlefield.

It was Ras Alula who secured the surrender of the rebel Walda Mikael after his treason with the Egyptians. The Emperor, true to his vow to forsake vengeance, conferred the title of Ras on the humbled rebel and made him vice-governor of Hamasien under the leadership of Ras Alula.[324] The alliance with Ras Walda Mikael would not last long though. Ras Alula would ensure that the Emperor banished him and his sons to Amba Salama. Ras Walda Mikael would be the last hereditary ruler to hold power in the Mareb Melash.[325] His lands and possessions were granted to Ras Alula.

A man of humble beginnings, Ras Alula was locked out of the Ethiopian nobility for his lack of Solomonic blood. His military deeds did not allow him to marry into

---

[324] Ibid., 23.

[325] Ibid., 25.

the nobility, and the gifts and lands granted to him by his sovereign could not change his social standing in the eyes of the other royal kingdoms. Nonetheless, he emerged in the era of great men as a legendary figure to be reckoned with. Ras Makonnen was justified in his concern.

CHAPTER NINETEEN

Ras Alula and the Defense of Zion

"I have found David my servant; with my holy oil have I anointed him: With whom my hand shall be established: mine arm also shall strengthen him. The enemy shall not exact upon him; nor the son of wickedness afflict him. And I will beat down his foes before his face, and plague them that hate him." – **Psalms 89:20-23**

Ras Makonnen remembered meeting Ras Alula. He was an impressive figure. Ras Alula had been given the honor of removing the stone from his cousin's neck at the ceremony of submission. Ras Makonnen saw Ras Alula again after he had distinguished himself in battle at the war of Kings between his cousin Menelik II and King Tekle Haymanot. Despite his own feats of bravery on the battlefield, Ras Makonnen was still a young warrior in comparison to the battle-tested Ras Alula.

At the conclusion of the battle of the two kings, Ras Makonnen witnessed Ras Alula being given the bulk of King Tekle Haymanot's arms, increasing his power and prestige. The aftermath of the battle of two kings showed Ras Makonnen how true power was wielded.

RAS ALULA AND THE WAR OF THE TWO KINGS

In June of 1882, King Menelik II and King Tekle Haymanot (formerly Ras Adal) faced each other on the battlefield. Menelik II remembered the King of Gojjam's presence at his submission ceremony to Emperor Yohannes IV and relished the opportunity to show him that he was not merely a defenseless vassal of the emperor.

Wise King Menelik II had spent the time since his submission conquering the southern lands of Ethiopia, and increasing his wealth and power in the process. His military campaigns brought him into conflict with the Oromo and Gurage kingdoms, which were no match for Menelik II's modern armaments and experience from decades of wars for the throne. Arsi, Sidama and Kaffa were forced to pay tribute to King Menelik II. He, of course, paid some of his newly attained tributes to Emperor Yohannes IV.

The Kingdom of Kaffa, a region known for its gold, ivory and hides, was becoming a major source of revenue for Menelik II. Kaffa was also famous for being the birthplace of coffee. In 1882, Tekle Haymanot decided to claim Kaffa as decreed by Emperor Yohannes IV. Ras Gobena, Menelik II's general in the region, found himself facing a king on the battlefield and sent word to his leader. Thus, the stage was set for an epic battle of kings.

Word of the coming battle spread quickly through the realm. The emperor sent word to his two vassals to submit their dispute to his council and avoid a costly war but his calls for peace went unheeded. On June 6, 1882, the war began. The fighting lasted a day. King Menelik II captured Tekle Haymanot, who was wounded, as well as two of his sons.[326]

Emperor Yohannes IV was right. The war was costly and 2000 of Menelik II's men met the angel of death that day. At the conclusion of the bloodshed, King Menelik II and his Shoan army emerged victorious and gained control of Gojjam. Menelik II announced his victory stating, "The King of Gojam defied me. I marched against him and took his crown... made him prisoner...took all his lands."[327]

The conflict was unavoidable in Menelik II's mind. He had already been benefiting from the resources of the Kaffa kingdom when Emperor Yohannes IV gave it to King Tekle Haymanot to balance Menelik II's growing power. Had he not defeated Tekle Haymanot, he would have lost a major source of income and dashed his hopes of one day challenging the emperor and claiming the title he believed destined to be his. The emperor was furious and his inner circle advised him to move immediately on Shoa to ensure that Menelik II did not get too powerful.

When Menelik II got word that Yohannes IV was on his way, he wrote to the emperor to reassure him that he was still loyal to the throne. The emperor ordered him to bring the captives of Gojjam to his camp, where he ordered them released on the spot. King Menelik II was also stripped of Wollo. Careful not to turn Menelik II to outright rebellion, the emperor allowed him to keep control of Kaffa but arranged to have some of Tekle Haymanot's weapons returned to him. The bulk of his

---

[326] Prouty, Chris. *Empress Taytu and Menilek II: Ethiopia 1883-1910.* 1986. The Red Sea Press, 2016, p. 23.

[327] Ibid.

arsenal was given to Ras Alula, who was also given King Tekle Haymanot's territory of Agaw Meder.[328]

Ras Alula was also charged with the responsibility of escorting King Menelik II's daughter Zawditu, who was given to Ras Araya Selassie Yohannes in marriage – the son of Emperor Yohannes IV. It was hoped that this union would unify Shoa and Tigray and help create a stable future for Ethiopia. The wedding took place in October of 1882 in an exhibition of royal splendor. Zawditu was only 8 years old; and Ras Araya Selassie Yohannes was 15. The wedding was expedited to cement the ties between the two royal houses and hopefully avoid a civil war that would implode the realm should Emperor Yohannes IV and King Menelik II be forced to go to war.

RAS ALULA AND THE EGYPTIANS

Ras Alula and Emperor Yohannes IV did not have much time to celebrate the nuptials as the Egyptian threat once again raised its head in 1883. It happened when Ras Alula, on his own initiative, destroyed an Egyptian company of soldiers sent to occupy Sahāti, a station in Egypt-controlled northern Ethiopia. It was a massacre of Egyptians and a potential diplomatic nightmare.

Ras Alula's attack had wider implications as Egypt was no longer under Ottoman control – it was now the domain of the British Empire. Fortunately, the British were under heavy pressure from the Islamic forces of the Mahdi in Sudan, where they had Egyptian forces under

---

[328] Erlich, Haggai. *Ras Alula and the Scramble for Africa, A Political Biography: Ethiopia & Eritrea 1875-1897*. The Red Sea Press, 1996, p. 36.

siege. Not wanting to engage in a war against Yohannes IV and the Mahdi, the British chose to negotiate a treaty. The British had adopted a policy of not engaging directly with the throne of Ethiopia since the Napier expedition. It appears that, since obtaining Emperor Yohannes IV's assistance on the Napier expedition, they had not maintained direct channels to him. Instead of reestablishing a direct channel with the emperor, the British chose to engage Ras Alula, who became instrumental in the subsequent negotiations, setting the groundwork for many of the terms of the eventual agreement. On June 3, 1884 the Ethiopians signed the Hewitt Treaty with the British government and Yohannes IV finally got the peaceful resolution with Egypt that he had been seeking since the Battles of Gundet and Gura.

In the immediate aftermath of the signing, the treaty was seen as a victory for Emperor Yohannes IV and Ras Alula. It would be the only treaty that the emperor signed with a foreign power. The flawed agreement pledged Ethiopia to assist with the Madhist threat in Sudan, while not securing the port of Massawa. The final terms of the treaty contained five major points:[329]

1. Differences between Egypt and Abyssinia would be mediated by the British government;
2. The Emperor would secure the withdrawal through his territory of East Sudan garrisons;
3. Free transit would be given through Massawa for all goods, including arms and ammunition, to and from Abyssinia, starting September 1, 1884;

---

[329] Gabre-Sellassie, Zewde. *Yohannes IV of Ethiopia: A Political Biography*. 1975. The Red Sea Press, 2014, p. 192.

4. Extradition of criminals between Egypt and Abyssinia; and

5. Assistance with the matter of consecration of bishops.

The Ethiopians would fulfil their terms with their Christian brethren in Europe to the letter. The British did not see things the same way and, a few months later, in November, the British would sit at the Berlin Conference and negotiate for the Massawa port and Ethiopia to be given to Italy. As the growing shadow of European colonization inched closer to the ancient realm, the Sudanese Madhists were also growing in strength and looking for territory. Ras Alula engaged and defeated them at the Battle of Kufit in 1885, as the Europeans continued to plot the division of Africa in Berlin. Ethiopia paid for that victory with many lives lost but also gained arms and experience that would serve them later.

Ras Alula established his headquarters in the village of Asmara and helped expand it into a regional center of activity. The years that followed, leading up to 1892, were characterized by interactions with Ethiopia's new neighbor, Italy, which had bought Massawa from the British and desired to stake a claim in northern Ethiopia. Things came to a head at the Battle of Dogali in January 1887, when a battalion of 500 Italian soldiers, on their way to reinforce the Italian's inherited position at Sahāti, were slaughtered by thousands of Ras Alula's army. This left a sour taste in the mouth of Italy but they were in no position then to avenge the loss.

In 1889, the Madhist threat returned and Emperor Yohannes IV was killed in the Battle of Matamma. Ras Alula was not only part of the inner circle summoned by the emperor to hear his dying words, which included his wishes for imperial succession, but he was also entrusted to care for Yohannes IV's heir. Dejazmatch Mengasha was adorned in the royal robes and ordered the army to retreat under the guise that he was his father. However, news of Yohannes IV's death had already leaked into the army. Sudanese gunners who were fighting for Ethiopia sensed that the tide had turned and they defected to fight with their countrymen. They carried news of the emperor's death to the Jihadists, rallying the army to swarm the scattered, retreating Ethiopians. Ras Alula and Dejazmatch Mengasha managed to escape but their once invincible forces were no more.

As Emperor Yohannes IV's death effectively removed Ras Alula's source of money and power, the legend of Yohannes IV was not sufficient to restrain the ambition of the other noble houses of Tigray. Tigray itself began to be split by the rival noble families, all claiming to be descended from the throne of King Solomon. There was Yohannes IV's family, there was the family of Ras Araya Dimtsu from Endarta, and there were the descendants of Sabagadis from Agame, headed by Dejazmatch Sebhat Aragawi. There was also Dejazmatch Seym, "Abba Gubaz," who was supported by forces outside of Tigray. Unfortunately for Emperor Yohannes IV's heir, the other houses refused to unite under his banner. The elite families of the Hamasien republic also refused to unite with Tigray. The recently arrived Kifu Ken, and the corresponding lack of food, further diminished Ras Alula's power as the remnants of his once powerful fighting force defected in favor of personal preservation.

The Italians were watching the weakness and division of the Tigray ruling families and, deciding to make good on their negotiations in Berlin, occupied Asmara in August of 1889.

Over the next three years (during the Kifu Ken), Ras Alula worked to strengthen the internal unity of Tigray. By January and February of 1892, Ras Mengesha and Ras Hagos marched south preparing to take on Emperor Menelik II's forces as it was rumored that Menelik II would lead his armies into Tigray to once and for all bring them under his control.[330]

Emperor Menelik II started his march toward Tigray, indeed. However, his intelligence (likely provided through his powerful Queen) let him know that it was not the time to engage with Tigray as they had managed to strengthen the pro-Tigrayan elements among the Amhara tribes. The Kifu Ken had also hit Tigray hard and there would be little food, if any, to support the imperial army on such a campaign. Menelik II was also facing trouble in the south, so he chose to halt his march in February and return to Shoa.

By March 1892, Ras Alula had managed to bring Dejazmatch Sebhat under the rule of Mengesha. The combined forces of Sebhat, Mengesha, Hagos and Alula were 10,000 battle-tested troops, remnants of the former imperial army, which easily included some of the best fighters within the realm.

The Italians, through their agent Gandolfi, gave 35,000 cartridges to Mengesha in a symbolic gesture of peace but the Italian support did not last. Gandolfi was soon replaced by General Oreste Baratieri, who was pro-Shoan.

By May 1892, Ras Alula and the now united chiefs of Tigray were assembled in his camp and pressing the

---

[330] Erlich, Haggai. *Ras Alula and the Scramble for Africa, A Political Biography: Ethiopia & Eritrea 1875-1897*. The Red Sea Press, 1996, p. 172.

Italians to give them weapons and grain. Their requests for assistance went unanswered. The Tigrayans had suffered tremendously under the Kifu Ken and could not wage war for the throne when they could not even feed themselves.

On July 3, 1892, days before the birth of Ras Makonnen's son in Ejersa Goro, Ras Alula sent word to the Italians that, despite their need for supplies, the Tigrayans would not raid the Italian controlled areas of northern Ethiopia.[331] He even captured an Ethiopian rebel who was fighting against the Italians, hoping that this would show his goodwill. Despite all his efforts, the Italians refused to give him an audience, unable to forgive the slaughter at Dogali. They wanted nothing to do with Ras Alula. History was against him. Power in Ethiopia had shifted to the highlands of Shoa.

For the baby boy born to Ras Makonnen, these developments were a blessing. They meant that his father, Emperor Menelik II's cousin, would have the power necessary to clear a path for him to join the ranks of great men who defined the age of priestly warrior kings following the Zemene Mesafint.

---

[331] Ibid., 180.

CHAPTER TWENTY

The Kingdom of Shoa

"And then the King of Ethiopia rose up to depart to his county and he came to his father that he might pray on his behalf, and he said unto him: 'Bless me, father,' and he made obeissance unto him, And the King raised him up, blessed him and embraced him, and said; 'Blessed be the Lord my God Who blessed my father David, and Who blessed our father Abraham, May He be with thee always, and bless thy seed even as He blessed Jacob and made his seed to be as many as the stars of heaven and the sand of the sea."

– Kebra Nagast[332]

The Evil Days could not have come at a worst time for the kingdom of Tigray. A weakened Tigray meant that Shoa had space to breathe and consolidate control over the other kingdoms. It meant that Emperor Menelik II had the chance to govern without the direct threat of one of the realm's most experienced and powerful fighting forces. For Ras Makonnen, it meant that he would not have to immediately face the powerful Ras Alula in a battle for the throne. If Ras Alula was one of the reasons for the success of Emperor Yohannes IV, then Ras Makonnen was one of the reasons for the success of Emperor Menelik II. In

---

[332] Brooks, Miguel F., comp., ed. and trans. *Kebra Nagast: The Glory of Kings*. 1995. Red Sea Press, 2002, p. 63.

1892, it seemed as though a clash of these two titans was inevitable. They were two generals, protectors of the throne and Ethiopian patriots.

Ethiopia would not allow these two giants of history to clash. The plagues and famine of the Kifu Ken was too much for any kingdom. For a time, the potentially devastating war between the Kingdoms of Tigray and Shoa was delayed as survival became the priority.

ETHIOPIA IN 1892

Ethiopia was a tired land in 1892. The Evil Days had taken a toll on the soil, the animals and the people. Years of internal wars, disease and famine weakened the population. People had lived on grubs and berries in the forests, and there were horrific rumors that some had turned to cannibalism![333] Yet, the Evil Days were not Ethiopia's only problem.

In 1892, Europe's shadow was cast over almost the entire continent of Africa. Ethiopia was the one geographic region that managed to maintain its own light with its long tradition as an independent empire and its fierce reputation as a jealous guardian of her independence. Despite that, the European shadow crept ever closer to Ethiopia's borders, threatening to add the realm to the ever-expanding colonial landscape.

The reigning Emperor Menelik II was a keen observer of world affairs. Although he claimed descent from the wise King Solomon and the great Empress

---

[333] Marcus, Harold G. *The Life and Times of Menelik II: Ethiopia 1844-1913*. Red Sea Press, 1995, p. 136.

Makeda, that was of little significance as he governed a struggling empire. The Emperor was working hard to answer the prayers of his people who, always strong in ancient faith, were then yearning for better days. He had already begun the thankless, sometimes bloody work of centralizing and unifying Ethiopia's fractured and warring kingdoms. As the latest figure in the age of priestly warrior kings, he was not unique in this vision. He was building on the work of Emperor Tewodros II (1818-1868) and Emperor Yohannes IV (1831-1889) before him. He stood on the shoulders and, at times, in the shadow of legends.

It was not easy ruling the cradle of civilization at that time. It seemed as if the empire was falling apart at the seams. Convincing autonomous kingdoms, some of which were neither Jews nor Christians, that their interests would be best served by accepting the King of Kings on the Solomonic throne as sovereign was no simple task.

THE KINGDOMS OF ETHIOPIA

Ethiopia gave life to several powerful kingdoms, which were in a never-ending power struggle. For thousands of years the realm existed in a state of constant change as its many kingdoms united and then divided over time. Smaller groups of peoples, not having the benefits of the latest military technologies, often fell victim to their better armed neighbors. The forging of empires was accompanied by bloodshed and the horrors of war.

The more powerful kings and Rases could marshal thousands of armed soldiers by sounding the drums of war within a few days' notice. This resulted in the realm being in a constant state of war as the Rases flexed their power. Ever blessed and resilient, Ethiopia managed to endure the culture of war, and the great kingdoms in 1892 included Tigray, Wollo, Begemder, Gondar, Harar, Afar, Gojjam, Kaffa, Omo, Lalibela and, of course, Shoa, where Emperor Menelik II and Ras Makonnen hailed from.

At the time, Menelik II had been emperor for only three years but, having grown up watching the modern history of Ethiopia unfold before him, he was wise beyond his 48 years. Born of royal Solomonic blood, high up in the holy mountains of Zion, his life was like a chapter out of an epic novel – the story of Shoa.

BIRTH OF SHOA

The Kingdom of Shoa's roots sprang from the great King of Kings, Emperor Lebna Dengel, who waged epic battles against Harar's own Imam Ahmad Gran. Consequently, the Emperor lost his life on the battlefield, leaving his offspring to continue the fight and, with the help of the Portuguese, emerge victorious. Emperor Lebna Dengel survived long enough to ensure the continuation of the Shoan royal bloodline.

RAS NAGASI KRETOS

The first acknowledged prince of Shoa was Nagasi Kretos, the grandson of Emperor Lebna Dengel. Starting out as a local ruler in Agancha, Nagasi was able to take advantage of the local disunity among the peoples surrounding Agancha and soon extended his rule into regions east of Manz. First mentioned in the chronicles of 14th century Emperor Amda Seyon, Manz was called "Manzehel." It was mentioned again in the royal chronicles of Baeda Maryam I.[334] Manz was a region that was known for its rebellious nature but its people were often accused of fighting each other more than external forces. The area was said to have no towns, and its proud families lived far apart. Whatever the case, Nagasi Kretos was able to exploit the weakness of this small province and place it under his rule.

Nagasi established his base not in Manz but on the border with Ifat. Needless to say, Ifat soon fell to his expansionist vision. Known as a powerful warlord, he traveled to the then capital, Gondar, where he was given the title of Ras. He received his Nagarit (or war drums) from the hands of the Emperor Iyasu I (1682-1706).

SEBESTYANOS

In his will, Ras Nagasi stated that his oldest son, Akawa, would inherit his throne. Ultimately, he was succeeded by another son, Sebestyanos, to whom he left only a silver cutlass, a spear and a gilded shield of rhinoceros's hide.

Akawa was gifted with the highest honor a father could give a son but he did not hold the throne for long. Drought and famine caused the people of Manz to question his administration and they staged a coup in favor of another son, Dana. All the same, not everyone was happy about the opposition to Ras Nagasi's eldest son. Already a shrewd navigator of royal intrigue, Sebestyanos moved to Merhabete, where he served as governor. He used the opportunity to put his father's inheritance to

---

[334] Huntingford, G.W.B. *The Historical Geography of Ethiopia.* The British Academy, 1989, p. 80.

work. With his cutlass, spear and shield, he marched his soldiers into neighboring lands and brought them under his brother's administration.

Sebestyanos shared his father's vision of an independent kingdom and he married into the Manz nobility to strengthen his claim on the area. He married into an Oromo family and continued waging war against the neighboring Oromo nations. As he grew stronger on the battlefield, he inevitably began to clash with his brother. His father's gifts of weapons seemed prophetic as he prevailed in battle over his brother's forces and declared himself ruler of Manz, claiming the title of Meridazmatch, meaning *fearsome commander*. This title would go on to be claimed by all the rulers of Shoa until the region's elevation to an independent kingdom.

During his reign, Sebestyanos began to impact and change the local culture and he established the towns of Doqaqit, Ayne and Eyabar.[335] He maintained several bases near present-day Ankober, openly showing his desire to acquire new territories.

MERIDAZMATCH ABIYE

Sebestyanos was succeeded by his son (or possibly brother), Abiye, who further strengthened his hold on Manz, Ifat and surrounding areas. All of the military activities in Shoa and southward expansion from its central mountain lands were not going unnoticed. Abiye aroused the concern of Emperor Iyasu II in Gondar. However, the emperor was also expanding his own empire. He was busy

---

335 Pankhurst, Richard. *History of Ethiopian Towns from the Middle Ages to the Early Nineteenth Century.* Wiesbaden: Steiner, 1982, p. 186.

fighting the Oromo kingdoms that had grown in number and filled the vacuum left by Imam Gran's jihad, so he had little time to launch an all-out war on the growing power and organization of the Shoan dynasty.

In return for a public act of submission, the promise of payment of regular tribute and military assistance, Abiye was allowed to continue his rule without interference and he was given the title of Mardazmatch. Confident with his seal of approval from Gondar, he established a base at Doqaqit and began the conquest of the Harr Amba area. Mardazmatch Abiya died in battle in 1743 against the valiant Karayu Oromo in a military campaign south of Ifat.[336]

MERIDAZMATCH AMHA IYASUS

Amha Iyasus succeeded his father, Meridazmatch Abiye, and continued the policy of expansion. He used his father's wealth to import some matchlock guns from Gondar so as to subdue the Oromo resistance. With his technological advantage, he won stunning victories that expanded Shoan control over the Christian territories of Manz, Tegulet, Efrata and Bulga. These victories only encouraged Amha Iyasus and he continued his expansion into the east and west against Gaddam, the Afar. He did not forget about his father's death on the battlefield and re-launched the war against the Karayu Oromo and Abichu Oromo to the south of Ifat.

It was Amha Iyasus who finally incorporated Ankober into Shoa, showing no mercy. It is written that he

---

[336] Marcus, Harold G. *The Life and Times of Menelik II: Ethiopia 1844-1913.* Red Sea Press, 1995, p. 8.

decimated the Oromo population between Debre Berhan and Ankober, and resettled the area with Amhara, even though he carried Oromo blood himself. Any peoples inhabiting the northeastern highlands not loyal to Shoa met the same fate. He also built a Christian church in Ankober, called Qeddus Giyorgis.

Meridazmatch Amha Iyasus ruled Shoa at the beginning of the Zemene Mesafint. He is credited with creating the Shoan policy of keeping some distance from the imperial throne by maintaining an un-utilized buffer zone between Shoa and the imperial territories. This isolated them somewhat from the powerful Yejju Oromo and the intrigue surrounding the throne of David. This strategy was successful, as so strong was Amha Iyasus's hold on the northeastern and central highlands that, when Amha Iyasus was called to Gondar to pay homage to the Emperor, he was treated like a sovereign king.

ASFA WOSSEN

In 1777 CE, a year after the 13 colonies of the United States of America declared independence, Amha Iyasus died and was succeeded by his son, Asfa Wossen. It was Asfa Wossen who confirmed his father's kingdom within an empire. Shoa now included Ifat, Ankober, Marhabete and Manz. Ifat included Gaddam and Efrata; Ankober comprised Debra Berhan and Bulga; Marhabete incorporated Gishe and Morat; and Manz contained Lalo Meda and Gera Meda.

The wealth gained from these incorporated territories allowed Asfa Wossen to appoint governors to oversee the various regions. As with many of the powerful princes of the Zemene Mesafint, Asfa Wossen ran his domain independently of the emperor's control in Gondar. Asfa Wossen, focused on expanding his domain, was not a micromanager and allowed his governors wide authority. His lack of personal attention to his provinces, and his decision to implement a regular tax on all the regions under his control, bred unrest and three rebellions that had to be put down, including one led by his heir.

Sometime after 1779 CE, Emperor Tekla Giyorgis marched his army to Shoa in a show of strength with hopes of securing Asfa Wossen's willing submission and payment of tribute. Asfa Wossen, not wanting to get entangled in a war with Gondar, gladly paid the tribute in exchange for the emperor leaving the Shoan highlands. It was the last tribute that Shoa would pay until Menelik II's father took the throne.

WOSSEN SEGED

Between 1808 and 1810, Asfa Wossen died and his son, Wossen Seged, took hold of the reins of power. Like his forefathers before him, he continued to strengthen the hold of the Shoan family branch in the highlands. Recognizing that Shoans were seen as conquerors, Wossen Seged began a policy of religious tolerance. He took the title of Ras and appointed non-Christian officials to Ifat-Agoba, Abarri Galla, Gullale and Abbichu Galla. He also introduced policies to facilitate the cultural and political assimilation of the population. His reforms were ahead of their time and were not widely supported by the nobility or the conservative church in whose eyes Muslims and pagans were not seen as equal to the children of Christ.

Wossen Seged claimed Solomonic heritage from both his father's and mother's bloodlines. He looked outside of Shoa and tried to strengthen the bonds between some of the other branches of the Solomonic dynasty. Like many progressive men before him and many after his time, Ras Wossen Seged was assassinated in 1813. As fate would have it, his life and example was not in vain.

KING SAHLE SELASSIE: THE FIRST KING OF SHOA

The leadership of Shoa passed to Sahle Selassie, Ras Wossen Seged's son. King Sahle Selassie cemented Shoa's place as an important center in the internal politics of Ethiopia, putting the Solomonic dynasty of Shoa on the map.

King Sahle Selassie was a great reformer known throughout the land for his benevolent rule and love of justice. He was bright, articulate and progressive. Most of all, he understood the importance of finance in building an empire. King Sahle Selassie was a student of his people's history and wished to reclaim Ethiopia's ancient borders from before the invasion of Imam Ahmad Gran. The church and his Christian subjects supported him in this vision. He was sure to build on the arsenal of his forefathers and, with a few hundred matchlocks, he brought Shoa's borders to the Awash river. Word of his conquest quickly spread throughout the land and several smaller kingdoms beyond the river submitted to him rather than risk full-on assault. These were Liban, Nono, Soddo and part of Gurage.

Managing to double the size of his father's territory, which he was sure was possible only with the help of the Almighty Creator, Sahle Selassie acknowledged his new land holdings and unmatched power by giving himself the title of Negus (King). It is doubtful that the emperor in Gondar could have opposed him. In any event, the title went unchallenged and Shoa began as a kingdom. By the height of his reign, his fame spread far beyond the borders of Shoa and European travelers began to take interest.

One of those European travellers was Major W. Cornwallis Harris who was a second lieutenant in the Engineers of the East India Company, Bombay Establishment. From 1841 to 1843, he led a British diplomatic mission from Bombay to Ethiopia to negotiate a commercial treaty. Major W. Cornwallis Harris traveled to King Sahle Selassie's Shoa in 1841 and described it:

> "As if by the touch of the magician's wand, the scene passes in an instant from the parched arid wastes [of the Afar desert] to the green and lovely highland of Abyssinia, presenting one sheet of rich and thriving cultivation...Birds warbled among the leafy groves, and throughout the rich landscape reigned an air of peace and plenty."[337]

In describing Ankober he says:

> "...the metropolis of Shoa, spreading far and wide over a verdant mountain...presented a most singular if not imposing appearance. Clusters of thatched houses of all sizes and shapes, resembling barns and haystacks, with small green enclosures and splinter palings, rising one above the other in very irregular tiers, adapt themselves to all the inequalities of the rugged surface...Connected with each

---

[337] Ibid., 11.

other by narrow lanes and hedge rows, these rude habitations, the residence of from twelve to fifteen thousand inhabitants, cover the entire mountain-side to the extreme pinnacle...Here on stands the palace of the Negoos, a most ungainly wooden palisades. They extend from the base of the summit, and are interspersed with barred stockades, between which are profusely scattered the abodes of household slaves, with breweries, kitchens, cellars, storehouses, magazines and granaries."[338]

Sahle Selassie's focus on not only warfare but economic development gained him riches beyond that of any of his forefathers. His living quarters were richly decorated with Persian rugs as well as guns mounted strategically on the walls.

When it was time to take a wife, he chose a noble woman from Marhabete, the same small town that gave refuge to his ancestor, Sebestyanos. He fathered four daughters and two sons. The eldest son was Haile Melekot.

HISTORY OF KING HAILE MELEKOT

In 1847, King Sahle Selassie declared Haile Melekot as his heir. On the verge of death, he traveled to Angolala to address a meeting of all the Oromo chiefs of Shoa and asked that they remain loyal to Haile Melekot in order to preserve the peace and prosperity of Shoa. His last act as King of Shoa was to travel to Debra Berhane and

---

[338] Ibid., 12.

proclaim his son King of Shoa. Only he and the Emperor in Gondar had the ability to confer this title.

King Haile Melekot attempted to strengthen Shoa by establishing an independent relationship with the British under the reign of Queen Victoria. While this attempt was not successful, it proved that Shoa had plans of being more than just a subject kingdom of the Emperor in Gondar. However, as fate would have it, both the Emperor and the King would have to bow before stronger forces. God and history had ordained that King Haile Melekot would not live to see his plans for Shoa or even his plans for his son materialize. He was to be the last Shoan king during the era of the Zemene Mesafint.

Shoa's wars of expansion were a part of its desire to be independent from the throne in Gondar but Ethiopia was a land of many thrones. Some thrones were stronger than others.

CHAPTER TWENTY-ONE

CHAPTER TWENTY-ONE

Shoa's Future in Captivity

"To every thing there is a season, and a time to every purpose under the heaven: A time to be born, and a time to die; a time to plant, and a time to pluck up that which is planted." — **Ecclesiastes 3:1-2**

In 1892, Ras Makonnen and the Shoan nobility sat at the top of the hierarchy of the Solomonic dynasty in Ethiopia. The independent Kingdom of Shoa was now the center of power in the empire. What had started as a small, independent kingdom under King Sahle Selassie was now home of the King of all the Kings of the realm. During the age of King Sahle Selassie, the Kingdom of Shoa had started to reach out to foreign powers to make independent connections. During the reign of Emperor Menelik II, all official foreign correspondence was initiated by the Kingdom of Shoa.

Ras Makonnen recalled that it was not long ago that the Kingdom of Shoa was in the same position as the other kingdoms of the realm, and was forced to give tribute to a more powerful kingdom. Ras Makonnen's childhood was spent as the citizen of a vassal kingdom. It was Emperor Yohannes IV's word that was absolute law. Ras Makonnen was a teenager when he met Menelik II and his cousin was already a powerful leader. Despite wielding considerable power, his cousin was not the most powerful man in the realm. Despite not being on the top of the totem pole, Ras Makonnen watched his cousin rebuild the Kingdom of Shoa and reclaim the prestige that was enjoyed during the reign of his grandfather, King Sahle Selassie.

Ras Makonnen watched Menelik II pick up where his father left off. He admired how Menelik II did not stop working until he sat on the throne of King Solomon and over all the kings of the other kingdoms. Ras Makonnen understood that the leaders of the other kingdoms would be thinking the same way and therefore he could not afford to get comfortable, not even for the birth of his baby boy. Ras Makonnen and his cousin were in the midst of a global Scramble and only the strong would be victorious. Ras Makonnen was well aware: just as the Kingdom of Shoa rose to power under an ambitious leader, it could also fall to one more ambitious as in the days of Tewodros II.

THE FALL OF SHOA

In 1855, about 37 years before the birth of the baby boy, both Shoa and Gondar stood in the way of Emperor Tewodros II's rise to power and unifying campaign. They had to be neutralized. With an army of 50,000 men, the emperor entered Shoa. Emperor Tewodros II met little resistance. Menelik II's father, King Haile Melekot was gravely ill by then and ultimately died before having a chance to face Tewodros II in battle.[339] His body was quickly buried by his followers.

Emperor Tewodros II admired the legacy of Shoa and he was looking forward to the honor of meeting the King or facing him in battle. When his imposing army of war-hardened soldiers marched into Shoa, inspiring awe in the highland inhabitants, Tewodros II did not believe that Haile Melekot had already died. He therefore ordered the King's body to be dug up and wept upon seeing it with his own eyes. It is written that Tewodros II ensured that Haile Melekot was reburied with all the honors due to a king, and he personally attended the funeral.

The Emperor's gesture demonstrated a sharp change from the pettiness of the era of princes, and also aided his mission to win the hearts and minds of his countrymen. His vision was to unify Ethiopia and he recognized Shoa's growing importance to the empire. He thus left the governance of Shoa to a Shoan, making Haile Melekot's brother the new governor.

In order to ensure that there would be no challenge to his throne from Shoa, the Emperor took the King's only son captive to remain a prisoner in his mountain fortress of Magdala. That son, whose birth name was Sahle Maryam, would join the other princes of the noble houses of Ethiopia and be instructed in the new vision of a united Ethiopia under Christ. At the tender age of eleven, he found himself away from his conquered homeland and at the beginning of his epic journey to the throne of the world's most ancient empire.

---

[339] Ibid., 18.

HISTORY OF SAHLE MARYAM

Sahle Maryam was born in the town of Ankober, where he spent his early childhood 8,500 feet above sea level in the clean, crisp air.[340] He was no stranger to war. Ankober itself was originally inhabited by Ethiopia's Oromo people who migrated to the region following the reign of Imam Ahmad Gran, until it was conquered by Sahle Maryam's Shoan ancestor, the "fearsome commander," Amha Iyasus. Meridazmatch Amha's wars with the Oromo population between Debre Berhan and Ankober meant that Shoa developed as a relatively advanced military society by Ethiopian standards.[341] Despite its tragic and bloody beginnings, prior to the Evil Days, Ankober, the Shoan capital, was a pleasant place by most accounts.

At Sahle Maryam's birth, his father was joyous at having a male heir, prophesying that his son would replace him as King of Shoa and enjoy a glorious reign. He also married the child's mother so as to legitimize the birth.[342] There is much disagreement about the origins of Sahle Maryam's mother but it is thought that she was of humble birth and worked in the palace. In a nation where genealogies for nobility are kept with biblical accuracy, it was difficult for scholars to find information about her background.

Sahle Maryam would indeed ascend the throne with a name that would justify the faith of Haile Melekot.

---

[340] Ibid., 7.

[341] Ibid., 17.

[342] Ibid.

However, it would be some time before that name became synonymous with the glory of modern Ethiopia.

THE CAPTIVE PRINCE

In 1855 CE, robbed of the normal joys of childhood, 11-year-old Sahle Maryam lost his father and he was taken prisoner by the mighty Emperor Tewodros II. He would spend the next stage of his life captive in the mountain fortress of Magdala in Wollo, 12,000 feet above sea level.

It was at Magdala where he learned the art of governance. As he became a man, he was surrounded by all the intrigues of a royal court, studying all he saw intently. Though captive along with the sons of other Ethiopian nobles, he was treated like a son by Emperor Tewodros II, once stating, "[Although] he killed my father and took me to his court, he always loved me as a son; he educated me with the greatest care, and almost showed for me greater affection than for his own son." Sahle Maryam went as far as to say that Tewodros II declared to him "more than once...[that I] would rule after him."[343] The emperor not only gave him the title of Dejazmatch but he also gave him the hand of his own daughter in marriage.

Despite receiving such good treatment, and also sharing in the Emperor's vision of a fully united Ethiopia, Dejazmatch Sahle was a proud Shoan. He viewed himself, first and foremost, as the heir to the throne of Shoa. Thus, when the opportunity presented itself, with help from a Muslim Queen of Wollo, he made his escape in 1865.

---

[343] Ibid., 23.

The loss of Dejazmatch Sahle enraged Emperor Tewodros II. In response to the assistance provided by the Wollo Muslim Queen, he had her son and his associates, who were captive, hacked to pieces in front of him. He also had some of the Amhara dignitaries beaten to death with bamboo rods. Despite his rage at the security breach, his deep affection for Sahle Maryam and his uncle (who remained behind) prevented him from retaliating against them.

The Emperor's continued bloodlust caused many members of his powerful army to desert him. Some of them joined Dejazmatch Sahle, helping to strengthen him as the newly established ruler of Shoa. Plus, having murdered the young Muslim prince from Wollo, he further alienated a powerful enemy and gave his former captive a powerful ally. The word of his brutality as an emperor spread throughout the countryside in the same manner as the legend of his good deeds toward the poor spread as an outlaw.

CHAPTER TWENTY-TWO

A Great Escape

"Blessed be the Lord, who hath not given us as a prey to their teeth. Our soul is escaped as a bird out of the snare of the fowlers: the snare is broken, and we are escaped. Our help is in the name of the Lord, who made heaven and earth." – **Psalms 124:6-8**

As Governor of Harar, Ras Makonnen had learned from Emperor Tewodros II that strength alone could not unite a nation. Though he was a great general and more than capable on the battlefield, he was aware that winning the hearts and minds of the people of Harar would take more than military victories.

A wrong decision could mean the life of his wife and newborn son. He was the leader of a Christian minority in a Muslim city. A well-planned rebellion could wipe his family off the map. Ras Makonnen knew the best protection against rebellion was to improve the standard of living of the poor and working class.

Ras Makonnen knew that despite his religious background, Emperor Tewodros II had lost sight of the core teachings of the gospel - the golden rule - *do unto others as you would have them do unto you*. His desire for unity at all costs had blinded him to his own brutality. In the end, it cost him his kingdom and his life. Had he worked on building relations with his fellow Ethiopians, as opposed to only crushing rebellions and dissent, he would have had support against the foreign invaders that sealed his fate.

Ras Makonnen knew his cousin would need the support of Harar and the other territories brought under the control of the central government in the coming conflict with Europe. It was with this in mind that Ras Makonnen waived his right to sit in judgement and allowed the Mullahs to govern their own affairs. He also built a new mosque for the city's Muslims. He was determined to build bridges and make Harar a model for the new Ethiopia.[344] Ras Makonnen also admired that Menelik II chose to not hold grudges against Emperor Tewodros II for depriving him of his freedom or for his acts of rage and murder. Instead, Menelik II chose to remember his *jegna* for his vision and his acts of kindness to a young prince of Shoa.

THE GREAT ESCAPE

It was late at night when the escape party made its move. As the rest of the fortress slept, Dejazmatch Sahle Maryam, assisted by his uncle Darge Sahle Selassie, slowly navigated the treacherous terrain that made Magdala such an excellent fortress. A wrong move in the dark could lead to a ghastly fall and a terrible death! Not until they finished the perilous climb to the southeast, reaching the high plateau of Wollo, did they finally breathe easier. It was daylight by the time they arrived at their destination.

---

[344] Mosley, Leonard. *Haile Selassie: The Conquering Lion.* Weidenfeld and Nicolson, 1964, pp. 27-28.

The entire countryside had ceased to support Emperor Tewodros II, so the escapees had a significant head start on any attempt to recapture them. By the time the emperor discovered what had happened, he looked out from his mountain fortress to see Sahle Maryam's party received by Wollo's rebel Oromo. There was little he could do but take out his frustration on his remaining captives.

It was another headache for Tewodros II, another crack in the united nation he was working so hard to build. His fits of rage had been increasing as his vision seemed to slip further and further from his grasp.

In addition to the head start, the Dejazmatch had made arrangements with one of the ruling families of Wollo to ensure his safe passage through to the kingdom of Shoa. Of all the leading families in Wollo, there was only one leader who could guarantee that safety with any certainty and, as was common in Ethiopia's history, that leader was a woman.

QUEEN WORQITU

She, who played that key role in Dejazmatch Sahle Maryam's escape was the Muslim queen, Queen Worqitu. She was a member of one of the proud Wollo Oromo families and had been angered by Emperor Tewodros II.

Ever since the news reached her of her son's death at the hands of the emperor, Queen Worqitu became a more fervent ally to the Dejazmatch. Having already assisted in his escape from Magdala by providing him with an armed escort, she would also provide warriors when he decided to march on Magdala in 1867 with his 30,000-strong army. The price for her loyalty was the Dejazmatch's support in ensuring that she would be the one in control of Wollo. By the time Sahle Maryam's army reached the Magdala area, Tewodros II was not there. The constant state of rebellion throughout the kingdom meant that the emperor's time was taken up with marching his armies to confront various uprisings. The young Dejazmatch decided not to wait at Magdala to engage in battle as he did not have adequate supplies for his massive, combined Shoan and Wollo army. Plus, he was not sure about the strength of Tewodros II's army.

Upon his return to Shoa, Dejazmatch Sahle Maryam was welcomed as the long-lost son of Haile Melekot. Fresh from commanding a massive army of men, and confident in his destiny, he declared himself King of Kings, Menelik II, and the fame of Shoa once again echoed throughout the Ethiopian realm.

THE RISE OF KING OF KINGS, MENELIK II

In 1868, when the British government finally decided to move against Tewodros II for imprisoning their nationals, Menelik II refused to help them. He also informed the British that he would not aid Tewodros II either, yet he would defend the borders of Shoa should the British attempt to violate them for any reason.[345] As the British invasion commenced, Menelik II camped his army in Wollo to await the outcome. His love for Tewodros II prevented him from being in Wollo until the invasion was concluded. He left Wollo at Easter to go to Shoa for spiritual rejuvenation.

---

[345] Marcus, Harold G. *The Life and Times of Menelik II: Ethiopia 1844-1913*. Red Sea Press, 1995, p. 29.

Meanwhile, Queen Worqitu never forgave Tewodros II for the death of her son. After the British turned the tide against the emperor, many members of his fleeing army were killed by the warriors of Wollo.

When the Queen died in 1868, Menelik II decided that it was time for the Kingdom of Shoa to control the Kingdom of Wollo. This would give him a reliable buffer zone against Tigray and the rising power of Dejazmatch Kassa. Unknown to Menelik II at the time was the fact that Kassa was on his way to becoming Emperor Yohannes IV.

Abba Wato of Wollo did not agree with Wollo being under Shoan rule and made it clear that it would not abide. However, Abba Wato did not have the strength to take on Menelik II's forces. When Dejazmatch Kassa became Emperor Yohannes IV, Abba Wato pledged allegiance to his throne, hoping to get protection from the powerful new emperor. That protection never came. Emperor Yohannes IV had to deal with external threats to his newly acquired realm and left Abba Wato to fend for himself.

Menelik II seized the opportunity and captured Magdala, imprisoned Abba Wato and appointed an ally as governor of Wollo – Mohammed Ali, a relative of Queen Worqitu. This alliance, like the province of Wollo itself, would have significant importance in years to come.

CHAPTER TWENTY-THREE
The Kingdom of Wollo

"Who can find a virtuous woman? for her price is far above rubies. The heart of her husband doth safely trust in her, so that he shall have no need of spoil. She will do him good and not evil all the days of her life." – **Proverbs 31:10-12**

Ras Makonnen's thoughts drifted to the well-being of his wife. She was not from Shoa. She was not born to a Christian father. While she was not raised with her father, his Islamic shadow would always hang over her in the eyes of some of Ras Makonnen's countrymen. However, as his lawful wife, she had always embraced Christ and suffered greatly in trying to produce a healthy child for his legacy. He loved her greatly.

He could only imagine her stress as she had previously lost eight children during childbirth. He knew she would be worrying about whether the healthy baby boy would survive. It was his duty to reassure, love and protect her. Their marriage was arranged but it had grown into a loving union. He had ensured that their union would not be common law, like that with his former wife, but be permanent and sanctioned by the Church. His union with her was an act to stitch together an empire. It was the custom of the realm in the 1870s and necessary to build the strategic union between the Kingdom of Shoa and the

Kingdom of Wollo. Dejazmatch Ali, ruler of the Woreilu Oromo clan, had now become a strategic ally. Similar to the Kingdom of Tigray, the Kingdom of Wollo was an important strategic center of power in the realm and a place that occupied a considerable amount of Ras Makonnen's mental resources.

King Menelik II's friendships in Wollo, and his eventual conquest of it, would impact the lives of Ras Makonnen and his newborn son in unexpected ways. It was during Menelik II's time in that province that Ras Makonnen first became aware of the eventual mother of his baby boy. He understood that his marriage to Yeshimebet was also Menelik II's way of showing his appreciation to his uncle Darge for his decades of service. King Menelik II would not have given his blessing for his cousin to marry just anyone!

WOLLO: THE BIRTHPLACE OF QUEENS

In 1892, moving south from the Red Sea would first put you in the Italy-controlled domain of the historic Axumite empire and the republic of Hamasien. Claiming their piece of the African cake as decided at the Berlin Conference, the Italians conquered these ancient kingdoms following the death of Emperor Yohannes IV in 1889 and declared their colony, Eritrea. Heading further south would lead into the highlands of the Kingdom of Tigray, where Emperor Yohannes IV and Ras Alula became legends. To the southwest of there lies the Kingdom of Begmender and, to the southeast, the Sultanates of the Afar and Harar. Nestled below Tigray, and bordering Begemder, Gojjam, Shoa and Harar, is the

Kingdom of Wollo, which would become renown for being the birthplace of powerful women. Like Harar, Wollo was lion country in 1892. The rarely sighted black-maned Ethiopian lion engendered both fear and respect in the local inhabitants.

Also like Harar, Wollo was a Muslim stronghold in Ethiopia and its ruling families were powerful and ambitious. Previously, it was a sanctuary for Emperor Yekuno Amlak and the revival of the Solomonic dynasty following the era of the Zagwe Dynasty. The Solomonic kings used the region until the time of Imam Ahmad Gran. It was there in Wollo that he burned the gold leaf-covered church of Mekane Selassie to the ground. Following the period of the Imam's conquest, and the Islamic fervor left in his wake, the region remained ruled by Muslims until the time of Tewodros II. (It was also in Wollo that Tewodros II made his last stand.) While he left his mark there, it was Emperor Yohannes IV who made the largest religious impact in Wollo with his policy of forced conversions for the tribal chiefs.

Bordered by powerful neighbors, the Ethiopians from Wollo were frequently major players in shaping Ethiopian history. As Harar is renown for birthing an extraordinary baby boy, Wollo is also remembered for being the birthplace of three extraordinary baby girls. One of those baby girls would become the mother of the baby boy and Ras Makonnen's wife, Woizero Yeshimebet.

A WOLLO PRINCESS, WOIZERO YESHIMEBET

Woizero Yeshimebet's date of birth is uncertain but she was probably born some time between 1862 and 1864. The wife and royal consort of Ras Makonnen, Woizero

Yeshimebet was a royal princess of Wollo, born in the Woreilu region in a place called Dolo.[346] She was born in the era of Emperor Tewodros II, the supreme ruler in Wollo and the entire realm at the time. Though small in stature, she was born as a child of noble birth from one of the centers of Ethiopia's power. Woizero Yeshimebet was destined to always be close to power.

THE FATHER OF YESHIMEBET

Her father was Dejazmatch Ali Aba Jiffar, whose title spoke to the power he held amongst the Wollo elite. Dejazmatch Ali Aba Jiffar began life in Gondor as a Muslim trader and chief of the Warra Illu clan of the Wollo Oromo tribe. Little more is known of him.

Dejazmatch Ali Aba Jiffar would surely have submitted to Menelik II during the latter's time in Wollo. The marriage of his own daughter, Woizero Yeshimebet, to Ras Makonnen (Menelik II's right hand man) would have secured a place of high regard in the Christian royal court for his family. It is not clear whether he had any say in their ultimate union, as his daughter was under the stewardship of Ras Darge. However, it is clear that Yeshimebet was his daughter and bore his last name, so he would have undoubtedly benefited from the union.

---

[346] Beresford, Deena-Marie. *Gurage! Gurage! Gurage! The Story of a Wollo Princess: Woizero Yeshimabet Ali AbaJifar.* Yeshimabet's Books and Things, 2019, p. 11.

THE MOTHER OF YESHIMEBET

Woizero Yeshimebet's mother was Woizero Wolete Ihata Giyorgis Yimeru, or Woizero Wolete Giyorgis for short. She was the daughter of a Gurage nobel, Ato Yimeru.[347] Fate would lead her to Wollo where she would give birth to a beautiful baby girl named Yeshimebet. Having a Christian mother and Muslim father was not the norm in those times and, according to oral history, Woizero Yeshimebet did not spend much time with her father. She and her mother, on the other hand, were inseparable. It was her mother's culture and connections that would shape her life and future family.

It is recorded that Woizero Wolete Giyorgis was traveling from Shoa to Gondor to visit a 17-year-old Menelik II in 1861. The reason for the visit is not clear but it would have been important as the journey was in the midst of Emperor Tewodros II's wave of conquest throughout Ethiopia. It may even have been rumors of Menelik II being in the area that inspired her journey. Whatever the case, Woizero Wolete Giyorgis was not able to have the meeting as Menelik II and his uncle, Ras Darge, were taken captive by Emperor Tewodros II in 1855. (In a time before modern means of communication, it is no surprise that she was unaware that they were prisoners at the time of her visit.)

Without a Shoan to protect her and her entourage in Wollo, Woizero Wolete Giyorgis was taken captive by Sheik Ali, a Dejazmatch who was the governor of Woreilu

---

[347] Ibid., 23.

at the time. Shortly after being abducted, Woizero Wolete Giyorgis became pregnant with Woizero Yeshimebet.

Once Menelik II built his power base in Wollo, and the tribal chiefs submitted to his rule, Woizero Wolete Giyorgis's Amhara roots and connections helped her secure freedom from Dejazmatch Ali. She returned to Shoa with her daughter in 1866 and soon became the consort of Menelik II's trusted uncle, Ras Darge Sahle Selassie, the very same uncle who aided his escape from Tewodros II.[348]

In addition to the intelligence, courage and beauty that he saw in her, Ras Darge's interest in Woizero Wolete Giyorgis might also have been due to her Gurage roots (through her mother). The royal families of the day were very much excited by a prophecy that a son born of a Gurage woman would inherit the imperial throne.[349] Indeed, Woizero Wolete Giyorigis bore him a son named Desta.[350] However, long before she would produce a male heir for him, Ras Darge took an infant Woizero Yeshimebet into his home and raised her as his own daughter. It was in the home of Ras Darge where Ras Makonnen is said to have first become aware of his future wife. It was Ras Darge who arranged that Ras Makonnen should marry Yeshimebet.[351] Those without inside knowledge – foreigners such as the French writer, Casimir Mondon-Vidailhet – assumed that Yeshimebet was Ras

[348] Ibid., 38.

[349] Ibid., 81.

[350] Prouty, Chris. *Empress Taytu and Menilek II: Ethiopia 1883-1910.* 1986. The Red Sea Press, 2016, p. 106.

[351] Ibid.

Darge's daughter. She was 12 years old when she was given to Ras Makonnen as a wife in 1878.[352]

WOREILU

Woizero Yeshimebet would not have been unused to the high altitude of Ejersa Goro, where she gave birth to the baby boy years later. Her birthplace and childhood home, Woreilu, was 9,000 feet above sea level. It was also an important location for Menelik II, who established it as a *ketema*, or garrison town, shortly after his escape from Emperor Tewodros II. Woizero Yeshimebet's hometown became a staging ground for Menelik II as he rebuilt the legacy of Shoa and his father. Woreilu was likely where Menelik II first interacted with Dejazmatch Ali, who he would have depended on to ensure the cooperation of the local population. His presence, along with his Wollo allies and large contingent of Shoan soldiers, attracted tradesmen and market people. From 1870 onward, the Thursday market in Woreilu was known as one of the best attended in Shoa. The industrious inhabitants of Wollo enticed soldiers and civilians alike with their goods and the market was particularly known for its products made from black wool.[353]

It was in Woreilu that Menelik II built his royal compound, which were several stone structures established on the east side of a hill. There were government administrative offices, a jail and a grand

---

[352] Beresford, Deena-Marie. *Gurage! Gurage! Gurage! The Story of a Wollo Princess: Woizero Yeshimabet Ali AbaJifar.* Yeshimabet's Books and Things, 2019, p. 81. The date of marriage has also been recorded as 1873.

[353] Ibid., 20.

banquet hall. From his royal *gibbi*, Menelik II could see the Wonchit gorges and enjoy the sunrise. He could also see approaching threats from miles away due to the defensible position of the compound, which became his principal staging ground for his military campaigns between 1871 and 1879. The *gibbi* was part of his strategy to bring the north of Ethiopia under his control, knowing that he could not truly be King of Kings otherwise. Ras Makonnen also spent considerable time in Woreilu for this reason.

After Menelik II subdued Wollo with the might of his Shoan military force, governor Mohammed Ali and the leading chiefs of Wollo made a formal submission to him in September 1876 at the feast of the Holy Cross (Masqal). At that meeting, Menelik II showed his tolerance towards Muslims and demonstrated his genius in diplomacy. He addressed his Christian followers and stated, "These people of Wollo, even though now Moslem, will become in two or three years our brothers by baptism, Do not hate them...do not be irritated if Moslem come into your homes."[354] The King's tolerant attitude did not prevent Mohammed Ali from burning down the newly constructed town in 1877. Tolerating Muslims was one thing but Menelik II did not tolerate dissent. He quickly brought the rebellious Mohammed Ali back into submission.

King Menelik II would use Woizero Yeshimebet's hometown as a staging ground for military campaigns into Gojjam and Yejju.[355]

Menelik II's demonstrated tolerance towards Muslims was in direct contrast to the attitude of his rival,

---

[354] Marcus, Harold G. *The Life and Times of Menelik II: Ethiopia 1844-1913*. Red Sea Press, 1995, p. 40.

[355] Beresford, Deena-Marie. *Gurage! Gurage! Gurage! The Story of a Wollo Princess: Woizero Yeshimabet Ali AbaJifar*. Yeshimabet's Books and Things, 2019, p. 21.

Emperor Yohannes IV, who maintained a policy of forced conversions for the ruling elite in order for them to continue in their positions of leadership. This helped to eventually strengthen his relationship with Mohammed Ali. To cement their alliance, Menelik II granted Mohammed Ali the towns of Woreilu and Borena-Sayint as part of his governorship. It could not have been known that Mohammed Ali's fate was to be inextricably linked to the life of the baby boy born in Harar.

FROM MOHAMMED ALI TO RAS MIKAEL

Mohammed Ali was born in Wollo in 1851, toward the end of the era of princes and the intermittent reign of Emperor Yohannes III. During this period, the real power was still held generally by the Yejju Oromo clans and the great Ras Ali in particular. The son of an Imam, Mohammed Ali grew into a powerful warrior and a shrewd and pragmatic leader.

Despite having sworn loyalty to Menelik II in 1876, and having proved his loyalty by engaging in a military campaign to subdue Gojjam, Mohammed Ali found his power slipping upon his return to Wollo. It appeared the rebellion started under Abba Wato still had support and the proud Muslim community was not convinced it should follow Menelik II, who appeared to be on the losing side of history against the increasing strength of Emperor Yohannes IV. Rather than lose his power base, Mohammed Ali chose to become the leader of the anti-Shoan revolt. He followed in Abba Wato's footsteps and sought the protection of the more powerful emperor. When his army burned down Menelik II's Woreilu base while he was away on a military campaign, that decision came at a high price. Emperor Yohannes IV was too busy to provide immediate protection for Wollo – he was, once again, distracted by other uprisings and external threats – and Menelik II exploited the opportunity, marching his army into Wollo and again bringing the kingdom to its knees.

Emperor Yohannes IV was not pleased. The stage was now set for an epic confrontation between Ethiopia's two powerhouses. Preparations were made in Shoa. The emperor marched his powerful army into position to put an end to the threat in those highlands once and for all. Both men knew that, should a battle take place, there would be heavy casualties.

Quietly, negotiations were started by the Church to avert the catastrophe. As it had done many times before in Ethiopian history, the Church was able to allow cooler heads to prevail and an agreement was finally reached. Part of the agreement granted Menelik II continued control over Wollo, provided that he built churches and converted the Oromo population to Christianity. This part of the peace accord was further expanded in 1878 at the Council of Boru Meda – it was decided by Emperor Yohannes IV, in consultation with the priest of the Orthodox Church, that all Muslim leaders in the realm would have three months to convert to Christianity or lose their positions.

Ever pragmatic, Mohammed Ali converted to Christianity and became Mikael. He then exerted his power and influence to help bring the largely Muslim Kingdom of Wollo to the love of Christ. For his loyalty he was given the title of Ras.

The original rebel, Abba Wato, also converted. He was baptized as Haile Maryam and given the title of Dejazmatch. Those who did not wish to accept Christianity left Wollo and fled to Muslim strongholds in

Harar, Metemma and Jimma. Menelik II himself was not a supporter of the forced conversions but he complied with the imperial decree and set out to convert the Muslim regions of the Kingdom of Shoa.

Menelik II was later deprived of his control of Wollo after battling his rival, Ras Adal, who had been elevated to King by Emperor Yohannes IV. Eastern Wollo and sections of southern Wollo were retained by Ras Mikael. However, the emperor gave the important northern Wollo (bordering Tigray) to his twelve-year-old son, Ras Araya Selassie. A marriage was arranged between Ras Araya Selassie and Menelik II's daughter, Zawditu, who was six years old at the time. The year was 1882.

In 1892, the ever practical Ras Mikael married another of Menelik II's daughters[356] and would go on to make his base in the first official town in Wollo, and its future capital, Dessie.

MENELIK II'S WOLLO CONNECTION

Aside from the relationships that Menelik II had established with Queen Worqitu and Mohammed Ali, he had also befriended another important member of the Wollo Oromo while captive in Tewedoros II's court. This was Lij Wale, a member of the Yejju family of Wollo. Lij Wale was the brother of Menelik II's future wife, Empress Taitu, another of the extraordinary baby girls born in Wollo. The Yejju families had been the central power behind the throne for the majority of the Zemene Mesafint.

---

[356] Caulk, Richard. *Between the Jaws of Hyenas: A Diplomatic History of Ethiopia (1876-1896)*. Harrassowitz, 2002.

Their influence stretched from the Kingdom of Begemder to Wollo and beyond.

Menelik II and Lij Wale bonded in captivity and their friendship would be one of the most significant in the life of the young prince. Menelik II could not have known but he and Lij Wale would one day be more than friends. They would be family.

THE BIRTH OF MENEN ASFAW

Menelik II's daughter was not Ras Mikael's only wife. During his Muslim life, Ras Mikael had practiced polygamy and had conceived children with his other wives. One of his daughters was Woizero Sehin Mikael.

In order to secure a powerful alliance with the ruling family of the fortress Ambassel, Woizero Sehin was sent with the blessings of her powerful father to marry Jantirar Asfaw Ali, the head of that family. On April 3, 1891 Woizero Sehin had a daughter named Woizero Menen Asfaw. This was the third extraordinary baby girl from Wollo, and one whose life would one day intersect with the life of the baby boy who would be born a year later in the mountains near Harar. In 1892, Menen Asfaw was a one-year-old infant and, like the other extraordinary princesses born in Wollo, she was enjoying the relatively comfortable circumstances of her birth into one of the noble families of Ethiopia. Woizero Menen spent the year with her mother in surroundings that were out of a fairytale. Her home was at the top of a flat hilltop surrounded by cliffs.[357] Woizero Sehin and her attendants

---

[357] Parnell, Anjahli, ed. and comp. *The Biography of Empress Menen Afsaw: The Mother of the Ethiopian Nation*, Roots Publishing, 2011.

would have taken Woizero Menen to experience the fresh, crisp mountain air of Wollo. Her destiny was inextricably linked to the baby boy.

Ethiopian noble women were often used to cement peace between warring factions or to strengthen royal houses who desired closer ties. Emperor Yohannes IV knew the power of these unions and asserted his newly affirmed power by convincing Menelik II to marry into the powerful Yejju family. The Emperor knew that Menelik II marrying a noble woman of northern stock would place someone with allegiance to the north in the house of his southern rival. Menelik II could not have known then: he was being blessed with a life companion that would help him solidify his legend while creating one of her own. He had long before recognized the power of the Yejju Oromo, and had earlier tried without success to marry into the dynasty and merge its power with Shoa. He was content to let the emperor feel in control but was more than happy to take the sister of his long time friend, Lij Wale - Taitu Betul - as his bride.

CHAPTER TWENTY-FOUR

A Priestly Warrior Queen

"I am a woman and I do not love war; but rather than accepting this I prefer war." – **Empress Taitu Betul**[358]

Wollo was not a region to be taken lightly. Just like Tigray, it had to be monitored closely, so Ras Makonnen spent much time in that kingdom. After all, it was the birthplace of both his and the Emperor's wives. Empress Taitu, in particular, loved Wollo.

Just as he tried to please his cousin, the Emperor, Ras Makonnen did his best to please the Empress. When she requested that he take care of some business for her in Jerusalem, he was happy to accept the request. He could still vividly remember his first trip to the holy city, Jerusalem. Aside from his joy in visiting the birthplace of Yeshua the Christ, he had been entrusted with a mission from Empress Taitu to secure the living arrangements of Ethiopian priests living in the holy city.

---

[358] Marcus, Harold G. *The Life and Times of Menelik II: Ethiopia 1844-1913*. Red Sea Press, 1995, p. 130.

Despite the power and prestige of his cousin, those in the know were aware that his empress also held considerable power in her own right. Menelik II valued her counsel above all others. Empress Taitu was brilliant and the major players in the realm were careful not to make an enemy of her. Ras Makonnen did everything in his power to fulfill her wishes.

Upon his arrival in Jerusalem, Ras Makonnen quickly realized that he had been tasked with an incredibly difficult mission. Jerusalem was under the control of the Ottoman Empire and they were not cooperative with an empire that had delivered them two stunning defeats on the battlefield. He was greatly concerned when, upon his return to Ethiopia, he had not been able to complete the task. Once back in Harar, he continued to press forward on the purchase of property in Jerusalem. Despite her disappointment, Empress Taitu appreciated his efforts and he gained a powerful ally. Ras Makonnen, well aware of the power she wielded, was happy to have her in his corner.

EMPRESS TAITU

It is not certain when she was born. Years as early as 1839 and as late as 1851 have been put forward as possibilities. In any case, by 1892, Empress Taitu was already a force to be reckoned with. The height of her glory was imminent but she had already proved herself a powerful conservative voice in the politics of the realm.

THE STRONG ROOTS OF TAITU

Taitu's father was Ras Betul Haile Maryam of one of the ruling Yejju Oromo families of Gondar. Her mother was also a noblewoman from Gondar. Taitu was raised knowing what it meant to rule.

Her bloodline highlighted how precarious Ethiopia's tribal distinctions were regarding the Solomonic throne. Even though she was Oromo, Empress Taitu's chroniclers made sure to emphasize her descent from Emperor Susenyos I, who reigned from 1606 to 1632. Her family was an offshoot of one of the daughters of Emperor Susenyos I, who had 25 children by several wives, illustrating how widely dispersed the Solomonic bloodline was among Ethiopia's highland nobility.

Emperor Susenyos I's reign was notorious, yet seldom spoken of in Ethiopian history. It served as a historical lesson on the consequences of allowing a foreign faith primacy in the holy realm. Emperor Susenyos I fell under the sway of the Portuguese, who had managed to gain a foothold in the country in the wake of Imam Ahmad Gran's jihad, maintaining a presence by leveraging the military assistance that they had provided to Ethiopia. Emperor Susenyos I actually converted from the Orthodox faith to Catholicism and, under the instruction of Jesuit priest, Pero Paez, proclaimed an end to the Orthodox faith. This sparked a religious uprising and 6,000 souls were claimed by the melee that ensued because of the emperor's attempt to place the throne of David under the jurisdiction of the throne of Saint Peter. Emperor Susenyos I was badly shaken by the harm he had caused to the realm and he abdicated the throne in favor of his son, Emperor Fasilides, once he ensured the restoration of Ethiopian Orthodoxy.

Emperor Fasilides led an Orthodox Christian revival in Ethiopia and went out of his way to repair the legacy of his family. Among his achievements were: the reestablishing of the historic connection between Ethiopian Christianity and the Coptics of the Holy See of Saint Mark in Egypt; the founding of the imperial capital of Gondar; and the building of stone bridges and a church, St. Mary of Zion, to house the Ark of the Covenant in Axum. Emperor Fasilides is also credited with establishing an embassy in India.

THE POWER OF THE YEJJU OROMO

Emperor Susenyos I's daughter became an ancestor to one of the ruling Rases of the Zemene Mesafint, Ras Gebre of Semen. He was Taitu's great-grandfather and was known for making the hunter-gatherer nations pay their tribute to him in gold. Ras Gebre's Yejju Oromo subjects were said to have stopped farming because his kingdom was so prosperous that there was no shortage of food and drink. It is more likely that war became the economy – his loyal subjects would have also made up his private army and be able to survive off the plunder that characterized the turbulent era of princes. Ras Gebre's reign began at nearly the beginning of the Zemene Mesafint and he ruled for 44 years.

Semen was Taitu's power base, the domain of her paternal grandfather, Dejazmatch Haile Mariam. It was a mountain range distinguished for being the home of Ethiopia's tallest mountain, Ras Dashan, plus the home of the Ethiopian Wolf, the legendary Ethiopian Ibex and bands of grazing Gelada Baboons. The bearded vulture with its 10-foot wingspan could also be seen soaring on the updrafts above the rugged mountain range. Dejazmatch Haile Mariam's sons and daughters were born in Semen, the land of their father. However, the people of Semen did not support them all.

ANTI-YEJJU MOVEMENT

There was a growing movement percolating in the northern mountains. The spread and relative prosperity of the Yejju Oromo began to create resentment among the non-Yejju. The growing anti-Yejju movement became increasingly problematic for Dejazmatch Haile Mariam's eldest son, Merso, and his brother, Betul (Taitu's father), who shared a mother of Oromo heritage.

The Tigrayan nobility were among those uncomfortable with the power of the Yejju Oromo, some even viewing them as usurpers from the time of Imam Ahmad Gran's jihad. They pushed back against Yejju dominance at every opportunity. When Dejazmatch Haile Mariam selected Merso to succeed him, his proud and loyal Semen officers rejected him with the reason that he would promote his mother's people and, thus, increase the power and influence of the Yejju. Instead, they chose another son named Wube to govern – he was blessed that his mother was a woman of status from Tigray. Merso and Betul were not so lucky, even though their mother was the daughter of the legendary Ras Gugsa. Ras Gugsa was so powerful during the Zemene Mesafint that he personally appointed the emperors in Gondar between 1800 and

1825.[359] Shortly after Ras Gugsa's demise, Ras Ali and his mother, Empress Manan, became Ethiopia's primary power brokers and dominant force. By 1832, it was Ras Ali who determined who would sit on the throne in Gondar. This did not sit well with the various branches of the Solomonic bloodline that made up the traditional highland nobility and only increased anti-Yejju sentiment.

Despite their ability to claim descent from two very powerful bloodlines, Merso and Betul perhaps sensed the changing tide against the Yejju Oromo and fled from Semen with their mother. They settled in Tigray, where their sister had married the ruler of Tigray, Sebagades. The brothers were sure that the strength of their ties to Tigrayan nobility would keep them safe. They were wrong.

Ras Wube's power grew in his father's kingdom and the same officers who advocated for his succession rode beside him to conquer Tigray from 1832 to 1836. He spared his brothers' lives but, perhaps because of their Oromo blood, he placed them in a position of servitude. This did not sit well with Merso and Betul. True to the era of princes, they rebelled. Being the grandsons of the great Ras Gugsa, they had options. They were able to join their cousin, the powerful Ras Ali.

Despite having converted to Christianity, the Yejju were part of the legacy of devastation wrought under Imam Ahmad Gran. Ras Wube tapped into the festering hatred of his countrymen and positioned himself as the champion who would rid the land of the Yejju Oromo, or the Yejju Gallas as was the common term at the time.[360] (The term *Galla* was seen as derogatory to the proud

---

[359] Prouty, Chris. *Empress Taytu and Menilek II: Ethiopia 1883-1910.* 1986. The Red Sea Press, 2016, p. 28.

[360] Ibid., 29.

Oromo people.) Furthermore, the living embodiment of the power of the Yejju was Ras Ali. He was a reminder to the highland Solomonic princes of their inability to control the throne of their ancestors. It was also rumored that Ras Ali was secretly still Muslim and required loyalists to make pilgrimages to the tomb of Imam Ahmad Gran. Despite all this, Ras Ali was too powerful to openly oppose, so Ras Wube allowed him to marry his daughter.

Ras Ali made his base Debre Tabor. A favored military campsite of Ras Gugsa, Ras Ali turned it into a bona fide small city from which Begemder, Gojjam and Wollo were all ruled. As his power grew, Ras Ali built churches and palaces, including one for his mother, Empress Manan Liban, which was only slightly smaller than his.

The growing importance of Debre Tabor was not going unnoticed by Ras Wube. He continued to build his strength in the mountains of Semen, training his men and making war in the high altitude. They were men of the mountain, hardy and tested. Once he was confident that his passionate army was up to the task, he decided the time had come to put an end to the Yejju and restore the power of the Solomonic dynasty in Ethiopia. With the arrival of a 21-year-old Egyptian Coptic Abuna, the first in decades, Ras Wube made the case that Ras Ali was a closet Muslim who needed to be relieved of his power. The church was now on his side. Ras Wube was ready to advance.

In one of the boldest moves of the era of princes, Ras Wube marched on Debre Tabor, the seat of Ras Ali's power. He found that the tide was on his side and Ras Ali's forces were defeated. Celebrations ensued and, in the drunken chaos, Betul and his elder brother Merso took advantage of an opportunity to capture Ras Wube. Soon, Ras Ali was restored to power. Grateful for their assistance, he allowed Merso to finally fulfil the wish of his father. Merso would now govern Semen. At last, he had won his life's greatest victory! Yet, it was short lived because, as it would turn out, Merso's biggest enemy was his own personality.

In his own gratitude, Merso traveled to Gondar to pay his respects to Empress Manan Liban but the meeting was a disaster. Perhaps, he was not aware who held the real power in the realm. Empress Manan was not aware of, nor did she approve, Merso's appointment as governor by her son. The fact that he had a reputation for being disrespectful to women did not help his cause. The meeting was not cordial and Merso could not hide his arrogance.[361] The fact that Merso's relationship was much better with his soldiers did not change the Empress's mind about him. She quietly moved to action. In the end, deals were made and the young Abuna was made to see things in a light favorable to Ras Wube, who was quickly restored to power. Arrangements were also made to have Ras Ali baptized by the young Abuna to dispel the Muslim rumors once and for all.

Before Merso and his brother could reach his new post, a messenger of Ras Ali arrived to inform him he was no longer governor. With the restoration of Ras Wube to the governance of Semen, Betul and Merso were put in chains. Being of royal bloodline, they were then given small districts in Gojjam to keep them out of harm's way. Betul parted ways with his brother, who had grown bitter and cruel, and he pragmatically decided to give his services to the powerful and resilient army of his cousin, Ras Ali. He fathered two boys and two girls – Taitu was his third born.

---

[361] Ibid., 30.

During the period of Taitu's birth, the power of the Yejju kingdom had reached its zenith. She grew up in an Ethiopia where the Yejju Oromo, via Ras Ali and Empress Manan Liban, decided which Solomonic prince sat on the throne of David and inhabited the ornate castles built by Emperor Fasilides.

Ras Ali maintained power by being constantly ready for war. As a soldier, Betul would have had to leave his wife to go on many campaigns. Being related to the powerful Ras Ali, Betul would be given the privilege of having his wife stay with the other noble ladies in a protected area, at the village of princesses.

THE PRINCESS VILLAGE

In Begemder, not far from Debre Tabor, was a village of aristocratic women – Mahdere Maryam. To enter, one needed special permission. Empress Manan Liban received audience at Mahdere Maryam and interacted with other ladies of nobility there. In a land where it was customary for people to walk barefooted, Mahdere Maryam was distinguished by the volume of noblewomen who wore Turkish slippers, and their beautiful footwear was matched by the beauty of their vegetable gardens. The village served as a sanctuary for both Ras Ali's wife and Ras Wube's daughter during the battle for Debre Tabor. It is also considered by some to have been the birthplace of Empress Taitu.[362]

Taitu's father, Betul, died in the Battle of Ayshal, one of the battles that ended the era of princes. Taitu was at a monastery in Gojjam at the time. Meanwhile, her

---

[362] Ibid., 31.

brothers were taken captive by Emperor Tewodros II to receive instruction with the other princes of the realm. This is how it is said that the future Emperor Menelik II first learned about Taitu. As he became close with her brothers, he enquired if they had a sister. Some chroniclers go as far as to say that he requested her hand in marriage but was denied because her family was hoping for a marriage to someone with close ties to Tewodros II. Being a prisoner from Shoa, he could not help them improve their position in the north.

Indeed, the Yejju knew how to play the game of thrones. Accordingly, Taitu's first marriage was to one of Tewdoros II's officers.

THE MARRIAGES OF TAITU

Her family's choice of husband proved hasty. Shortly after their wedding, he offended Tewodros II and found himself in chains. Young Taitu was forced to walk behind the army on foot, also chained at the wrist, and cook for the soldiers like a peasant. This was in extreme contrast to her upbringing in Mahdere Maryam.

Following such disgrace, she married two other high-ranking men – Dejazmatch Tekle Giyorgis and the governor of Yejju, Jantirar Udie. Both these marriages were also chess moves orchestrated with family consultation and both men were divorced when appropriate, although it could be precarious to be a noblewoman over a certain age without a husband. Single women could fall victim to the dreaded zar demons. According to local folk tales, the zar demon looked like a handsome, light-skinned Ethiopian but could cause physical and mental illness.

The marriage to Jantirar Udie, who was the guardian of the mountain fortress of Ambasel in Yejju, provided refuge after Tewodros II died. Taitu was safe when the war of the Dejazmatch versus the King of Kings took place. After Emperor Yohannes IV emerged victorious, Taitu's husband (a loyal governor of Tewodros II) was imprisoned and she was allowed to return to her mother who resided with her new husband at the monastery of Debre Mewi.

Taitu did not stay at the monastery for long and ended up marrying again, this time to Kegnazmatch Zikargatchew. He was the brother of one of the most powerful women in Ethiopia, the beautiful and cunning Bafena, whose claim to fame was that she was the love of the powerful King of Shoa, Menelik II. Intellectually, the Kegnazmatch was no match for his new wife. Taitu could read and write Amharic and Ge'ez, and she was versed in the sacred texts of the empire. She was a poet, a masterful chess player and could play instruments as well. Intimidated by his noble spouse, Kegnazmatch Zikargatchew resorted to physical assault in an effort to impose his will on her. Telling her jealous husband that she was going to travel, Taitu gathered valuable property and servants, and she escaped to her brother in Yejju.

In 1882, Taitu first met Menelik II. Following the battle between the King of Shoa and the King of Gojjam, the two combatants were called to the court of Emperor Yohannes IV. The victorious Menelik II was being reprimanded for fighting a war not authorized by the throne. Taitu had traveled to the emperor's court to inquire about some of her men who had been serving Menelik II, and whose fate was now at Yohannes IV's mercy. She was likely impressed by the power demonstrated by Menelik II and, as the wife of his consort's brother, she would have been able to view the Shoan king in a new light. Menelik

II was impressed by her family and the durability of the Yejju Oromo. His enduring friendship with her brother, Wale, was also a major factor of his attraction.

With his vision of a united Ethiopia in mind, Emperor Yohannes IV was interested in Taitu's northern pedigree and links to Tigray. A marriage to Taitu may prevent Menelik II from ever considering making war with the north. Negotiations over her retainers in the care of Menelik II ended in an agreement of marriage. Kegnazmatch Zikargatchew's marriage to Taitu was forgotten in favor of the more powerful suitor. Bafena, his sister, had fallen out of favor with powerful members of the nobility though Menelik II was still under her spell. Though Menelik's II was enamoured with Bafena, he did all that he could to win the heart of the more impressive Taitu, knowing that she was disgusted by his relationship with Bafena. Taitu initially rejected his efforts. Menelik II remained confident, after all he was King of Shoa and a priestly warrior king in his own right. Taitu did not make him wait too long.

THE POWER COUPLE: TAITU AND MENELIK II

When Emperor Yohannes IV pushed strongly for Taitu's marriage with King Menelik II, she had already been married three times. The emperor was aware that Taitu was very proud of her northern Semen and Yejju roots, and that her presence at the royal court of Menelik II would balance the influence of Shoa throughout the empire. Upon their marriage in 1883, Taitu was crowned Queen of Shoa.

The marriage removed the power of Menelik II's previous consort, Bafena, who had been suspected of masterminding a previous plot against Menelik II. She was divorced and exiled to a remote village to live out the rest of her days. The only child they had together was handicapped and not eligible in the eyes of Shoan nobles to succeed Menelik II on the throne.

In 1889, Queen Taitu was at her husband's side when he was crowned Emperor in the Shoan highlands. (This was a departure from tradition as emperors were typically crowned in Axum, near to the Ark of the Covenant.) Two days after his coronation, Taitu herself was crowned Empress.

If Emperor Menelik II was a priestly, warrior king, then Empress Taitu was a priestly, warrior queen. Her first task was to build a church at Mount Entoto and she also quickly gained a reputation for charity. A French man, Father Ferdinand, is recorded as saying of Taitu, "She has studied the psalms of David, is an enduring woman and gives charity to the poor."[363]

In 1890, when Ras Makonnen traveled to Europe and Jerusalem, Empress Taitu entrusted him with money to buy property in Jerusalem that would serve as a base of operations for Ethiopian priests making pilgrimage to the holy land. During his stay there, Ras Makonnen selected a property, paid the purchase price and left instructions with the Italian consul in Jerusalem for the conclusion of the transaction. Empress Taitu was not pleased that, upon his return to Ethiopia, he had not yet secured the deed for the property.[364] Diligent as always, Ras Makonnen wrote to the consul from Harar, to follow up on the progress and ensure that the house was registered in the name of

---

[363] Ibid., 43.

[364] Prouty, Chris. *Empress Taytu and Menilek II: Ethiopia 1883-1910*. 1986. The Red Sea Press, 2016, p. 117.

Empress Taitu.[365] He was informed that the Turkish governor of Jerusalem ruled that Ethiopian subjects were not permitted to own property in the holy city. The Turkish government was likely not pleased with the two humiliating defeats their armies suffered by Emperor Yohannes IV.

Strengthening the ties between Jerusalem and Ethiopia was a priority for Empress Taitu and she committed her time and resources accordingly. She sent her trusted priest caretaker to ensure that the Orthodox faith would have a presence in the city where Yeshua preached his gospel. Unfortunately, Ethiopians were not respected by the authorities and her priest representative was thrown in jail after walking into a police station and slapping the police chief. (He would later inform his royal patron that he was disrespected and mocked by the chief on a public street.) The Empress sent another priest, this time carrying a letter with the imperial seal, charging the Italian consul with rectifying the situation and taking care of the property ownership with the Turkish government.

THE NEW FLOWER

As demonstrated by her loyalty to her church, Empress Taitu was an Ethiopian patriot in every sense of the word. By 1892, she was firmly in control of the Ethiopian royal court, holding just as much power as her husband. That year, while Menelik II was away on a military campaign, she moved the capital from the mountains of Enttoto. Enttoto was cold, rainy and windy, and it did not agree with Empress Taitu's health. She preferred to frequent the

---

[365] Ibid.

hot springs in the valley below. Although she did not openly oppose her husband's choice of Enttoto, she simply moved herself and her attendants down to the warmer climate of the forested valley. As early as 1886-7, while Menelik II armies battled in Arussi and Harar, Queen Taitu spent her time in the valley. She would have the imperial craftsmen build her a *katama* there.[366] By 1892, even Menelik II spent most his time there and the surroundings became full of the tents and lodgings of people who had business with the imperial court. A new capital was born.

It was Taitu herself who had named Ethiopia's new capital, Addis Ababa (meaning *new flower*), which would become the center of government for the ancient realm as it made its transition into modernity. It is ironic that an empress with northern roots would forever shift the throne of David from the northern coastal region southward to the central highlands.

Empress Taitu was confident in the history, land and religion of the Ethiopian realm, and she made great efforts to preserve Ethiopia's legacy for future generations. She worked to increase her husband's power and influence, and defended him against all challengers, great or small. Many Europeans discovered that disrespect for Menelik II in any form was not tolerated in her presence.

In fact, Empress Taitu was very distrustful of Europeans, remembering the disastrous results of her ancestor, Emperor Susenyos I's trust in them. In 1892, she carefully watched the growing number of Europeans in the land and she remained suspicious of their activities throughout her reign. She could feel the clouds of

---

[366] Marcus, Harold G. *The Life and Times of Menelik II: Ethiopia 1844-1913*. Red Sea Press, 1995, p. 220. A *katama* is a type of dwelling.

colonialism gathering on the horizons of her beloved kingdom.

CHAPTER TWENTY-FIVE

Ras Makonnen's Heir

"Once have I sworn by my holiness that I will not lie unto David. His seed shall endure for ever, and his throne as the sun before me. It shall be established for ever as the moon, and as a faithful witness in heaven. Selah." — **Psalms 89:35-37**

Every May, Ras Makonnen traveled with his family to the mountain village of Ejersa Goro, escaping the many diseases that were common within the cramped confines of Harar at that time of year. There, amidst the clouds at approximately 2780 meters (or 9120.23 feet) above sea level, he built a traditional Ethiopian home overlooking the fertile valley. The air was thin, clean and crisp, and Ras Makonnen could truly enjoy the beauty of the land that he had given his life to serve and defend. In 1892, he traveled to Ejersa Goro early with his pregnant wife, Woizero Yeshimebet, and he prayed that the cleaner environment would provide better conditions for child birth.

Ras Makonnen loved Ethiopia as only a warrior who had fought for a land could. Having had the opportunity to travel abroad, he was just as aware as any of his fellow Ethiopians that his land was ancient and her indigenous culture precious. A brilliant military strategist, he was also well aware that the land was facing a threat greater than ever before. His mind was heavy with the burden that his knowledge of the world had given him.

It was his total love for Ethiopia that made places like Ejersa Goro so special to Ras Makonnen. In that setting, he was able to clear his mind and strategize in preparation to meet future challenges.

AN HEIR FOR RAS MAKONNEN

In 1892, it was widely believed that Ras Makonnen was a contender to be named by his aging cousin as heir to the throne and that, one day, the ancient realm of Ethiopia would be his to govern. Despite the speculation, Ras Makonnen was confident of only one thing: the Almighty's will would be accomplished. He prayed that the tender mercies of the Almighty Creator would bless him with a male offspring. If neither he nor Menelik II produced a lawful heir to complete their work, there would be great danger that 3000 years of history would come to naught and that Europe would prevail over their beloved realm.

While the Almighty did bless Sarah, Abraham's wife, late in life against all odds, Empress Taitu had no children and was well advanced in her years. Ras Makonnen was therefore joyful when Woizero Yeshimebet gave birth to a son. Yes, he already had a son who he loved but that son was not a lawful heir. His mother was not Ras Makonnen's lawful wife via an Orthodox Church marriage ceremony. Plus, Ras Makonnen's spirit told him that his first son was not the one who would ensure Ethiopia's success. He trusted his spirit. (The full extent of his spirit would be fully revealed on his death bed in his final command to his generals.) Although he clearly knew that overwhelming odds faced his land, his unwavering faith did not allow him to feel fear. This second son would show the enemies of the throne the might of the Almighty's covenant. It was the boy's enemies who would fear him. After all, he had survived from the womb of Woizero Yeshimebet.

Ras Makonnen had met his wife in the house of Ras Darge. Since then, eight children had died before or after emerging from her womb. Still, he treated her with kindness as his spirit told him that there was something special about her. He trusted his spirit and he truly loved his wife.

During his time in Harar, the elders and astrologers told Ras Makonnen that this ninth child in Woizero Yeshimebet's womb was special. This child would bring peace to Ethiopia and the world. They instructed him to remove the child from his mother as soon as possible after birth as there were powerful forces seeking to destroy him. This was the only way that the child would live and claim his destiny.[367] Ras Makonnen, cautious about putting his full trust in the words of men, was a man of deep faith. He listened to his elders and especially remembered their pronouncements when he witnessed the powerful bursts of thunder and lightning on the night of his son's birth.

On July 23, 1892, in that small mountain village of Ejersa Goro, off the Kombolcha road in a small, traditional wattle and daub house "with a certain Indian appearance about its outside veranda,"[368] as the Earth was satisfied with rain, the boy child was born.

---

[367] *Man of the Millennium: Emperor Haile Selassie I.* Directed by Tikher Teferra, 2008.

[368] Sandford, Christine. *The Lion of Judah Hath Prevailed.* 1954. Research Associates School Times Publications, 1998, p. 25.

A NAME FOR THE BABY BOY

Ras Makonnen was aware of the fear and trembling that the weather caused in those gathered at the compound. He also recalled the sayings of the elders and astrologers about the fate of the child. Accounting for these factors, and knowing that Ethiopia's challenges would require a strong and fearless leader to face them, Ras Makonnen named his newborn son Tafari (or Teferi), meaning *one to be feared or respected*.

Ras Makonnen was hoping that the Almighty would grant him a son with leadership qualities. As an educated man who traveled outside of Ethiopia's boundaries, he knew firsthand that times were changing. Acutely aware of the threat from Muslim Jihadists, it was clear to him that the balance of power in the world had tipped in favor of Europe and her insatiable appetite for resources and territory. Ethiopia would need visionary leadership in order to retain her precious freedom and independence.

The European kingdoms were the real masters beyond Ethiopia's borders, surrounding the realm on all sides. The British were in Sudan and Somalia, the Italians were in Eritrea and Somalia, and the French controlled Djibouti. Ethiopia was the only country on the entire continent without European overlords calling the shots. Ras Makonnen prayed unceasingly for the Creator to send relief for his beloved land. He was very familiar with the psalm written by his family's great forefather, King David of Israel: "Ethiopia shall soon stretch out her hands onto God." This gave him strength in times of adversity. He was certain that the Almighty, the Merciful Creator, would surely protect Ethiopia against all foes, and for all time.

Receiving news that his child was born alive, knowing that he now had a living heir and seeing the strong, lively baby boy anointed with oils, the prophetic words of the Harar elders began to weigh heavy on his mind. Ras Makonnen was already planning to train his son to uphold the covenants of David and his forefathers, and to maintain Ethiopia in her Christian faith.

CHAPTER TWENTY-SIX

Emperor Menelik II's Challenges

"By the KEBRA NAGAST we know and have learned that most certainly the King of Ethiopia is honourable...that he is the King of Zion, the firstborn of the seed of Shem...that the habitation of God is in Zion, and that He breaketh the might and power of all his enemies and foes..." – **Kebra Nagast**[369]

After ensuring that Woizero Yeshimebet was okay, Ras Makonnen walked to his mule. Satisfied with the health and safety of his heir, it was time to return to his governing duties. Leaving some of his best and most loyal warriors behind to provide protection for his wife and son, his gun bearer and the majority of his soldiers who had surrounded the compound accompanied him on his journey to Harar. The royal procession was forced to move cautiously in the falling rain and the slow journey gave Ras Makonnen time to think about the multiple internal and external threats facing his beloved country.

---

[369] Brooks, Miguel F., comp., ed. and trans. *Kebra Nagast: The Glory of Kings.* 1995. Red Sea Press, 2002, p. 128.

INTERNAL CONFLICTS: WAR OF THE THRONES

Notwithstanding the fact that Ethiopia's external enemies were a constant threat, it was Ethiopia's internal conflicts that most concerned Emperor Menelik II in 1892. He held no illusions about the ambitions of the European powers surrounding his kingdom but he had been dealing with them for decades and viewed them as a necessary evil because of their access to modern armaments and technology. On the other hand, a united Ethiopia could vanquish any foe. Divided, Ethiopia would meet the fate of every other mighty African kingdom.

Upon the death of Emperor Yohannes IV, Menelik II had taken the title of King of Kings, quickly crowning himself Emperor and assuming supreme power in the realm. Shoa had finally completed its transition from subject state, to independent kingdom, to vassal state, to home of the Negus Negast. The center of power had shifted from the north to the central highlands of the mountainous realm.

Under Emperor Menelik II, Ethiopia's kingdoms were made provinces and organized under the direction of the most powerful Rases. Most of the Rases claimed some direct connection to the line of King Solomon and King David. As is always the case with history, their greatness was often dependent on which side of the sword one happened to be on. Some Rases ruled their provinces as tyrants, while some, as in the case of Ras Makonnen, ruled as enlightened statesmen. All were warriors and all were expected to lead their loyal armies into battle. As powerful as they were, their influence was nowhere near that of the

Rases during the Zemene Mesafint. Those days were over and power was now centralized with the throne.

While each Ras respected his counterparts, they were by no means always amicable with each other. If they submitted to the rule of Emperor Menelik II, it was only because of his unmatched military strength. Certainly, the Rases of Ethiopia were well trained and tested warriors and the Zemene Mesafint had shown the great houses that family name did not assure title in Ethiopia. Leadership ability had to be proven in each generation.

MENELIK II, THE THRONE AND THE COVENANT OF KING DAVID IN ETHIOPIA

Sensing the danger that surrounded Ethiopia when he took the throne, Emperor Menelik II quickly and aggressively moved to centralize the country. The internal politics of Ethiopia in 1892, as always, orbited around the realm's connection to the royal bloodline of King Solomon and the throne of King David. Menelik II made it clear throughout the realm that, while the family of the deceased Yohannes IV also claimed descent from King Solomon and the Queen of Sheba, it was through the females of the dynasty. He asserted that his own claim to the throne was based on male descent from Emperor Legna Dengel. This was more in line with the prophecy and the divine promise given onto King David – it was based on the uninterrupted, direct male lineage. Therefore, the claims of the House of Shoa were at least equal to those of the elder Gondar line of the dynasty.

Like his predecessors, Emperor Tewodros II and Emperor Yohannes IV, Emperor Menelik II was very much aware that there had ceased to be a king from the line of David in Jerusalem centuries ago. The curse revealed to King Solomon in the Kebra Nagast had come to pass. Jerusalem had been conquered by Islam. Unlike Tewodros II, Menelik II did not have an obsession with leading an army to liberate Jerusalem from the Turks. He was more appreciative of the geopolitical implications of the Solomonic bloodline in Ethiopia. He was motivated by a vision of the priestly, warrior king on the throne of David, uniting the Christians of the world. Menelik II would seek to accomplish this not through war with Europe but through diplomacy.

Ethiopia was in a truly unique position among the nations of the world. The Kebra Nagast states that Rome, the seat of Western Christianity, was home to one of the sons of King Solomon. However, Rome maintained no connection to the throne of Solomon. The Pope, who was Rome's highest spiritual authority, claimed to rule Christendom from the throne of Peter. Meanwhile, the Italian monarchy descended from the House of Savoy, tracing its origins to a 10th century family in the Savoy region of Italy. They made no claim to be heirs to the throne of King David. The Savoy family was thought to originate in the Saxony region of Germany and was renown for diplomatic skill, plus accumulated wealth and power through control of the mountain passes of the Alps.[370]

Ethiopia, the land of the Queen of Sheba, was the only land to be found where King David's offspring had been blessed to continue the legacy of his throne. It was the only land where the Almighty's promise to Judah by his father, Israel – and confirmed to King David – had been fulfilled and maintained. This reality was the foundation for spiritual life in the Ethiopian highlands and it was this

---

[370] "Savoy." *Catholic Encyclopedia*. Robert Appleton Company, 1913.

reality that made Ethiopia peculiar in the eyes of the world. Traveling through Ethiopia in 1892 was like traveling through the pages of the Bible. Emperor Menelik II was not as spiritually inclined as predecessors like Tewodros II and Yohannes IV but he did learn firsthand the power of the clergy from his time in Tewodros II's court. He also governed upon a priestly foundation. As a devout Orthodox Christian himself, he attended church regularly. The psalms of David were often sung by the Orthodox priests and monks throughout Ethiopia and Menelik II knew very well the promise that the Almighty swore onto King David, which David had memorialized in a psalm and sang to the people of Jerusalem:

> "The Lord hath sworn in truth unto David; he will not turn from it; Of the fruit of thy body will I set upon thy throne. If thy children will keep my covenant and my testimony that I shall teach them, their children shall also sit upon thy throne for evermore."[371]

Like his predecessors before him, Emperor Menelik II was quick to let foreign governments know of his royal lineage. To this end, all of his correspondences had the same words written across the top – *The Lion of Judah has prevailed* – signaling the triumph of prophecy over the will of men.

MENELIK II'S MARCH ON TIGRAY

Domestically, the legend of Yohannes IV still lingered in Tigray and the word filtering back to Emperor

---

[371] Psalms 132:11-12

Menelik II was that the former emperor's son, Ras Mengesha, and his trusted general, Ras Alula, were building strength in the north. This could not be permitted. Menelik II knew that it was in his best interest to crush them before they could gain too much momentum. He needed to ensure the loyalty of Tigray, which was one of the gateways to the coastline and the rest of the outside world. So, in 1892, he began a military advance on the famed northern province.[372]

As he made the slow march north, Emperor Menelik II must have thought about the many times Emperor Yohannes IV had marched on Shoa with his notorious, well-armed Tigrayan cavalry. Now, the tables had turned. He was the King of Kings in Zion. Still, the people of Tigray were fiercely independent and did not enjoy taking orders from outsiders. In their leaders' eyes, Tigray was an independent kingdom and not a province or subject kingdom.

Ras Mengesha had, indeed, rallied the Rases of Tigray with Ras Alula's help, building a united front to challenge Menelik II's power.[373] The memory of his father inspired a lot of support among the powerful families of the kingdom. They, like Ras Mengesha himself, believed the throne of David was rightfully his to control. Without their support, Emperor Menelik II would not be able to govern the realm effectively.

---

[372] Erlich, Haggai. *Ras Alula and the Scramble for Africa, A Political Biography: Ethiopia & Eritrea 1875-1897*. The Red Sea Press, 1996, p. 172.

[373] Ibid.

THE IMPORTANCE OF TIGRAY

Tigray was a crucial part of Ethiopia. Losing Tigray and its coastal access would have created problems with the importation of weapons, which Menelik II knew would be necessary to defend against any future foreign aggressors. More importantly, he would lose a tremendous spiritual blessing as he would not have access to Axum and the Ark of the Covenant. These would have to remain a part of his empire. As recorded in the Kebra Nagast, in the minds of Ethiopia's Orthodox Christians, it was the Ark of the Covenant that helped assure Ethiopia's freedom for thousands of years. Therefore, it was the Ark of the Covenant that would ensure Ethiopia's survival in the looming European invasion. To Ethiopia's faithful, the Kebra Nagast was fact. Every church in the empire contained a replica of the Ark. For any King of Kings, Tigray was non-negotiable.

These strategic and spiritual considerations compelled Emperor Menelik II to lead a sizable army to pacify this part of the empire. However, his army never reached the borders of Tigray. As Menelik II marched through his empire, the full extent of the Kifu Ken became apparent. The road to Tigray was devastated by the Kifu Ken and was in no position to sustain such a large army. With internal problems also happening in Shoa,[374] Emperor Menelik II was forced to turn back on February 17, 1892. Wise and cautious as always, he decided to secure his base.

---

[374] Ibid.

CHAPTER TWENTY-SEVEN

The Kingdom of Rome

"The kingdom of Rome was the portion and domination of Japhet, the son of Noah. They planned and they made twelve great cities, and Darious built the greatest cities of their kingdom. Antioch, Tyre, Parthia and Rome, and those who reigned dwelled there; and King Constatine built Constantinople after his own name... the sign of the Cross having appeared to him during the battle in the form of stars cut in heaven, he was delivered out the hands of the enemy; and from that time onwards the Kings of Rome made their habitation there." – **Kebra Nagast**[375]

Ras Makonnen was constantly advising his cousin not to overcommit his resources in fighting internal rivals. They must always be aware of and prepared to face the European threat. His cousin was intensely curious and interrogated him about his trips to European capitals. All out war with Tigray would play into European hands.

Despite not wanting to focus solely on local conflicts, uprisings continued to occur in the realm where the kingdoms were fiercely independent. The kingdoms to the south were actively rebelling. The conquest of the mighty kingdom of the Arsi Oromo was not going well and

---

[375] Brooks, Miguel F., comp., ed. and trans. *Kebra Nagast: The Glory of Kings.* 1995. Red Sea Press, 2002, p. 100.

resources had to be redirected to address the uprising. In 1887, one of Menelik II's uncles and trusted generals, Ras Darge, allegedly committed atrocities in order to psychologically break the kingdom's resistance.[376] It only strengthened the resolve of the resistance. To make matters worse, the people of Arsi chose Islam *en masse* rather than convert to the religion of the imperial court that sought to invade their kingdom. The relationship between Christians and Muslims in the expanding empire was once again on shaky ground.

Despite the strength of Ethiopia's independent kingdoms, Ras Makonnen knew that they would be no match for what he had seen in Europe. Their successful resistance against Menelik II would only mean that they would become a part of a European colony. The expert Arsi horsemen could not withstand European machine guns and other forms of modern warfare.

There were no good options. Peace was a luxury not afforded to the imperial court during the Scramble for Africa and the Evil Days. The European threat was real. The Scramble for Africa was real. Ras Makonnen ensured that Emperor Menelik II was well aware of the facts that faced Ethiopia should they choose to be passive during the Scramble.

---

[376] A., Mohammed. "Aanolee: 'A Tragedy on Which Ethiopian Sources Are Silent'." *OPride.com*, 8 April 2014, https://www.opride.com/2014/04/08/aanolee-mutilation-a-tragedy-on-which-ethiopian-sources-are-silent/.

THE RISE OF ROME

Ethiopia's distinction of being the only historically Christian state in Africa did not go unnoticed outside of its borders. Her internal politics were of much interest as indicated by the growing presence of foreigners visiting the country. To the countries of Europe, Ethiopia's Solomonic history made it an exotic, potential African acquisition. To Europe, Africa was the dark continent. It was a cake to be devoured.

Finally ready to activate their territorial claims made at the Berlin conference, the Italians consolidated their colonies in 1890 and declared one autonomous colony called Eritrea. Burning with the desire to bring Ras Alula to justice, they saw it as their duty to strengthen the new emperor, Menelik II, and crush the Tigrayan nobility that had been responsible for the massacre of their troops at Dogali. During Emperor Yohannes IV's reign, Menelik II had maintained consistent communication with them, having learned the usefulness of foreign connections from Yohannes IV himself. In their view, Emperor Menelik II was their man in Ethiopia and they expected that his ascendancy to the throne was a green light for them to execute their full control over Ethiopia. A student of both Tewodros II and Yohannes IV, Menelik II had other plans.

Following Yohannes IV's death, along with the drought and devastation of the Kifu Ken, Ras Alula and Ras Mengesha were in no position to maintain their massive, inherited army. As the days passed, desertions increased. The Italians viewed this as an opportunity and, in December 1889, General Baldassare Orero arrived in Massawa with a mission to take over the Red Sea

Garrison. Soon, Ras Alula and Ras Mengesha were forced to leave their base at Adwa to find provisions to feed their army – there would have been no hope to rebuild the power of Tigray otherwise. General Orero and his army (including some Ethiopian Italian allies) got word of this development and entered Adwa on January 26, 1890. Unfortunately, General Orero miscalculated the response of Emperor Menelik II.

The emperor viewed the Italian action as an act of aggression. Adwa was well into Ethiopia's territory and he had given the Italians no permission to march into that area. Both Ras Makonnen and Menelik II's Italian advisor, Count Antonelli, objected to the move as a violation of the Treaty of Wichale, which Ethiopia had recently entered into during Ras Makonnen's trip to Italy. Meanwhile, word of the occupation spread fast. Tigrayan leaders quickly accused Emperor Menelik II of selling out their kingdom to the Italians, adding insult to injury when the Kifu Ken had already started devouring the land. In reality, the emperor's hands were tied and he could not march his massive army into drought-stricken Tigray.

The Italian incursion finally convinced Ras Mengesha to submit to Emperor Menelik II on March 15, 1890 – he nor Ras Alula had the strength to fight both the Kifu Ken and the Italians. The growing boldness of the Italians was deeply troubling to the emperor but, ultimately, he benefited from their maneuver. Being the astute statesman he was, Menelik II realized that the foreigners would be useful in controlling internal threats. With this in mind, he entered into the Convention of Denghelt, an agreement that provided for exile for Tigrayans who had been hostile to Italian interests and to the appointment of a Shoan governor. The Italians would also assist in suppressing revolts and disarming the proud

Tigrayans.[377] By signing this agreement with Italy, Emperor Menelik II also decreased the likelihood that Italy would enter into an agreement with his rivals. Again, he learned the lesson from the British Napier expedition of how a foreign power could change the internal balance of power.

Emperor Menelik II also requested that his Italian advisor become the civil governor of Eritrea. He wanted an Italian known to him in power. Once appointed, Count Antonelli was successful in getting General Orero to back off his aggressive policies.

While some Italians felt that their nation should seek to take over Ethiopia through peaceful trade, others among them wanted a more muscular posture toward Ethiopia, which they viewed as inferior. In 1891, Colonel G.B. Luciano campaigned for Eritrea to be a military settlement and further added, "I have no intention of degrading the Abyssinian race, strong, intelligent and noblest among the indigenous peoples [of Africa], but I insist that in many respects we are superior to it, especially as to civilization, and we would not renounce the supremacy of the white race over these peoples."[378]

As the Kifu Ken raged on and desperation ensued, Emperor Menelik II requested that the Italians provide supplies for Ras Mengesha and his starving army. General Orero complied with 60,000 francs' worth of grain.

---

[377] Marcus, Harold G. *The Life and Times of Menelik II: Ethiopia 1844-1913*. Red Sea Press, 1995, p. 121.

[378] Ibid., 122-123.

THINGS FALL APART

The relationship between Ethiopia and Italy changed when Emperor Menelik II received replies from the foreign leaders he wrote upon ascending to the throne of David. Queen Victoria wrote:

> "We note further Your Majesty's intention to send someone to us hereafter to discuss matters of common interest to our Kingdoms. Inasmuch, however, as the Italian Government have notified to us that by a Treaty concluded on the 2nd of May last between Italy and Ethiopia, 'it is provided that...the King of Ethiopia consents to avail himself of the Government of...the King of Italy for the conduct of all matters which he may have with other Powers or Governments,' We shall communicate to the Government of our Friend...the King of Italy copies of Your Majesty's letter and Our reply."[379]

The German emperor's reply echoed Queen Victoria. Both replies were displeasing to Empress Taitu, confirming her dislike of foreigners and their designs on Ethiopian territory. Emperor Menelik II was equally concerned. However, the conditions of the Kifu Ken prevented any forward action. For now, the status quo would have to remain.

The weakened position of his empire did not stop Emperor Menelik II from summoning the Italian

---

[379] Ibid., 124.

representative, Count Augusto Salimbeni, to his court to explain how the Italians had corrupted the translation of their agreement. After some time there, Salimbeni concluded, "...if we wish to maintain the Mareb frontier we must rely on bayonets and cannon."

Empress Taitu told her husband:

> "[Emperor Yohannes IV] never wanted to cede an inch of territory: he fought against the Italians [and] he fought against the Egyptians for this [principle]; he died for this, and you after such an example, wish to sell your country? Who will [want to] tell your history?"[380]

When Count Salimbeni tried to explain the Italian position, an unimpressed Taitu coldly replied, "Poor devil! The others have made complications and they send you to put them right!"

The Empress was right not to trust the Italians. While Salimbeni was trying to satisfy the royal court with sweet talk, General Orero was attempting to negotiate directly with Ras Mengesha about the northern border with Eritrea. Emperor Menelik II wrote a diplomatic letter to the King of Italy requesting that the error in the Wichale agreement be rectified. He wrote another letter to Eritrea stating, "If I call myself King of Kings of Ethiopia, it is because I have added Tigre to my kingdom; and if you will take [land] up to Mareb, what is left for me?"[381]

Also, the Italians had given him a bank loan of 2,000,000 lire and the bank made an error in fixing the rate and time of repayment, calculating from June 1, 1891

---

[380] Ibid., 125.

[381] Ibid., 127.

rather than the true date in July 1892. This further cemented the suspicions of Empress Taitu and other anti-Italian nobles in the royal court. It seemed as if the Italians were plotting at every turn to cheat Emperor Menelik II out of his newly acquired empire.[382] The situation was deteriorating rapidly.

Italy tried to calm the situation by dismissing General Orero, who they stated had acted outside his mandate in negotiating with Ras Mengesha. His replacement was General Antonio Gandolfi. They also dispatched Count Antonelli to try to reach some accord but his audience at the palace with Menelik II and Taitu did not go as planned. The royal couple exchanged opportunities to give the Count a piece of their mind. So forceful and passionate was Emperor Menelik II's admonition that he lost his voice by the end of the exchange.[383]

At one point, the Count presented a proposal that "the Emperor of Ethiopia undertakes not to accept the protection of any other power. If he should do so, he will always give preference to the government of H.M. the King of Italy." Empress Taitu then informed the Count, "I am a woman and I do not love war; but rather than accepting this I prefer war." The Count did his best to remove the objections from the proposal but Menelik II would not make any decision without the advice of his most trusted advisors. Accordingly, he summoned Ras Makonnen from Harar.

It was January 20, 1891 when Menelik II made the decision to honor the Ethiopian translation of the Wichale agreement. This was not pleasing to the Italians as it

---

[382] Ibid., 129.

[383] Ibid., 130.

caused a huge embarrassment for them in Europe, opening the door for a stronger European country to enter and take over their piece of the African cake. Count Antonelli and Ambassador Salimbeni decided to try forcing a declaration from Menelik II – they announced that they were leaving the court to return to Italy. The emperor knew that Ethiopia could not risk war with Italy during the Kifu Ken, so he attempted to delay their departure and informed them that he wished to remain in good standing with Italy.

On February 3, 1891 the Italians received a letter from Ras Makonnen in Amharic text. On February 6, the Italians were invited to sign statements about the frontier and the article in contention. Finally! As the Italians signed the agreement, they felt vindicated by their perseverance. In order to avoid any accusations of continued treachery, the Italians requested that the interpreter should come from Menelik II. It was agreed. However, after days passed without seeing the interpreter turn up, the Italians decided to do the work themselves and used the Italian embassy interpreter, Ato Yosef. This is when they noticed the word "sarraza."

ETHIOPIA OUTSMARTS THE ITALIANS

"Sarraza" - in their excitement over reaching a deal, they had glossed over this word for days without realizing what it meant. They searched for a translation and could not find any, until Ato Yosef informed them that the word meant "cancel" or "annul." After further discussion and research, they realized that the inclusion of the word meant that the contested Article XVII had been abrogated.

In fact, the signed agreement stated, "...as you told me that Article XVII... should be annulled by a common accord, and as you asked me to give you a favourable response to the good understanding between Ethiopia and Italy, we have annulled the Amharic text as well as the Italian text of Article XVII."[384]

The Italians had been outmaneuvered at their own game! Their feelings of superiority were dashed against the mountainous terrain of the Ethiopian highlands. Count Antonelli, who had felt close to Ras Makonnen and the royal family, now felt betrayed. He ran to the palace and requested an audience with Ras Makonnen, who heard him patiently and then asked to take the letter to Emperor Menelik II. Count Antonelli agreed but cut his signature and seal from the agreement, upsetting the ever-composed Ras Makonnen who considered it an attack against the crown. Realizing that he needed to humble himself or risk serious consequences, Count Antonelli explained that he had not touched Menelik II's signature or seal. After some time, he was permitted audience with the emperor, who was sitting in the presence of some of the most powerful nobility in the realm – Empress Taitu, Ras Mengesha Atikem, Ras Makonnen and Grazmatch Yosef. Count Antonelli pleaded his case and that of his country, explaining that the act of the Ethiopians was an offense to the King of Italy himself.

Emperor Menelik II treated the irate Italian as he would a child caught in his own deceit. He lectured:

> "You know the Amharic language perfectly, and you well know that what you have written in the Italian text is not at all what you discussed with me. You look to me to give you support against the consequences of your own personal faults... if you wish us

---

[384] Ibid., 133.

to understand each other, find something to replace this article which is positive for both countries, and let me know it. I am completely ready to accept it, because I wish nothing but friendship. But if you tell me: it is impossible, there is nothing but acceptance, with good or bad grace, of what is written in the Italian text, my response is this: I can scarcely accept such a proposition."

Count Antonelli's response was to leave the country. He would place all the blame for the impasse on Emperor Menelik II.

ETHIOPIA REPELS ALL INVADERS

Meanwhile, millions of Ethiopians were dying. The Kifu Ken had gripped the land and large groups of people from the north began to take the road heading south in search of food and pasture. Emperor Menelik II deployed his soldiers into the fields to farm and he provided them and provincial governors with farming equipment.[385]

Despite the crushing famine, Menelik II could not shake the sense of foreboding regarding his disagreement with the Italians. Wanting to give them no pretext to invade Ethiopia during such trying times, he demanded that his Ethiopian subjects find a way to repay the Italian loan. He divided the 2,000,000 lire loan among the various kingdoms and provinces and urged them to produce tax revenue equivalent to their size within his kingdom. He also demanded that they produce revenue on top of that,

---

[385] Ibid., 136.

sufficient to provide the country with 2,000,000 more in taxes.[386] The additional funds were to be used to import relief supplies from the coast.

To survive the demands of the Kifu Ken, Ethiopian expansion to the south was increased and the tribes bordering Shoa and Harar were raided continuously for supplies. Ras Makonnen led the charge from Harar, extending Ethiopia's reach far into the Ogaden.

While the Emperors and Rases of Ethiopia were, at times throughout its history, bitter rivals, they all had one thing in common: they believed in the Kebra Nagast's declaration that, with the Almighty's aid, all Ethiopia's enemies could be repelled or contained. Egypt (under the banner of the Ottoman Empire), Sudan (under the banner of the legendary "Mahdi") and Italy (waving the banner of Western Christianity) – all had attempted to invade or encroach on Ethiopia in recent times. All were defeated. As far as the Ethiopians were concerned, Ethiopia was Zion, the Almighty's peculiar treasure, and it was protected by the powers of the Ark of the Covenant and the covenant of David. Ethiopia would always remain free under the Creator's divine aid. This belief, along with the power of the Church, maintained national unity in times of nationwide crisis. With the Kifu Ken raging and the Italian threat looming, the Rases were compelled to work with the powerful Emperor Menelik II rather than outwardly oppose him.

In 1892, both the Ottoman Empire and the Mahdi of Sudan had been defeated without the full participation of all Ethiopia's kingdoms. However, Ethiopia was by no means out of the woods regarding the defense of her ancient borders. Her traditional adversaries, the Ottomans

---

[386] Ibid.

in Egypt and Mahdists in Sudan, both fell down before the growing power of the Europeans, not strong enough to resist their unparalleled military strength. Now, it was Europe that controlled all the territories bordering Ethiopia.

As Ras Makonnen made his way from the mountains of Ejersa Goro down into the walled city of Harar, thoughts of Italian intentions were certainly on his mind. Aside from the threat of rebellion within Harar or from the surrounding countryside, there was the looming threat from Italy. He not only had the protection of his cousin, the emperor, and his loving wife to consider, but he was now also responsible for protecting his new heir. It seemed like only a matter of time before Ethiopia's interests and Europe's interests would come into direct conflict.

CHAPTER TWENTY-EIGHT

The Year was 1892

"He shall have dominion also from sea to sea, and from the river unto the ends of the earth. They that dwell in the wilderness shall bow before him; and his enemies shall lick the dust. The kings of Tarshish and of the isles shall bring presents: the kings of Sheba and Seba shall offer gifts. Yea, all kings shall fall down before him: all nations shall serve him. For he shall deliver the needy when he crieth; the poor also, and him that hath no helper. He shall spare the poor and needy, and shall save the souls of the needy. He shall redeem their soul from deceit and violence: and precious shall their blood be in his sight. And he shall live, and to him shall be given of the gold of Sheba: prayer also shall be made for him continually; and daily shall he be praised." **– Psalms 72:8-15**

There is no record of Ras Makonnen speaking out explicitly against white supremacy. However, it is clear that Ras Makonnen and his countrymen had little trust of foreigners. The justification for his distrust was all over the continent of Africa and even the world-at-large.

THE WORLD IN 1892

The year 1892 marked a turning point for humanity. The world was changing. A social cancer – the philosophy of white supremacy – was spreading around the world. Most of the world's people were being squeezed by the unrelenting grip of foreign colonization or facing indirect foreign rule economically and politically. Africa, Brazil and the Caribbean, in particular, were being swallowed by ravenous foreign appetites as the major powers of the day sought resources to feed their unprecedented, steadily growing levels of consumption. Indigenous cultures were being systematically destroyed by these forces behind Western expansion.

In Africa, European governments were busy implementing their agreements from the Berlin Conference. The Church in Europe also saw Africa as an opportunity for wealth and expansion, and missionaries began flooding into the continent. Church and state interests were aligned. This was the period when the Westernized Bible and the gun were introduced to countless millions of Africans who had spent centuries isolated from the rest of the world.

WAR IN THE CONGO

In February 1891, thousands of miles away from the highlands of Ethiopia, the infamous King Leopold II of Belgium sent one of his trusted officers, Major Guillaume Van Kerckhoven, and nineteen other of his finest officers to subdue the northern Congo and portions of the Nile.[387] The 500-strong expedition, with its mechanized methods of murder, was ordered to quickly bring the northeastern Congo under Belgian rule and then journey up the Nile to capture more territory. It was characteristic of the type of missions that were ordered from distant European capitals during the colonial period.

Major Guillaume Van Kerckhoven's mission was disastrous and ended in his death but he managed to carve a path of death and destruction before his passing. On these missions, the colonial powers murdered countless Africans with the aid of the machine gun. Living on the continent, Africans relied on ancient warfare methods, and praised their warriors for their skills in sword-to-sword combat. Major Guillaume would have studied various African army tactics, such as those of the mighty Oyo Empire in West Africa, who prided themselves in not using guns on the battlefield until late in the colonial period.[388] Their well-armored warriors were masters with their swords, yet they, like the Congolese warriors he encountered, were no match for the terrible barrage of bullets unleashed from the Gatlin, Winchester and other weapons that had revolutionized the age-old art of killing.

The major's mission also helped to ignite the Congo-Arab War of 1892 in the Congo between Belgian interests and the Black Arab slave traders who controlled the region then. Sefu, the son of the famous Zanzibar slave trader, Tippu Tip, launched a full-scale attack on the Europeans and their allies on November 19, 1892. Backed by 10,000 soldiers armed with outdated weapons, they

---

[387] Lewis, David Levering. *Race to Fashoda: Colonialism and African Resistance*. Henry Holt and Co., 1987.

[388] Stride, George T. and Ifeka, Caroline. *Peoples and Empires of West Africa: West Africa in History, 1000-1800*. Nelson 1971, p. 301.

were no match for the modern rifles of the Europeans. After a strong rain rendered their gunpowder loaded muzzle-loaders useless, Sefu's stronghold was stormed, resulting in 600 dead on the battlefield, 2000 to 3000 killed or drowned in the river, and at least 1000 men taken as prisoners of war.[389] Sefu and the rest of the survivors disappeared into the dense jungle that characterized the Congo.

BRITISH CONQUEST OF NIGERIA

The Belgians were by no means the only Europeans who were advancing in Africa in the year of Ras Makonnen's baby boy's birth. The British conquest of Ijebu-Ode on May 22, 1892 marked another major extension of colonial power, this time into the Nigerian interior.[390] The Kingdom of Ijebu was a stronghold of the Yoruba, laying claim to an important trade route between Lagos and Ibadan. The Maxim guns of the British armed forces ensured that it was quickly added to the British colony of Southern Nigeria.[391]

From the late 1700s until the 1850s, the Yoruba Oyo Empire city-state of Lagos arose as a major slave port.[392] The Yoruba were using war to rebuild their empire

---

[389] Pakenham, Thomas. *The Scramble for Africa: White Man's Conquest of the Dark Continent from 1876 to 1912.* 1992. Perennial, 2003, p. 443.

[390] See: http://en.wikipedia.org/wiki/1892

[391] Lloyd, Peter C. "Ijebu." *African Kingships in Perspective.*

[392] Ojo, Olatunji. "The Organization of the Atlantic Slave Trade in Yorubaland, ca.1777 to ca.1856." *International Journal of African Historical Studies*, vol. 41.1, 2008. "Slave production in the interior raised exports from Lagos tenfold, making it West Africa's leading

after suffering a stunning defeat from the neighboring Nupe Kingdom in 1535.[393] The Yoruba had been driven into exile and had learned from the defeat – a more disciplined and centralized Oyo Empire emerged. As war raged in West Africa, the Oyo Empire found a profitable way to deal with their prisoners of war. It would later be revealed that they had made a deal with the devil, which allowed the Yoruba kings to amass significant wealth for a time. The renowned Oyo generals and their cavalry ensured a steady stream of prisoners for trade with the Europeans whose settlements had dotted the coast. The benefits of their deal did not last and, by 1892, the Yoruba kingdoms were almost all vassals to their former trade partners.

The conquest of the Kingdom of Ijebu-Ode in 1892 continued the colonial wave sweeping Nigeria. The tipping point had been the fall of the centralized power of the Oyo Empire. While not all Yoruba were part of the Oyo Empire, it represented the pinnacle of Yoruba power until it was weakened by internal intrigue. The Europeans exploited the divide and, without a united adversary to oppose their designs, they were able to continue their Scramble without abatement in the Niger Delta. By 1852, after a successful attack on Lagos, the British had installed

---

slave port. The most accurate trade figures are found in the Trans-Atlantic slave voyage database (TSD), which put the number of slave exports between 1776 and 1850 at 308,800. Of that number, only 24,000 slaves were shipped before 1801, while 114,200 and 170,600 were sold during 1801–25 and 1826–50, respectively. Exports from Badagry lagged far behind, with about 37,400 slaves sold during 1776–1860."

[393] Cartwright, Mark. "Oyo Empire." *World History Encyclopedia*, 2 Apr 2020. https://www.worldhistory.org/Oyo_Empire/

a British-friendly Oba to rule over the city.[394] The former Oba then fled to Ijebu.

After securing Lagos, European influence in Nigeria grew for decades. That being the case, the powerful Awujale, the traditional ruler of Ijebu, found his power threatened in his own land. In order to assert his strength and cut the power of Europeans, he stopped all trade to Lagos.

In May 1891, the British sent their acting governor, Captain C.M. Denton C.M.G., backed by an army of Hausa troops, to negotiate the reopening of the passage. After the application of some pressure, the Awujale agreed and trade was resumed in January 1892. The British agreed to provide an annual payment of £500 to compensate for lost customs revenue.[395] The distrust was high among the Yoruba and word began to spread about European designs for Africa. A white missionary was denied passage through the Ijebu kingdom and sent back to Lagos.[396] His denial of passage violated the agreement struck with the Awujale, and this became the pretext for war that the British were waiting for.

The use of force was authorized. The British had learned from their previous wars on African soil and began to mobilize troops from the Gold Coast, Sierra Leone,

---

[394] Smith, Robert S. *The Lagos Consulate, 1851-1861*. University of California Press, 1979, pp. 26–31.

[395] Tayo, Ayomide O. "How a Christian Missionary Caused the Expedition of a Great Kingdom." *Pulse Nigeria*, 8 Dec. 2017, https://www.pulse.ng/gist/pop-culture/british-ijebu-war-how-a-christian-missionary-caused-the-expedition-of-a-great-kingdom/er9tc4y.

[396] Omipidan, Teslim. "Battle of Imagbon: The British-Ijebu War of 1892." *OldNaija*, https://oldnaija.com/2019/04/04/the-british-ijebu-war-of-1892-the-battle-of-imagbon/.

Ibadan and even Lagos. Being in a state with a history of war, it was not difficult to recruit Africans to fight for the British cause. Many who would fight for the British were Africans residing to the north, who had escaped enslavement by the Yoruba.[397] The Ijebu were not short on enemies.

The British and their machine guns landed in Nigeria on May 12, 1892 with 450 men. They added another 186 to that number with recruits in Lagos. The Ijebu were prepared with 8,000 soldiers, most of whom had only old rifles to defend their kingdom.[398] The British war strategy was to win by any means, and they burned down every Ijebu village they encountered.[399]

The Ijebu readied for the assault. Their mystics enchanted the river but not even the most potent Yoruba *juju* could stand against the sweeping tide of European imperialism. Modern armaments won the day. The machine guns were merciless and 900 men lost their lives.[400] The Awujale had no choice but to surrender.

Less than two months before the birth of the baby boy in the Ethiopian highlands, one of the last remaining Yoruba strongholds had fallen to British control.

FRENCH CONQUEST OF BENIN

On November 17, 1892, two days before the Congo-Arab War began, French troops occupied Abomey,

---

[397] Ibid.

[398] Ibid.

[399] Ibid.

[400] Ibid.

the then capital of the Kingdom of Dahomey in modern day Benin. The Dahomey were one of Africa's mightiest tribes and their subjugation was an ominous signal for the rest of free Africa. Still, the writing was on the wall from over a decade before that.

The war with France that started in 1890 was only the final blow to a mighty kingdom already in decline. The Dahomey, like the Oyo, had benefited from the Europe-run slave trade and subsequently struggled against the Scramble. Starting in the 1840s, the British imposed blockades against the kingdom to prevent the exportation of Africans. The growing power of the kingdom was a threat to British interests in Nigeria.

Africans also rose against the Dahomey. Abeokuta, a city-state founded as a place of refuge for Africans escaping Dahomey's slave traders, handed the Dahomey a stunning military defeat in 1851.[401]

Ultimately, the British and the Yoruba were not Dahomey's downfall – it was the French who would bring down the powerful kingdom.

King Behanzin of Dahomey tried in vain to stop the expanding French influence over his kingdom and surrounding areas. His armies and public relations were no match for a French war machine that highlighted the Dahomean practice of human sacrifice as a means of painting Dahomey's culture as savage.[402]

To the Dahomey, it was the French who were the true savages as they cut down the sacred trees in Oueme

---

[401] Yoder, John C. "Fly and Elephant Parties: Political Polarization in Dahomey, 1840-1870." *The Journal of African History*, vol. 15, no. 3, 1974, pp. 417–432.

[402] Rummel, R. J. *Death by Government*. Transaction Publishers, 1994, p. 63.

and Zou as part of their war strategy.[403] The French's modern armaments, bribery and other military tactics proved very problematic for the Dahomey in the end.

Had the kingdoms of Africa come together against the European threat, they would have surely triumphed against the Scramble. Separately, on the other hand, they were no match for Europe's advanced military technology. Had Menelik II called the King of Dahomey for assistance in 1892, King Behanzin would have been in no position to render aid. The same was true for most of the continent's great kingdoms and their rulers.

THE MIGHTY TRIBES HAVE FALLEN

On July 4, 1879, the British had won a decisive victory against the legendary Zulus of South Africa, establishing a firm foothold in the southern part of Africa. By 1888, the British agent, Cecil Rhodes, had traveled north and tricked King Lobengula of Zimbabwe into granting him the mineral rights to his lands. As Ethiopia entered the Kifu Ken in 1889, Cecil Rhodes was able to secure a royal charter for the British South Africa Company – he had the blessing of Queen Victoria needed to secure British interests in Zimbabwe.[404] Death was to follow.

Cecil Rhodes spent 1892 preparing to send a group of white settlers into the middle of Matabeleland. They would have the protection of the well-armed British South Africa Police. What they did not have was the blessing of

---

[403] See: https://en.wikipedia.org/wiki/B%C3%A9hanzin

[404] Farwell, Byron. *The Encyclopedia of Nineteenth-Century Land Warfare: An Illustrated World View*. W. W. Norton & Co., 2001, p. 539.

King Lobengula to settle in his kingdom. So, the stage for war was set.

During the same period of British conquest over South Africa, the British war machine was active in West Africa. On February 4, 1874, the mighty Ashanti abandoned their capital, Kumasi, in the face of the advance of British troops. The British found a massive palace complete with a library of books in many languages. Like most conquerors, they burned the palace to the ground. By July that year, the Asantehene (King of the Ashanti) signed a treaty obligating the Ashanti to pay reparations for the war. The proud Ashanti kingdom was forced "to pay the sum of 50,000 ounces of approved gold as indemnity for the expenses he has occasioned to Her Majesty the Queen of England by the late war."[405] In 1891, the British would add insult to injury when they demanded that the Ashanti become a British protectorate. The stage was being set for Yaa Asantewaa and the Ashanti resistance that would characterize the decade following the British's disrespectful request.

As the number of pockets of free people in Africa shrunk, the vast tracts of land connecting Ethiopia's highlands looked more and more appetizing to the Europeans who grew increasingly ravenous by 1892.

THE UNITED STATES IN 1892

In the Western Hemisphere, the descendants of Africans living in the United States of America were routinely being tortured and brutalized, especially after the

---

[405] Goldstein, Erik. *Wars and Peace Treaties: 1816-1991*. 1992. Routledge, 2005.

reconstruction movement that followed the American Civil War had collapsed and given way to Jim Crow. On record, 71 white people and 155 black people were lynched there in 1892. The white people were often lynched by other whites because they assisted black people in their communities, and many more lynched black people were not officially recorded.

Bessie Coleman, the first African-American female pilot, was only just born on January 26, 1892. Homer Plessy, another African-American, was arrested on June 7 for the crime of sitting in the "whites only" section of a train car. Later that year, on October 12, the USA's Pledge of Allegiance was recited in unison for the first time by students in public schools to mark the 400th anniversary of the Columbus Day holiday.[406]

In 1892, while Menelik II was struggling to recover from the Kifu Ken, Black American citizens were living a more malicious and prolonged version of evil days. For Black Americans, their evil days came in the form of racial terrorism, which had been persisting for hundreds of years. At the same time that the United States was persecuting its people of African descent, it also began to open its doors to the world. On January 1, 1892, it began to accommodate predominantly European immigrants through Ellis Island in New York.

JAMAICA IN 1892

In 1892, a stonemason named Malchus Garvey was working hard in Jamaica to provide for his large family.

---

[406] The words "one nation under God" were not yet added and would not be added until 1954.

Having many children, he was blessed to have the means to provide for them with a trade that was always in demand. His wife, Sarah Richards, was a domestic servant and dutiful mother. From humble beginnings, she was the daughter of indentured farmers. She had also experienced loss in childbirth, so she took particular care in raising her two surviving children, especially her youngest, Marcus.

Marcus Garvey, then a 5-year-old toddler of above average intelligence, was born in the parish of Saint Ann in 1887. His birthday was August 17, the same day as Menelik II, and his destiny would one day intersect with that of Ras Makonnen and Yeshimebet's son – the baby boy born in the highlands of Ethiopia. For the time being, young Marcus was being influenced by his rural surroundings.

As a stonemason, Malchus could afford the finest education for his children that money could buy, and they were even able to interact with neighboring white children. His youngest son's dark complexion did not go unnoticed among the rural elite though. Marcus was too young to notice. He would later write:

> "As a child, I went to school with white boys and girls, like all other Negroes. We were not called Negroes then. I never heard the term Negro used once until I was about fourteen... It was then that I found for the first time that there was some difference in humanity, and that there were different races, each having its own separate and distinct social elite. I did not care about

separations after I was told about it... I simply had no regrets."[407]

Marcus's lack of racial awareness as a child would positively impact his self-confidence – he would grow to feel in no way inferior to his white counterparts. His father's wealth meant that his family had more money than many of their humble neighbors. Malchus Garvey was an educated man who kept a collection of books and believed in the power of the written word. His love for education would leave an indelible mark on Marcus, who would emerge on the world stage as a man with global scope. Garvey was far more privileged than the rest of his countryfolk in Jamaica and those across the Caribbean.

Hard times had hit the Caribbean region. The exports of sugar in Jamaica itself had dropped dramatically, from 1,053,000 CWT in 1838 to 378,000 CWT in 1890, a 64 percent drop.[408] The decline of the sugar industry led to major hardships for Jamaica's African population. A rise in unemployment was leading to high numbers of people fleeing the island to seek greener pastures. The rate of male employment between 1891 and 1911 would fall from 19,206 to 13,153.[409]

The sugar situation in Jamaica was also giving rise to increased banana cultivation. Many plantations started switching to banana production and, by 1899, fourteen of eighteen plantations in the parish of Saint Thomas made the transition.[410] Thus, while Emperor Yohannes IV and

---

[407] Nicholas, Tracy. *Rastafari: A Way of Life*. Frontline Books, 1996, p. 12.

[408] James, Winston. *Holding Aloft the Banner of Ethiopia: Caribbean Radicalism in Early Twentieth-Century America*. Verso, 1998, p. 17.

[409] Ibid.

[410] Ibid.

then Emperor Menelik II asserted his dominance in the Ethiopian highlands, Jamaica began its ascent to becoming the number one banana producer in the world between the years of 1870 and 1929.[411]

This period of Jamaican history was characterized by the disenfranchisement of its African descendants and the consolidation of its land into the hands of large European landholders. In many respects, the condition of African Jamaicans was worse than during the period of slavery. One of the steps backward was in medical care as post-slavery employers were no longer responsible for medical treatment and most African Jamaicans could not dream of affording the attention of a medical doctor.[412]

This period of decline also came with the migration of Jamaica's rural population to the capital city, Kingston. Many of the new inhabitants there were pushed into domestic work and those who could not find domestic work had to hustle, trade or join the ranks of the growing long-term unemployed. By the time the news of the little boy born in Harar would reach this capital city, it would be full of impoverished Africans in need of hope. Yet, not even the greatest futurist could have predicted that the news of Ras Makonnen and Woizero Yeshimebet's baby boy, reaching this faraway island, would change the world forever.

EASTERN EUROPE IN 1892

Closer to home, powerful forces were at work in Eastern Europe. With the rise of a unified Germany

---

[411] Ibid.

[412] Ibid.

coupled with the rise in Italian power, the concept of Slav nationalism was working on the people who were under the thumb of the Austro-Hungarian Empire. A great, future personal friend of the baby boy was born in Kumrovec (Austria-Hungary) on May 7, 1892 – Josip Broz Tito, furute president of Yugoslavia and champion of the non-aligned movement.

AN END TO ETHIOPIAN ISOLATION

For hundreds of years since the invasion of Imam Ahmad Gran, Ethiopia had developed largely without outside interference. It was an island of tradition in a world of change but things started to change by 1892. Ethiopia was now beginning to embark on a journey that would forever change the face of the modern world as well as history's perception of Africa.

When faced with the option between integrating with the wider world and isolation, Ethiopia normally chose the latter. However, with the visit of Ras Makonnen to Italy in 1888, Emperor Menelik II had signaled his plan to change the status quo. Not since Zara Yaqob's delegation to Italy in 1441 and Fasilides's ambassador to India in 1664-5 had an emperor attempted to send a formal delegation to an outside power.

Menelik II had no choice. The tide was turning, and not in favor of Ethiopia or Africa. The events of the Berlin Conference had made it impossible for the emperor to maintain an isolationist policy. Even though not a single African was at the table in Berlin, Ethiopia registered how it would respond to Africa's division at the Battle of Dogali in 1885, and by proving unwilling to give in to European demands for control.

It could not have been known then: the son of Ras Makonnen and Woizero Yeshimebet born in the holy mountains of Ejersa Goro would grow to become a man who would usher Ethiopia into the modern world, stand against fascism, change the face of education and progress in Ethiopia forever, give birth to a global following and provide the foundation for the united nations of Africa.

By the end of 1892, the same baby boy, Lij Tafari, was healthy and growing stronger by the day; and he would need his strength. The Italians had not forgotten the humiliation of defeat on the battlefield. Emperor Menelik II's refusal to accept Italy's protection over Ethiopia was taken as a slap in the face that would not be tolerated. Although young Tafari defied the odds and survived his first few months on Earth, his tranquil existence in Harar would be short-lived. War was on the horizon.

CHAPTER TWENTY-NINE

The Birth

"Behold, the days come, saith the Lord, that I will raise unto David a righteous Branch, and a King shall reign and prosper, and shall execute judgment and justice in the earth." **– Jeremiah 23:5**

Lij Tafari was born into struggle. With his very first breath of air outside of the womb, he was crowned a victor over the power of death. As if in divine celebration, his first cries were "drowned by a spectacular cannonading of thunder and [the] torrential downpour."[413] Of his eight brothers and sisters who attempted to enter the world before him, all died during the birthing process or shortly thereafter. Thus, the successful birth of Lij Tafari to his mother, Woizero Yeshimebet, could easily be considered a divine miracle. He alone survived! Yeshimebet's heart filled with hope as her son showed all the signs of being a healthy baby boy. The warm, life-renewing energy of a mother's love flooded the room, adding to the effect of the new rains and the lightning and thunder.

The women who attended the bedside of Yeshimebet raised their voices in the traditional Ethiopian praise. The men in the village sounded their rifles in

---

[413] Mosley, Leonard. *Haile Selassie: The Conquering Lion.* Weidenfeld and Nicolson, 1964, p. 23.

jubilation as "cattle [were] killed and tej and talla [made] ready."[414] There would be a feast and celebration for two nights.

Yeshimebet did not have that much time to spend with Tafari. He was passed to the attendants as soon as he was determined healthy, then passed outside the house and taken to a wet nurse. Ras Makonnen had followed the elders' advice and temporarily removed the boy from his mother to ensure his survival.

Even though there were rumors that Yeshimebet was cursed, she was indeed blessed. As a member of the nobility, her surroundings were extremely clean. The multiple attendants present made sure, for this birth, that extra precautions were taken.

Ras Makonnen was a man of faith who believed in science. He ensured that the backward practices that permeated Ethiopian culture at the time were not permitted to be used on his beloved wife. No expense was spared to bring in the best available doctors to attend to her. Ras Makonnen was open to modern advancements in childbirth and was willing to trust these advancements over questionable traditional practices. It was a delicate balance. Some traditions were deeply embedded in Church ritual and not all could be abandoned.

BIRTH RITUALS IN ETHIOPIA

Lij Tafari's birth was prior to the introduction of modern hospitals. According to tradition, many Ethiopian

---

[414] Ibid.

mothers were expected to spend 40 days in a small, smoke-filled hut bonding with their newborns. This was especially true for women of nobility, who were not permitted to exercise or move about. Many mothers and babies died after the birthing process as the lack of movement (and lack of sanitary environment for many) meant they were more susceptible to some deadly infection or another. Working class women who followed their husbands traveling with the imperial court experienced a generally different reality, especially during times of war. Some of them were forced to have their children on the roadside or in temporary camps typical of this nomadic lifestyle. It was strenuous to carry their babies while carrying their loads, yet these mothers likely benefited from the fresh air and exercise that life on the move provided.

Woizero Yeshimebet was not able to see or bond with her baby boy during her time of isolation. As a noblewoman – no less, the wife of Harar's governor – she was not in a smoke-filled hut. Instead, she was in a small traditional wattle and daub house. She also had the finest physicians in the realm. Childbirth was a period of uncleanliness and therefore a time that required separation from the general community. She was blessed to have attendants to see to her needs.

Due to her poor track record of birthing children who lived, Yeshimebet was seen as carrying some form of curse. In 1892, many of the curses attached to unsuspecting mothers were the results of traditional practices that contributed to high infant or mother mortality. Chief among these practices were child marriages and the corresponding pregnancies of very young teens and even pre-teens. Many traditional remedies for ailments associated with the birthing process also added to the dangers. For instance, to relieve birth pains, sulphur was burned in the birth hut.[415] Another example is the use of butter during the birth ritual to ease the child's arrival into the world. Midwives would rub butter on the bellies of expecting mothers and then place them on a smooth stone also lathered in butter. Butter was also placed on the tongue of the newborn to ensure a pleasant voice.[416] (After birth, babies were bathed daily and rubbed in butter.) Other women were encouraged to put on dirty clothes for the birthing process. These various practices might have increased the risks of infection significantly.

Koso (supposedly sold by Emperor Tewodros II's mother) was also used by mothers near the time of birth. They would take the bitter herb to prepare their bodies for childbirth. Unfortunately, some mothers or midwives would give koso to the newborns, risking internal rupture as their newly formed digestive systems were not equipped to deal with the herb's strong purging qualities.[417]

Diapers were non-existent in the ancient realm and mothers had to creatively deal with their babies' waste. Chafing was prevented by using finely ground clay or powdered, burnt cow dung. This was applied to their armpits and between their thighs.

Some regions also practiced circumcision, both male and female.[418] This ancient custom also presented major problems for children's health, especially in instances when the knives used were not sterile. In poorer tribes, knives would be replaced by sharpened glass or a

---

[415] Prouty, Chris. *Empress Taytu and Menilek II: Ethiopia 1883-1910*. 1986. The Red Sea Press, 2016, p. 32.

[416] Ibid., 33.

[417] Ibid.

[418] Ibid., 32.

sharp stone.[419] The circumcision ceremony took place on the 8th day for boys and anywhere between the 15th and 80th day for girls. Only prayer and urine were used to guard against infection during the dangerous procedure. Little girls in Ethiopia perhaps did not have as drastic an experience as their counterparts in parts of Sudan and Somalia, not counting the Afar and the Somali who lived historically within Ethiopia's borders, who also practiced clitoridectomy, infibulation and excision. In the Christian highlands, according to some customs, little girls were subjected to the trimming of their labia minora.[420] The wound from the circumcision was packed with butter and ashes from a cloth burnt for the occasion, and was said to heal relatively quickly in the absence of infection. Generally, the side effects from this custom were internal infection, trauma, plus difficulty in urination and menstruation.[421]

The rationale for the custom of circumcision was that it was thought to control the female sex drive and improve the chance that she would make it to her wedding night as a virgin. Virginity was prized in Christian Ethiopia and females were often used as bargaining chips or as a means to balance power within the realm. A virgin daughter was worth much more to a family than a daughter who already had sex. If there was no blood produced from the breaking of the hymen on the marriage night, the newly wed wife could be beaten and sent back to her family with the demand that any dowry paid be returned.

It is not known whether Woizero Yeshimebet endured female circumcision. However, it is known that

---

[419] Ibid., 34.

[420] Ibid.

[421] Ibid., 33.

she endured isolation from her child. As a mother with a history of losing children, she may have been encouraged to cut a piece of her newborn's ear and swallow it, shave half of her head before delivery or wear a sliver of iron to keep Satan and his angels of death at bay.[422] For many who followed the ancient traditions of the realm, these were insurances against the death of a new child.

Upon entering the world, newborns in some regions were birthed into a wicker basket that was padded with either straw or flour.[423] A careful midwife would then pick up the baby, who would then be washed in cold water until clean. Some midwives would then use their hands to mold the head and face of the baby, gently massaging and pressing on the baby's head to ensure it would grow into a handsome child and then an adult.

On that fateful day, July 23, 1892, Woizero Yeshimebet had given birth to a baby boy. She knew it was a boy because the attendant women, in keeping with their tradition, took great pride in shouting out the baby's sex at the moment of birth. After being taken from her, baby Tafari might have been taken to his father, who would have placed the tip of a lance in his mouth to ensure that he would grow with courage.

For the governor of Harar, the birth of a healthy baby boy meant that the surrounding countryside was treated to a symphony of rifle fire, the customary seven times to announce the birth of the governor of Harar's baby boy.[424] Lij Tafari was then taken to his maternal grandmother, Woizero Walatta Giyorgis, to give him an additional chance of survival. The wise elder would take

---

[422] Ibid., 34.

[423] Ibid., 33.

[424] Ibid., 34.

care of him until his mother could be cleared of any potential curses.

CHAPTER THIRTY

The New Name

"Him that overcometh will I make a pillar in the temple of my God, and he shall go no more out: and I will write upon him the name of my God, and the name of the city of my God, which is new Jerusalem, which cometh down out of heaven from my God: and I will write upon him my new name." – **Revelation 3:12**

After 40 days of prayer and careful observation to make sure the child remained healthy, the time arrived for Lij Tafari to be baptized and receive his baptismal name. Now reunited with his mother, and still under the attentive care of his grandmother Woizero Walatta Giyorgis, he would first have to make the journey from the beautiful mountains of Ejersa Goro to the city of Harar. There he would be baptized according to the Orthodox tradition in the Coptic church recently built by his father. Ras Makonnen had made all the necessary preparations to see that his son would receive proper blessings. He sent word to his wife, as well as a contingent of his most trusted warriors to ensure a safe arrival. Due to pressing business in Harar, Ras Makonnen had previously left Ejersa Goro and was not able to accompany them on their journey. He did not have much time to spend with his son during the month or so since his birth. However, he already noticed a quiet strength in the boy. It would be up to the church to give Tafari his Christian name.

The rains had continued since that fateful day of July 23 and the blessing of water made the journey from Ejersa Goro to Harar slow and difficult. Dirt paths turned into red mud, then into mighty torrents of red water. It was as if all the blood that was lost during the Evil Days had seeped out of the ground and was washing away from the land. Despite the conditions, the journey was triumphant and the ceremonial order was painstakingly kept with six members of Ras Makonnen's camp at the head of the procession. Each man, carefully selected for the occasion, sounded a different note on his curved one-note horn.

Following the players of instruments was Harar's deputy governor, Fitawrari Banti, dressed in "a crimson coat and velvet hat, his pony richly ornamented, a silver shield on the saddle bow, spear carriers running at his side."[425] The deputy governor was given the honor of walking before the decorated carriage of Woizero Yeshimebet, followed by baby Tafari in his carriage with a striking silver embroidered canopy. Only a month old, Lij Tafari's presence was already accompanied with majesty.

Ras Makonnen knew that word traveled fast within the cramped confines of Harar, and that his wife's paternal family were Oromo Muslim nobility well known in the walled city. He intended to make the baptism of the only surviving child from her womb a day to remember in Harar. He would also show the people that a Christian could love, honor and respect a woman born to a Muslim father, and this would further solidify local respect for his leadership.

---

[425] Mosley, Leonard. *Haile Selassie: The Conquering Lion.* Weidenfeld and Nicolson, 1964, p. 23.

The people of Harar could hear the procession long before they laid eyes on it. Rifle fire rang out in homage to the blessing that the Almighty had bestowed upon the land and upon Ras Makonnen. Some of his finest fighting men fanned out from the procession upon arrival, dressed in colored shirts with leopard or lion skins carefully draped over their shoulders, lion manes around their heads and curved swords clanking in announcement to all within earshot. (The lion manes symbolized The Lion of Judah. Each warrior was required to kill a lion before he could be considered a man.) Skilled warriors on horseback, considered among the finest warriors in all Ethiopia, galloped with the procession, kicking up red sprays of mud as they neared the city. Behind them were the enslaved attendants, hired attendants and women assigned to fulfill the needs of Yeshimebet. They rhythmically chanted – "lelelelele" – as their ancestors had done before for as long as any living Ethiopian could remember. Their haunting voices carried on the wind along with the loud, continuous gunshots.[426]

Birth was celebrated by all in Ethiopia. The chief at every village greeted the procession and offered *talla* beer for the multitude and *tej* for the officers on horseback. The villagers all bowed their heads as the procession passed by. Some of the women and children clapped and cheered.

Just outside the walls of Harar, Ras Makonnen waited patiently on his horse. He, too, had heard the procession and was eager to lay his eyes on his son once again. When Tafari's carriage arrived, he picked up his son. The cloth in which Tafari was wrapped was covered in red mud stains and Ras Makonnen could not help but notice the striking color and quietly ponder the

---

[426] Ibid.

significance. He turned his horse around and proudly led the procession into the city with his baby boy in his arms.

It was a day of great joy. The Muslim chiefs arrived from the surrounding countryside to pay their tributes. Emperor Menelik II sent many gifts for Tafari. Ras Makonnen offered up praises to the Almighty for bringing his child to this moment alive.

HOLY BAPTISM

Baptism is the first of seven sacraments of the Ethiopian Orthodox Church. It is the door through which the faithful in Christ enter the body of Christ (the Church). It is through this door that the faithful are able to partake in the other sacraments.

Tafari would be immersed in water three times in the name of the Holy Trinity – the Father, the Son and the Holy Spirit. He could be baptized only once in his life. As Yeshua the Christ was baptized by John the Baptist, so are his followers in the Orthodox Church baptized. Baptism represented Tafari's spiritual birth. He would partake in the death and resurrection of Christ. As an infant unable to talk, his father would answer for him before he could receive the baptism. Following centuries old ritual, the priest would ask Ras Makonnen to ensure that Lij Tafari would renounce Satan and all his works.

Tafari would then receive a new name, one different from his family name. The choice of a suitable name would typically be given first to the parents. On this day, Ras Makonnen would not choose. He had no doubt that his baby boy was special. The child had defied death and made it to his 40th day and baptism. It could only be the power of the Father, his son Christ and the Holy Spirit that protected his child. It could only be the might and power of the trinity that allowed his son to be born with the rains, and for his first cries to be saluted with thunder and lightning. Before Ras Makonnen could suggest a name, the attendant priest made the declaration.

Undoubtedly, the priest knew of the fate of Tafari's brothers and sisters, of his birth at the start of the rains and that Ras Makonnen was a favorite to succeed Emperor Menelik II as emperor; and he knew that the boy was Makonnen's only legitimate heir. Therefore, the priest declared that the boy's name would be a name used by none before him, a name from the ancient Ge'ez language. Tafari's new name would be Haile Selassie, meaning *the might of the trinity*.

"I baptize you in the name of the Father and the Son and the Holy Spirit; your name is Haile Selassie." The priest's voice echoed throughout the stillness and the people gathered stood in awe of the majesty of the occasion. The new name would echo throughout the ages.

REVELATIONS: THE RAS TAFARI

Decades later, 7,668 miles (12,341 kilometers) away, a population of exiled people of African descent would celebrate the moment of Tafari's birth as a holy day. These people, called by the name Ras Tafari, would first rise in the distant island of Jamaica. The first adherents were working class and followers of a man named Marcus Garvey. They studied the Bible with unmatched fervor. They would adopt the name Ras Tafari based on their interpretation of scripture and declare that they were the people destined to receive the redemption promised therein. The elders of the faith would connect the coming of Lij Tafari to their redemption from the tribulation of the trans-Atlantic slave trade. It would be proclaimed:

> "But now thus saith the LORD that created thee, O Jacob, and he that formed thee, O Israel, Fear not: for I have redeemed thee, I have called thee by thy name; thou art mine. When thou passest through the waters, I will be with thee; and through the rivers, they shall not overflow thee: when thou walkest through the fire, thou shalt not be burned; neither shall the flame kindle upon thee. For I am the LORD thy God, the Holy One of Israel, thy Saviour: I gave Egypt for thy ransom, Ethiopia and Seba for thee. Since thou wast precious in my sight, thou hast been honourable, and I have loved thee: therefore will I give men for thee, and people for thy life. Fear not: for I am with thee: I will bring thy seed from the east, and gather thee from the west; I will say to the north, Give up; and to the south, Keep not back: bring my sons from far, and my daughters from the ends of the earth; Even every one that is called by my name: for I have created him for my glory, I have formed him; yea, I have made him."[427]

For those Africans exiled to the islands, redemption for a people "called by my name" meant that they, too, would claim what they saw as the new name, Haile Selassie I, Ras Tafari. Even their location, so far from their native Africa, was also explained in prophecy. They would refer to the prophet Isaiah, who prophesied, "Then it will

---

[427] Isaiah 43:1-7

happen on that day that the Lord Will again recover the second time with His hand The remnant of His people, who will remain, From Assyria, Egypt, Pathros, Cush, Elam, Shinar, Hamath, *And from the islands of the sea.*"[428]

The elders of this peculiar faith, in their examination of Woizero Yeshimebet and her troubles with childbirth, would later refer to the prophet John who authored the Book of Revelation and make mention of "a woman clothed in the sun" who, "being with child cried travailing in birth." They would explain the deaths of Yeshimebet's earlier children by referencing the "wonder in heaven," the appearance in the vision of John of "a great red dragon, having seven heads and ten horns, and seven crowns upon his heads." The vision revealed to John that this dragon had a "tail [that] drew the third part of the stars of heaven, and did cast them to the earth: and the dragon stood before the woman which was ready to be delivered, for to devour her child as soon as it was born."[429]

The spiritual dragon prevailed against all but Tafari. After all, he was the one to be feared. Ras Tafari all over the world would note that John's vision confirms Tafari's victory in saying that the woman "brought forth a man child, who was to rule the nations with a rod of iron" and that this "child was caught up to God, and to his throne." These same Ras Tafari would connect the fact that Ethiopia was the only land on Earth that held the tradition of possessing the seat or throne of King David, which the Almighty promises to rule from. (Hence, "...caught up to God, and to *his* throne.") They would say this with no knowledge of the prophecies of the elders and astrologers who advised Ras Makonnen.

---

[428] Isaiah 11:11

[429] Revelation 12:1-5

However, in 1892, these things were not to come to pass for another 38 years. For now, only Ethiopia's Emperor Menelik II, Ras Makonnen and the small Christian community of Harar rejoiced over the birth of Woizero Yeshimebet's healthy baby boy. That year, the future and final emperor of the world's oldest nation state was born into the last remaining sanctuary of free land in Africa.

Much later (during his own painful exile in Britain), Emperor Haile Selassie I, King of Kings, Conquering Lion of the Tribe of Judah, Elect of God and Light of the World, reflected on his birth, saying only, "I was born on the 16th of Hamle 1884 [23rd of July 1892] in the year of John, at Ejersa Goro, not far from Harar."[430]

---

[430] Selassie, Haile, I. *My Life and Ethiopia's Progress: The Autobiography of Emperor Haile Sellassie I, King of Kings, Lord of Lords, Conquering Lion of Judah*, vol. 1. Frontline Distribution International, 1999, p. 14.

The story of Lij Tafari Makonnen will continue in...

Haile Selassie I's Ethiopia, Volume Two:
The Journey to Dejazmatch During the Scramble for Ethiopia

- Chapter One (Preview) -

"The wolf also shall dwell with the lamb, and the leopard shall lie down with the kid; and the calf and the young lion and the fatling together; and a little child shall lead them." – **Isaiah 11:6**

The youth of Addis Ababa were in awe! They were witnessing a 13-year-old child leading an army out of the city. Not just any army, it was one of the most powerful armies in the entire realm. The soldiers, some wearing headdresses with lion manes, looked both ferocious and disciplined as they marched through the well-worn dirt roads of the Ethiopian capital city. The teenager leading them was Ras Makonnen's son, Dejazmatch Tafari, no doubt the most powerful child in all Ethiopia.

Addis Ababa was in mourning that day. The angel of death had claimed the life of the great Ras Makonnen. He had passed away suddenly, leaving the empire and its royal family a massive diplomatic void. Far and wide, the nobility wept at the loss of Ras Makonnen. In the city of Harar, where he once governed, the news of his death shook the populace. Sadness became the status quo. As the customary period for mourning came to a close, the officers of Ras Makonnen received a message from the King of Kings, Emperor Menelik II saying, "Come at once with Tafari, his son, for it is before me at Addis Ababa that the lamentations for Ras Makonnen's 40-day mourning are to be held."[431]

Upon receiving the official communication, preparations were made for the long march from Harar to Addis Ababa. It was the rainy season and the trek would not be easy as there were no paved roads or motor vehicles. Horses, mules and foot were the main modes of transportation.

Death had already claimed the life of young Tafari's mother, Woizero Yeshimebet, and now his father breathed no more. Still unsatisfied but unable to prevail against Tafari himself, death's angel turned its attention to Ras Makonnen's prized army and stalked the columns of soldiers on their march. Many of them died along the journey. Great men who had distinguished themselves in battle were now casualties of the long distance to Addis Ababa.

With the rainy conditions came countless standing puddles of water, which in turn became breeding grounds for mosquitos. Malaria ravaged the travelers' camps during the night and, without the benefit of modern medicine, the mighty soldiers were no match for the Lord of Flies and his armies of mosquitos.

The march to Addis Ababa to honor Ras Makonnen became an Ethiopian march of tears as death after death shook the marching soldiers. The massive army of Ras Makonnen reached Addis Ababa on April 26th 1906.

Addis Ababa was already flooded with soldiers, foreigners and nobles who came to pay their respect to the

---

[431] Selassie, Haile, I. *My Life and Ethiopia's Progress: The Autobiography of Emperor Haile Sellassie I, King of Kings, Lord of Lords, Conquering Lion of Judah*, vol. 1. Frontline Distribution International, 1999, p. 23.

great Ras. The King of Kings, Emperor Menelik II spared no expense and had ordered massive tents be sewn together to provide some relief from the incessant rain. The beleaguered army from Harar joined the imperial army that was assembled in their full splendor. The nobility assembled on one side of the tent and the armies of the Emperor and the nobles assembled on the other side of the tents. The soldiers from Harar were shown where their camp would be. The large army was led a good distance away from the large white tent and set up their camp. After resting a few days and watching the other armies, dignitaries and peasant farmers arrive, the ceremonies were ready to begin.

On April 30, 1906, forty days since the passing of Ras Makonnen, priests from Addis Ababa's monasteries were joined with priests from the surrounding countryside for the purpose of providing prayers of absolution for the mass of Christians who gathered to show respect for the great Ras. Their chanting filled the large clearing and brought some spiritual relief to the sadness that gripped the realm. Following their priestly duties, the priest then made their way to the large white tent. It was time for the feast to begin. Menelik II was known for his feasts and Ras Makonnen's funeral feast was no exception.

The nobility, the Rases and Dejazmatches, assembled in the tent and watched as the priests feasted and shared their food with the many poor who patiently waited for their share. The wealthy nobles, inspired in part by the piety of the priests, also gave alms to the throngs of poor that had gathered for the spectacle. It was only appropriate as Ras Makonnen was known for his support of the church and kindness to the poor.

While the priests nourished themselves and the poor, Emperor Menelik II and his royal court moved into position on the massive field. A seat befitting for a king was brought for him to sit on. His army, the most powerful army of all the kingdoms assembled before him. They were joined by Ras Makonnen's soldiers from Harar and the thousands of other well wishers who had come to show their respect for Ras Makonnen.

Young Dejazmatch Tafari was humbled by the outpouring of love being shown for his father. According to the customs of Ethiopia, on the 40th day of mourning, those gathered for the deceased mourn as they would on the day of death. The young prince watched as men of distinction began to bring out his father's belongings to be presented in front of Emperor Menelik II and his army.

Both men and women wailed as they brought out Ras Makonnen's robes and his Ras's crown. Still more warriors brought forward his medals and his battle arms. Tears flowed like the mighty Blue Nile as Ras Makonnen's trusted horses and mules, decorated in golden harnesses, were paraded slowly before the army and nobility. The soldiers were reminded of Ras Makonnen's valiant defense of Ethiopia against the Italians and the stunning victory delivered against the Europeans that had shocked the whole world. The sight of such majesty gave one of the mourners courage. They stepped forward and shouted a dirge for all to hear:

"The telephonist, when he announced his death, was wrong; It is not Makonnen but the poor died."[432]

Dejazmatch Tafari was touched by the dirge and outpouring of love his father was receiving. He would never forget what he saw. It was whispered through the capital, Addis Ababa, that never in living memory had

---

[432] Ibid., 14.

anyone received such lamentations. Ras Makonnen was loved by the empire.

Following the funeral, Emperor Menelik II gave the order for the military to disperse. They were to return to their homes in the surrounding countryside. Addis Ababa could not feed or house such a large fighting force for long.

The following day, the armies of the Emperor and the great Rases pulled up their camps and slowly began to leave the great field. Emperor Menelik II's workers came and took down the large white tent and efforts were made to clean the refuse left in the field; however, there was one section of the field that could not be cleaned.

Theories began to spread through the dirt roads of the capital. Everyone had something to say. Ras Makonnen's army had not followed the order to disburse and instead quietly held their position in their camp. No one knew for certain why they had disobeyed a direct order from the Emperor. Accordingly, Emperor Menelik II's court attendants sent a messenger to inquire as to why the army was not moving. They were shocked with the response given by one of the generals. The general stated, "It is to escort to his camp our master's son, Dejazmatch Tafari."[433]

At the palace, Emperor Menelik II was still crushed with grief. He had lost not only a great general and advisor, but his cousin who had grown up in his care since he was a young boy. Emperor Menelik II was concerned about the emotional state of Dejazmatch Tafari. As his mentor and *jegna*, the great Emperor Tewedros II had cared for him, he would ensure the care of young Dejazmatch Tafari. Dejazmatch Tafari was a peculiar teenager. He did

---

[433] Ibid., 25.

not speak much and carried himself like a church elder. He made those around him nervous as the maturity of his actions and his youthful age seemed to be in perpetual conflict.

Word of what Ras Makonnen's general had said reached Emperor Menelik II and Empress Taitu. Dejazmatch Tafari was summoned to the royal chambers. Emperor Menelik II wanted Ras Makonnen's son to remain with him in the palace. Dejazmatch Tafari's calm demeanor and resemblance to his father gave Emperor Menelik II great comfort. However, he knew the passion of Ras Makonnen's soldiers as he had fought on the battlefield with some of them on more than one occasion. He knew they would not leave and violate their oath to their fallen leader. Emperor Menelik II made the decision to allow Dejazmatch Tafari to be escorted back to the camp by the soldiers.

Upon receipt of the Emperor's blessing, the soldiers left the field and streamed into the city to the palace to provide royal escort to Dejazmatch Tafari. Emperor Menelik II watched the young prince closely and was surprised he looked unimpressed by what was happening on his account. An army of enormous power was now his to command. Were it anyone but the son of Ras Makonnen, such a display would not be permitted. Quickly, word of the army's arrival within the city's borders spread and the inhabitants of Addis Ababa came out of their habitation to watch the spectacle.

The observers watched as Dejazmatch Tafari took his place among the army like someone born to rule. His face showed no fear or concern, only quiet confidence. As they moved through the city towards their camp the well trained columns of soldiers were joined by friends of Ras Makonnen. Out of the ashes of the death of Ras

Makonnon the phoenix of Dejazmatch Tafari was rising before the eyes of an entire city. No one moved. All eyes were glued on the small teenager at the head of a powerful army. An army that included both Christians and Muslims. Astonishment took hold of the city because of the size of the military escort.

Later Dejazmatch Tafari was told by his generals and his father's close friends that the common belief was that Emperor Menelik II and Empress Taitu allowed him to maintain control over his father's army because they would grant him the governorship of Harar. His advisors were wrong. Dejazmatch Tafari's time to govern Harar like his father had not yet come.

In order to understand how a teenager became the most powerful leader in Ethiopia outside of the Emperor, it is essential to return to 1893 to continue the story of the boy whose first cries were drowned by thunder and the only child who survived from the womb of Woizero Yeshimebet. During the period between 1893 and Ras Makonnen's death in 1906, Dejazmatch Tafari would bear witness to the impact of the greatest most significant war of the Scramble for Africa as well as experience both tragedy and triumph. In 1893, the story of the rise of Dejazmatch Tafari Makonnen was just beginning and being carefully shaped by the progressive ideas and wise mind of his father, Ras Makonnen, and thus we return to the walled city of Harar in 1893...

Index

A

Abarri Galla, 285
Abbichu Galla, 285
Abbot Yohannes, 129
Abeokuta, 362
Abiye, 282, 283
Abomey, 361
Abraha, 33
Abraham, iii, 32, 135, 146, 147,
148, 149, 151, 152, 153, 154,
155, 156, 157, 158, 159, 160,
161, 162, 165, 166, 167, 168,
174, 176, 177, 229, 277, 331
Abrahamic, 50, 113
Abuna, 124, 125, 126, 222, 246,
320, 321
Acts, 175, 192, 217, 218
Adal, 55, 72, 249, 250, 251, 258,
269, 311
Adam, 70, 104, 108, 139, 140,
146, 156, 167, 187
Admah, 152
Afar, 94, 280, 283, 287, 302, 375
Afran Quallo, 27
Africa, 5, i, ii, iv, vi, viii, ix, x, 2, 6,
7, 8, 10, 12, 13, 14, 15, 17, 19,
21, 24, 26, 29, 30, 35, 36, 45,
57, 63, 64, 67, 68, 69, 70, 71,
73, 74, 76, 77, 78, 80, 81, 83,
84, 85, 96, 97, 101, 102, 103,
104, 105, 106, 108, 109, 110,
111, 113, 114, 115, 116, 117,
130, 134, 135, 136, 137, 139,
140, 141, 142, 152, 186, 189,
196, 200, 220, 227, 228, 229,
233, 237, 239, 263, 271, 273,
275, 278, 340, 343, 344, 346,
355, 356, 357, 358, 359, 360,
362, 363, 364, 369, 370, 383,
385, 393
African, 5, 6, i, ii, iii, vi, vii, viii, ix,
x, xi, 5, 6, 7, 10, 12, 13, 14, 16,
17, 18, 19, 20, 21, 44, 45, 64,
69, 70, 71, 72, 73, 74, 76, 77,
79, 80, 82, 83, 84, 94, 95, 101,
102, 104, 107, 109, 110, 116,
118, 119, 120, 121, 123, 125,
133, 135, 137, 138, 139,140,
141, 142, 143, 144, 145, 147,
158, 178, 189, 200, 237, 260,
302, 336, 344, 350, 357, 358,
360, 362, 365, 367, 368, 369,
382
Afro-Asiatic, 137, 147, 149
Agame, 274
Agancha, 280
Agaw, 94, 124, 125, 126, 127,
228, 236, 271
Agoba, 285
Akan, 136
Akawa, 281
al-Bakri, Shaykh Umar Abadir,
24
Alexandria, 124, 168, 196
Ali, Asfaw, 312
Ali, Mohammed, 258, 300, 308,
309, 310, 311
Alo, 26
Alula, 6, 102, 197, 261, 262, 263,
264, 265, 266, 268, 271, 272,
273, 274, 275, 276, 277, 302,
340, 344, 345
Amba Salama, 266
Amda Seyon, 280
Amda Tsion, 231
Amha Iyasus, 283, 284, 293
Amhara, 6, 46, 60, 61, 94, 242,
275, 284, 295, 306

For more information and works of Kwasi Bonsu, Esq.,
visit **www.dejazmatchkwasi.com** or scan this QR code:

For more books published by Bookman Express, visit
www.bookmanexpress.pub or scan this QR code: